Political Keywords

Political Keywords

Using Language That Uses Us

Roderick P. Hart
University of Texas at Austin

Sharon E. Jarvis
University of Texas at Austin

William P. Jennings
University of Cincinnati

Deborah Smith-Howell
University of Nebraska–Omaha

New York   Oxford
OXFORD UNIVERSITY PRESS
2005

Oxford University Press

Oxford   New York
Auckland   Bangkok   Buenos Aires   Cape Town   Chennai
Dar es Salaam   Delhi   Hong Kong   Istanbul   Karachi   Kolkata
Kuala Lumpur   Madrid   Melbourne   Mexico City   Mumbai
Nairobi   São Paulo   Shanghai   Taipei   Tokyo   Toronto

Published by Oxford University Press, Inc.
198 Madison Avenue, New York, New York 10016
www.oup.com

Oxford is a registered trademark of Oxford University Press

Library of Congress Cataloging-in-Publication Data

Political keywords : using language that uses us / Roderick P. Hart . . . [et al.].
       p. cm.
     Includes index.
     ISBN 0-19-516238-2—ISBN 0-19-516239-0 (pbk.)
       1. Rhetoric—Political aspects—United States. 2. United States—Politics and government.
     I. Hart, Roderick P.

     P301.5.P67P65 2005
     808′.001′4—dc22
                                                                              2004041597

Printing number: 9   8   7   6   5   4   3   2   1

Printed in the United States of America
on acid-free paper

CONTENTS

FIGURES

TABLES

Political Keywords

The Possibilities of Language

It is said that all men are created equal in the United States, but that is not true for words. Some words are better than others, which is to say, they work harder, get more done, demand more respect. Americans become obedient in the presence of such words, words like *national defense* or the *Fourth of July* or *lower taxes*. It is almost impossible to champion these concepts and not win the day. Cultural historian Richard Weaver called such phrases God Terms, words that so concentrate the mind that no other thoughts can be thought.[1] Devil Terms, in contrast, words like *communism* or *inflation* or *al Qaeda,* are so disturbing that their mere mention casts a pall over an otherwise pleasant day. Words like these do our thinking for us, says Weaver, blotting out their alternatives. Such words also stir up emotions. To use them is to make a raw bid for influence.

Power is often associated with language. Much to the dismay of the French, for example, English has become the universal language of business, and that has been a boon to U.S. and British corporations alike. English also rules the Internet, and that marginalizes literally billions of people. Similarly, recent immigrants to the United States learn about language and power when they seek work with broken English as their only ally. Even after one gets a job, the story of language continues: Television announcers are required to lose their regional accents; electoral ballots are available only in English; ebonics is treated as a national joke; parents prohibit their children from speaking Spanish, thereby distancing them from their grandparents. The story of language and power persists: The *New York Times* is written for the elite, the tabloids for the great unwashed; wealthy students do better in spelling bees than do poor children; a typographical error on a job résumé is seen as a moral failing, not a technological one.

But language is also dynamic. In the 1980s, for example, rap lyrics were associated with illiteracy and gangsterism, but the 1990s changed all that when the music infiltrated white youth culture. This sort of "mainstreaming" can be a natural process (*kleenex* and *xerox* began as brand names rather than generics), but mainstreaming can also be manipulated. During the 2003 Iraq war, for example, the Bush administration lionized the *coalition forces* who fought the war even though the troops were largely from the United States. The administration also referred to *weapons of mass destruction* because it sounded more fearsome than the technical *chemical and biological agents*.[2] On other occasions, a term like *feminism* can be reviled in one era (the 1960s) only to become a God Term in the 1970s and 1980s. Ironically, researchers now tell us that *feminism* has lost its cachet among young career women who find the concept too ideological for the "blended" lifestyles they desire.[3] Given the speed with which language preferences change, it is not surprising that the National Institutes of Health recently put out an advisory telling researchers to eschew such terms as *sex workers, abortion,* or *transgendered* when making grant applications during a Republican administration.[4]

This book takes words seriously. It reports many years of research focused on keywords, words that preempt our thought patterns. When publishing his masterwork, *Keywords,* in 1976, British theorist Raymond Williams pulled together some thirty years of notetaking about the words people use unthinkingly. Williams observes, for example, that to be *cultured* today means pursuing the fine arts rather than animal husbandry (the term's original referent). Why such changes? Words shift when culture shifts, said Williams, and culture shifts when economic systems shift. So, for example, ordinary words like *democracy* and *patriotism* come to discipline us ("You believe in democracy, don't you?") because they undergird capitalism itself. But capitalism lets some people get very rich at the expense of others. What justifies such disparities? Williams' answer: Society becomes a linguistic machine encouraging ordinary citizens to keep capitalism alive via their daily utterances. He observes, for example, that the term *anarchist* originally meant one with a mild distaste for state control but took on a radicalized meaning so the State would be preserved. Because capitalism must continually reproduce itself, it turns *charity* (originally Christian love) into a loathsome "handout" and it makes the *consumer* (originally someone who was overindulgent) a cultural icon. In addition, says Williams, when we think of *development* today we think in economic terms, not in terms of self-fulfillment or moral education.

Williams' theory is laden with Marxian presuppositions, so his story of language is only one of those available. We will tell a different story here, one that focuses not so much on language meanings but on the work words do. We concentrate here on mainstream American politics, especially that occurring during the last half of the twentieth century. This is not a large swath of time, but it is an interesting one. Our data-collecting begins just after World War II and ends just prior to the Iraq War. Sandwiched between these conflicts were those of Korea, Vietnam, Grenada, the Balkans, and the Persian Gulf. Overseeing these struggles was a roughly equal mix of Republican and Democratic presidents who could not have been more different: a general, an engineer, a movie actor, a war hero, a habadasher, a football star, a Rhodes scholar, a grade school teacher, and two career politicians. These men—they were all men—confronted such complexities as nuclear weaponry, AIDS, cloning, airport security, and environmental pollution and insidious social calamities as well: racism, sexism, religious intolerance, illiteracy, and persistent poverty at home and abroad. But 1948 through 2000 were also magnificent years for the American people: Their brethern flew to the moon, built parts of a space station, discovered the structure of DNA, invented the Internet, created an extraordinary system of higher education, and developed VCRs, cell phones, DVDs, and talking refrigerators.

The subtitle of this book is "Using Language That Uses Us," and we take that functional title seriously. We will trace how eight political keywords have been employed during the last fifty years, paying special attention to the functions they serve. We will track what *politics* now means to modern commentators, how the *president* is used by schoolteachers to inculcate values in the nation's children, and why an innocent word like *government* sometimes gets people so upset. We will ask how the *people* are referenced in political talk and how the *media* portray themselves. We will also look at the work done by political *parties,* political *promises,* and political *consultants* because, together, they shed special light on modern elections.

Our approach here will differ from those taken by other commentators. Unlike historians, we will not detail the biographies of those who shaped the American political experience. Unlike sociologists, we will not examine the demographic, economic, and regional forces determining how power is distributed in the United States. And unlike many political scientists, we will not use survey data to explain how Americans respond to social change. Instead, we will look at the language of political "elites," people like politicians, the press, educators, authors, and so on, and ask what it can tell us about our lives and times. This approach does not let us account for the effects of modern communications, but it does shed light on recent cultural and political history. Words cannot tell us everything we need to know, but they can tell us what we do not know and what must be discovered. As a result, this book has questions as well as answers.

WORDS AS QUESTIONS

Political Keywords follows in a long line of inquiries into the nature of public language. Foremost among these thinkers was Ralph Waldo Emerson, who observed that "we infer the spirit of the nation in large measure from language, which is a sort of monument to which each forcible individual in a course of many hundred years has contributed a stone."[5] Emerson's image is a fine one: a culture being built stone-by-stone, with each citizen lending a hand. But there is also the story of Babel. As we learn in Genesis 11, the Lord was displeased with His people and therefore uttered a fateful decree: "Let us go down, and there confound their language, that they may not understand one another's speech." And so it was.

And so it is. Some of our greatest battles are now fought on the field of language, with "essentially contested concepts" dividing people from one another. In the 1960s, for example, Martin Luther King, Jr., fought with Malcolm X over whether *progress* was being made by African Americans. Thirty years later blacks and whites argued about *justice* in the wake of the O. J. Simpson trial. Political theorist William Connolly asks the question this way: "Is a 'lockout,' a 'blacklist,' a 'blackball,' or 'social excommunication' importantly different from a 'boycott'? What is the point of marking off such differences? What of refusing to draw such lines?"[6] Because people share understandings *imperfectly*, says Connolly, they continually struggle over a core set of concepts. But because they *share* these understandings imperfectly, they "are provided with some common leverage for limiting the range within which these contests can rationally proceed."[7] In other words, in struggling over *progress* and *justice* as they did, African Americans reconstituted themselves as African *Americans*, thereby honoring the most sacred term of all in the U.S. lexicon.

Because they are often a site of struggle, a society's keywords inevitably point to its deepest values. Take *democracy*, for example. As Russell Hanson reports, our conversation about that term "has degenerated into a veritable babel in which all participants speak past, rather than to, one another."[8] According to Hanson, American history has seen fundamental transformations of its central constructs over the years, with *republicanism* moving from a negative term (belligerent rejection of the status quo) to a positive one (the people controlling their own destiny).[9] In like manner, members of political *parties* were once seen as dangerously incendiary; a hundred years later the *two-party system* has become a cultural icon. And when it comes to *democracy* itself, says Hanson, the term moved from a moral concept to a fundamentally economic one, a "way of life" rather than a "way of valuing." As James Farr declares, "political concepts do not have an agency or life apart from the political actors who use and change them."[10]

People become part of the same polity when choosing among a common batch of candidates, and they can also become part of an interpretive community. But interpretations often differ among people, and that puts pressure on the community. As Robin Lakoff notes, it is natural for African Americans to speak of slavery as their own special *holocaust*, but Jewish Americans see the matter differently, striving mightily to reserve that term for their own historic experiences. "Victims of both slavery and the Nazis want to hold on to the mystique of their [own] words," says Lakoff, but the fact of the matter is that "nobody retains a copyright on words."[11] Deprived of such copyrights, we wrangle constantly, and that causes the ground beneath our feet to shift. Francis Beer notes, for example, that *reason* is a universally respected notion. But because that term is polysemous, because the heart also has its reasons, charges of "unreasonableness" are constantly hurled during political debates. Words, says Beer, "do not come with a set of instructions."[12]

Keywords are important because they arise out of our cultural past. When such words change, it often means something large is afoot. Richard Merritt provides an interesting example. After doing a detailed study of colonial newspapers in New England, Merritt found a gradual, but insistent, alteration in the national self-references used during the early 1700s. Allusions to *His Majesty's colonies* predominated in the early period but eventually gave way to *the American colonies*. What is especially important, says Merritt, is that these semantic changes occurred before actual political separation.[13] "Our response to the world is to make a text about it," says James Boyd White, and so changes in rhetorical behavior often preview fundamental political changes.[14] "The surest sign that a group or society has entered into the self-conscious possession of a new concept," says Quentin Skinner, "is that a corresponding vocabulary will be developed."[15]

Throughout this book we will use keywords as a kind of cultural barometer. In doing so, we follow in a line of productive scholarship. Richard Anderson has shown, for example, how the language of the streets quickly infiltrated the discourse of post-Soviet Russians, thereby signaling that both a political and a rhetorical revolution had taken place.[16] Nancy Fraser and Linda Gordon have tracked the concept of *dependency*, observing that it was originally associated with the saintly traditions of church and family but, as market economies developed, became linked to weakness and do-nothingness.[17] Daniel Rodgers notes that Americans now make sharp distinctions between *communities* and *special interests* even though these terms have a common root. It is politics, not linguistics, says Rodgers, that sanctifies the former and vilifies the latter.[18] Along these same lines, political strategist Frank Luntz observes that Republicans have completely (and unwisely, in his opinion) ceded ownership of *compassion* to the Democrats even though that concept occupies a hallowed place in the Christian lexicon (advice that George W. Bush quickly adopted).

Political Keywords will focus on functional terms, not abstract concepts, and that makes it different from previous studies. Celeste Condit and John Lucaites, for example, have done an exhaustive study of the genealogy of *equality*, finding that at various points in American history it has been used both by proponents and opponents of affirmative action.[19] This is not completely surprising, says Daniel Rodgers, since "large" words like *equality* are extraordinarily versatile for those outside the power structure. "The keywords of American politics," he says, "were words for the open air. From the Revolution on, American political writers knew the imperative of words big enough to mobilize the broad mass of citizens upon which their experiment in a kingless government depended."[20]

Perhaps because these words are so large, Americans have fought over them from the beginning. The American dialogue has largely been one about *rights*—how widely can they be disbursed? when is disbursing them dangerous?—and responsibility—to whom is it owed? how can it be properly manifested? Schoolchildren, churches, legislatures, the Veterans of Foreign Wars, the ACLU, and others debate these questions constantly, proving that a culture becomes a culture when it restricts its disagreements to a narrow range of concepts. The American people are one such people.

WORDS AS ANSWERS

Words are important because even though they are completely arbitrary, people tend to overlook their arbitrariness. Most people, that is, stand by their words, taking umbrage when their name is mispronounced even though their name is merely a random set of phonemes and morphemes. What people call their groups is also important to them, and it is also fabricated. As Dorothy Noyes observes, words like *folk, nation,* and even *race* are neither static nor genetically constituted.[21] What a group is—and who is part of that group—can change radically over time. Groups are "social imaginaries," says Noyes. Whether a person calls himself a Southie, a Bostonian, a Bay Stater, a New Englander, an Easterner, or an American is largely a result of socioemotional ties. The more cosmopolitan a person is, the broader will be that person's referents.

Each keyword contains a network of associations, calling up different memories and imaginings.[22] The *Southie,* for example, is Irish; the *Bostonian* a Red Sox fan. The *New Englander* is rather staid; the *American* energetic. Each label tells its own story. Each opens up a different emotional domain. The *Southie,* for example, will never vote Republican; the *Bostonian* may well do so. As Thomas McLaughlin says, "Using a term commits you to a set of values and strategies that it has developed over the history of its use. It is possible to use that term in a new way, but it is not possible to escape the term's past."[23]

Tracking keywords is therefore important for several reasons. A group's preferred words expose its distinct psychological makeup—its fears, anxieties, and sources of excitement. Keywords also reveal latent assumptions. Uwe Poerksen notes, for instance, that the term *information* had an interesting cultural history as it passed from the schoolhouse ("becoming informed") through science ("information units") and into the world of commodities ("information bank"). Popular terms like this become "an inspirational text," says Poerksen, "the sound alone fascinates."[24] Mike Emmison tells a similar story about *economy.* Over time, says Emmison, politicians have made it seem as if economic forces lie beyond state control, as if the economy is "on no one's side." As a result, "unpopular political decisions and policies can be taken and justified whilst avoiding the charge of class- or self-interest," thereby insulating politicians from the very bills they have passed.[25]

Over time, keywords pick up different referents and sometimes contradict their origins. Thus, a word itself may continue to be spelled in the same way, thereby giving it a "nominal continuity," but the vitality of language ensures that "every kind of extension, variation, and transfer" are brought to bear on that word over time.[26] As a result, dictionaries are useless for studying keywords because their nuances never stand still. A term like *middle class,* for example, seems to designate the middle third of the population, but surveys show that as many as 80 percent of the American people feel included in its embrace. *Middle class* has lost its economic meaning and now signals a socially desirable ordinariness, an ordinariness that lets wealthy Americans and those barely above the poverty level feel a certain kinship. Odd as that may seem, it makes sense in a mottled nation like the United States where Christians and Jews, Anglos and Hispanics, and straights and gays instinctively look for a place of purchase, a middle ground.

Throughout this book, then, we will focus on both the continuities and discontinuities of keywords. In doing so we will be indebted to the work of Raymond Williams. But Williams was only marginally interested in practical politics (our special focus here) even though he was very much interested in cultural politics. Williams tells his story this way: Having returned from serving in the military during World War II, he arrived on the Cambridge campus only to feel socially disconnected. He spoke the same language, of course, but his language meant something different to him than it did to his Cambridge classmates. Perhaps it was because he was Welsh, perhaps because he was from the working class, perhaps because he had just served in an artillery regiment. Whatever the reason, his English was not their English.

With that as his starting point, Williams began a lifelong study of the "deep politics" undergirding language practices, especially literary practices. Writing at that same time in the United States was Kenneth Burke. Burke was a polymath, a restless intellectual who transcended all disciplinary boundaries and who managed during the course of his career to put over six million words in print in fourteen books and hundreds of essays, lectures, poems, stories, and even a modest novel. Like Williams, Burke was attracted to Marxian thinking but, unlike Williams, he told other tales as well. Burke was especially interested in the power of language, in the hierarchies and counter-hierarchies it superintended, in the myths it nurtured and made popular. Like Williams, Burke was affected by World War II. One of his most brilliant essays deconstructed what he called "the rhetoric of Hitler's battle," showing how the führer used primal strategies to galvanize his fellow Germans.

But unlike Williams, Burke took a *rhetorical* approach to language, the approach to be adopted here. That is, Burke was more interested in the specific situations in which people found themselves. He examined how newspaper journalism became capitalist propaganda; how Shakespeare appealed to the everyday tastes of theatergoers; how religious dramaturgy set people up for feelings of guilt and redemption; how Franklin Roosevelt cozied up to big business even while excoriating them. When Burke looked at language he did not find ideology as much as he found appeals aimed at specific people with specific susceptibilities. Political rhetoric involves the "dancing of an attitude," said Burke, a playful attempt to inveigle oneself in the life of another. Using that perspective, Burke showed how Hitler used German history, German religion, German art, German folklore, German iconography, and German mythology to create the *volk* needed to do his bidding. Some may call politics hypocritical, said Burke, but it is better to think of it as a "prayerful use of language" designed "to sharpen up the pointless and blunt the too sharply pointed."[27] To look at keywords from Burke's perspective is therefore to examine the interpretive pressure they place on audiences. For Burke, politics must be dramatized to have suasive power.

Our work in this book has a third debt to pay as well—to political scientist Harold Lasswell. Lasswell was born five years after Burke (in 1902) and, like Burke, was interested in the psychodrama of politics. Like both Burke and Williams, Lasswell was deeply affected by his wartime experiences, in his case as director of war communications research at the Library of Congress from 1939 to 1945. But unlike them, Lasswell was a preeminent social scientist (especially a content analyst) who did his research by creating analytical templates and then systematically applying them to a large set of texts. Burke was also interested in discovering textual patterns (he called them "proportions"), but Lasswell did two things Burke would never have done: (1) He trained coders to analyze texts in the same way each time (thereby increasing the reliability of his research), and (2) he calibrated how often certain linguistic patterns were found in the corpus under study. Lasswell's masterwork, *Language of Politics: Studies in Quantitative Semantics,* is a fine example of what can be learned by turning words into numbers and back again.

Political Keywords is thus indebted to Raymond Williams' constructs, to Kenneth Burke's perspective, and to Harold Lasswell's methodology. This is an uncommon trinity, but together they will guide our audit of contemporary American discourse. Content analysis makes gathering data fairly easy, but interpreting those data is hard. Sometimes, for example, a president's personal background will best explain why he said what he said, while at other times one must factor in the influence of the working press or the chattering classes in Washington. At still other times cultural forces, especially mass entertainment, influence a speaker, as can the political calendar, the current geopolitical situation, the political rituals of the day, and the lobby groups that constantly posture and shout. All these forces, alone and collectively, affect what politicians say and why.

"To understand the political life of a community," says William Connolly, "one must understand the conceptual system within which that life moves."[28] Language inevitably informs these conceptual systems, but language also poses questions for us. For example, why did Elvin Lim find that references to *fate* have become less frequent in presidential speech during the last hundred years while references to *reform* have gone steadily upward?[29] Why does Paul Zernicke report that sitting chief executives refer to the *presidency* more often when confronted with crisis and controversy?[30] And why does Amy Pierce report that political *mandates* are claimed by presidential victors regardless of their level of victory; and why is that even truer for those who receive *less than* 50 percent of the vote?[31] Clearly, political keywords tell a complicated story. We shall try to unravel some of those complexities here.

WORDS AS SIGNALS

No book can do everything, and this book is no different. We focus here on only eight keywords and restrict ourselves to the last fifty years of American politics. The words we have chosen are quite ordinary ones, words like *government, party,* and *media,* because we wanted to get as close as possible to everyday politics. We could also have focused on *Congress* or the *Supreme*

Court, but that would have moved us in a more bureaucratic direction. We could have studied the great concepts of democracy—*freedom, justice,* and *revolution*—but we have not done so for two reasons: (1) Numerous scholars have already investigated such matters, and (2) everyday words often have more influence than these lofty abstractions. The keywords we have chosen are plain ones, words so taken for granted that they seem devoid of mystery. Still, we will look for mysteries here.

Our methodology will differ a bit from chapter to chapter, but our overall goal will not: to provide quantitative assessments of which keywords are used and why. The texts to be examined include campaign speeches, newspaper coverage, civics textbooks, scholarly book titles, presidential pronouncements, congressional hearings, and popular magazines. During the last ten years these materials have been entered into computerized databases at the University of Texas that now contain some twenty-five thousand texts. Chapters 2 and 3 have used the Titles Database; chapters 7 through 9 used the Presidential Tokens Database; and the remaining chapters have used a combination of the American Freedom Library Database[32] and the Campaign Mapping Project database (which contains a variety of speeches, ads, debates, news coverage, and letters to the editor from 1948 to 2000).[33] Our work proceeded by searching for the relevant keywords and then noting the source, date, authorship, and circumstances surrounding the text in question. In most cases the passage bracketing the keyword was then subjected to various coding procedures (to be detailed in subsequent chapters) to account for its contextual features.[34]

Content analysis lets the researcher develop subtle understanding of verbal behavior, but it cannot determine its effects. Other scholars using other methods are better equipped to do that. Here, we do what content analysts do best: take note of unusual linguistic frequencies and explain why those patterns have developed. In that sense, content analysis is rather like molecular pharmacology: It cannot alone determine which drug works best (only experimentation can do that), but it can record with great precision the blood chemistry resulting from particular drug regimens. Molecular analysis, that is, is also part of science—the science of description.

Our story begins with *politics* itself. Unit 1 describes how the very concept of politics is being transformed in the academy. For example, scholars have moved from studying the "politics of Churchill" to the "politics of the family" as various disciplines appropriate that concept to fit new social realities. In popular culture we now hear phrases like "gender politics," "identity politics," and even the "politics of baseball." But what do these new appropriations do to our understanding of traditional politics? If a concept comes to mean everything does it eventually come to mean nothing? Or does the migration of *politics* from the institutional to the cultural realm mean that more emancipatory social relations will soon follow?

This unit draws on a voluminous database of some four thousand book and article titles to track such dispersions of meaning. Chapter 2 explains

how during the last thirty years politics has moved well beyond the institutional realm as authors have opened up entirely new fields of study. Topics
such as religion, education, and health barely registered as political issues in
the 1950s but today are implicated in nearly 20 percent of our contemporary
discussions. In addition, authors are shedding new light on long-ignored
issues and marginalized peoples. But what has happened to the State during
this age of political expansion? Is it still visible? still powerful? When the personal becomes political, what does that imply for traditional understandings
of civic participation and political knowledge?

Chapter 3 follows up by examining the context within which *politics* is discussed. It assumes that phrases like "the politics of Woodrow Wilson" or
"the politics of Great Britain" are plain enough, but that things get strange
when politics goes metaphorical. By carefully tracking the "families of
images" used in book and article titles, we discover both martial and communal metaphors ("the politics of boxing" versus "the politics of suburbia"),
images of growth and decline ("the politics of modernism" versus "the politics of aging"), of domesticity and freedom ("the politics of cooking" versus
"the politics of exploration"), and of magnitude and depletion ("the politics
of Westward expansion" versus "the politics of bankruptcy"). The surprising thing, however, is that even though the political domain has increased
dramatically in recent years, these metaphorical patterns stay constant. As it
turns out, it makes little difference whether authors hail from diplomatic
studies or cultural studies, sociology or literature. The assumptions they
make about politics are remarkably alike. What does that tell us about the
world of political relations? about the limits of human imagination? about
the durability of raw political forces? Chapter 3 addresses these questions.

Unit 2 focuses on the three dominant forces of modern politics—*government,* the *mass media,* and the *people*—entities that are constantly in dialogue
with one another. The mass media, for example, no longer just report what
government does but also put pressure on the nation's leaders. In response,
the latter hires a phalanx of crafty aides to "get out the story" before it can
even be imagined by White House reporters. Citizens take all of this in—via
the web, via talk radio, via cable television—and react with a kaleidoscope
of emotions ranging from cosmic outrage to sheer, unadulterated boredom.
Somehow, out of this dialogue a democracy is fashioned.

Chapter 4 acknowledges that the American people have always had an
uncertain relationship with government. Numerous observers have argued,
for example, that the United States is unique because it lacked a recognizable
center of political life from the beginning. The Constitution came along to
make government functional, but public trust proved harder to generate,
which may be why John Adams wistfully hoped that Americans would form
"an unshaken attachment" to their government. Has Adams' wish been fulfilled? Has government become a lovable thing? If not, it is not for want of
trying. During the past fifty years American presidents have mentioned *government* continually, making it the fifty-third most commonly used word in

American politics, a frequency rivaling such common tokens as *at, an,* or *these*. But what do presidents say when saying such things?

This chapter examines governmental references contained in campaign speeches, inaugural addresses, and State of the Union messages during the last fifty years. We examine the ascribed relationships people have with their government, the defenders and opponents of governmental activity, the alleged effectiveness of governmental practices, and the qualities associated with ideal governance. Generally speaking, we find that rhetoric and reality move in opposite directions. We find, for example, that even though the budget of the federal government (as a proportion of GDP) has steadily declined, the rhetorical focus on government has only increased. We find, too, that those who run the government (e.g., campaign incumbents) rarely mention it, while challengers speak of government constantly. But our most important finding is that *politicians themselves* are more than eager to detail the inadequacies of government. This approach lets them cozy up to a cynical electorate at campaign time, but what are the long-term effects of such practices? Are politicians ensuring that popular governance cannot stay popular for very long? This is neither a simple nor an unimportant question.

Perhaps because they have become increasingly influential, the mass media are also dependable whipping boys in American politics. When politicians are in trouble these days, they often "run against the media" to regain electoral support. But what do reporters say about their own industry? Do they see themselves as part of the political system or distinct from it? What special obligations do they accept, what licenses do they cherish?

To answer such questions, we searched for references to *the media* and *the press* in eight thousand articles published in eight major newspapers during presidential general campaigns from 1948 to 2000. Over four thousand such occurrences were found and over six hundred coded (via stratified random sampling techniques). Not surprisingly, these references increased over time, perhaps paralleling the media's growing economic and political clout. While authors like Thomas Patterson have noted that the media's voice has become increasingly dominant over time (as shown, for example, by the decreasing sound bites accorded government officials in nightly newscasts), we find a more complex pattern.[35] Yes, the media do focus more on their own industry but they do so by quoting others, making the press something of a bashful giant. But they also succeed in making campaign coverage itself a standard trope of political reportage. Not surprisingly, Republicans are especially media-phobic, a malady dutifully reported in the nation's press. This keeps alive the old chestnut of "media bias," a chestnut lacking reliable scientific evidence. In any event, the Fourth Estate is no longer an estate apart but one drawn inexorably into the very center of American politics.

Also at the center of politics are the *people*. But who are they, really? For some observers, that is an impertinent question. The American people are hardly one entity, they will claim, since Americans are demographically diverse, religiously unsettled, and politically conflicted. No nation as complex as the United States, they will argue, can ever be reduced to a simple phrase, and, if it could, that phrase would be philosophically bankrupt. And yet politicians constantly make allusions to the *people,* whoever they might be. "The people are with me on this," says the campaigner, as if trying to describe and change the electorate simultaneously.

Chapter 6 shows that these language forms become especially popular during moments of national crisis. Using transcripts of remarks made by members of the U.S. House of Representatives, we analyzed collective tokens used during the Clinton impeachment proceedings and after the September 11 terrorist attacks. Both sets of remarks were compared to a large database of normative addresses to discover how the people were "hailed" during turbulent moments.

We find that not all crises are alike. House members spoke quite differently on these two occasions, with the people's emotional strength being singled out after September 11 versus their logical qualities during impeachment. Too, the political parties responded differently to the events but, surprisingly, completely switched roles between impeachment and September 11. But perhaps our most important finding is that the American people are ultimately seen as quite functional. They have their beliefs and values, yes, but they mostly want business to be business. American crisis rhetoric is thus more sober than emotional, as if merely reflecting on the *people* reminds politicians that rhetorical excess must be avoided. In these and other ways, American pragmatism continues to be reinscribed into the political life of the nation.

Unit 3 presents several different examinations of how the *president* is featured in political discourse. It seemed logical to focus on the chief executive since the presidency has always been the centerpiece of U.S. scholarship and gets so much media attention as well. But we also look here at how presidents themselves refer to their predecessors in office. Our timeline is a rich one: All presidential addresses from Harry Truman through Bill Clinton have been examined for allusions. We also look at a large collection of eighth-grade and high school civics textbooks, as well as references to the chief executive in *Time* magazine between 1945 and the present. The result is a broad-based study of the contours of American politics.

Chapter 7 shows how central the *president* has become in civics education, with textbooks consistently (and increasingly) using presidential allusions to instill basic values in the nation's youth. The "textbook president" inscribes a person-centered model of governance, one that features majestic incumbents taking heroic action. Textbook writers seem unable to think of the nation apart from those who govern it, sometimes overlooking abiding principles, canonical documents, international compacts, administrative units of government, and the vicissitudes of time, circumstance, and geography. The sheer number of presidential allusions suggests as much. But what are the consequences of a personalized view of governance? Can a society unaccustomed to thinking beyond its leaders stay in touch with its principles?

Worse, do such patterns ultimately lead to voter alienation and a sense of inefficacy? After all, if the president is the end-all and be-all of politics, what is left for the citizen to do?

Chapter 8 illustrates what happens when the mass media—exemplified by *Time* magazine—reflects on the presidency. Rather surprisingly, they adopt a centrist view of governance by emphasizing the transient nature of incumbency and, hence, the underlying stability of American political systems. The magazine also features presidential personalities, thereby circumnavigating troublesome philosophical and ideational matters.

Chapter 9 concludes our study of presidential allusions by looking more closely at their strategic uses. We find, for example, an insulating function being served when Ronald Reagan speaks at a White House luncheon celebrating FDR's centennial birthday, or when Gerald Ford dedicates a statue to Harry S. Truman. Such events let the chief executive cast himself and his programs as part of a continuous story, a natural outgrowth of processes long since set in motion. In short, while innocent in appearance, presidential tokens can become powerful signals of political circumstance, telling us which policies are popular and which are challenged in the electoral marketplace. Shakespeare may have had Hamlet decry, "Words, words, words," but, in politics, words are sometimes all there is.

Given how expensive and noisy elections have become, it is only fitting that we conclude our discussion of keywords by examining their rhetoric. If we are to believe contemporary scholarship, a "continuing campaign" has emerged in the United States, with presidents now plotting their second administration even while taking the oath of office for their first. So, for example, campaign guru Karl Rove became a fixture in the Oval Office from the very start of George W. Bush's presidency, with some wags suggesting that no policy decision or legislative effort was made by Bush without first calculating its impact on his reelection campaign. The Clinton administration operated little differently, which is why media specialists now outnumber policy specialists in the White House by two to one.

We will take three very different looks at the campaign, with chapter 10 being the most traditional. There we explore a distinctively American ambivalence about political partisanship, examining over a thousand references to *party* found in the remarks of political candidates and journalists. We key especially on what parties have come to mean in the United States, finding that such references have decreased over time but not quite in the way political scientist Martin Wattenberg might have predicted (who has described the American people's increasing antipathy for political parties).[36] Presidential candidates have indeed curtailed their use of such tokens, generally "runing away from the party" during the general election. The result is the modern, celebrity-oriented campaign. Journalists, too, have decreased their use of such tokens but not as much as have the candidates. While party ID may no longer be the useful "cognitive shortcut" it once was for voters, the media keep the concept alive, even as citizens themselves fall in love with the mythical *independent*. Our data show a rhetorical resurgence of the *party* since 1980, perhaps suggesting that parties are the constants and candidates the variables. Parties endure because they write checks but also because they simplify a world—politics—that is in constant need of simplifying. There are rhetorical attractions in that.

Chapter 11 focuses on the promises made by politicians. Given the popular disgust with politics these days, that may seem an unusually vacuous topic. But the story of political promises is an interesting one and its questions are compelling: When do candidates make promises, and why do they think they will be effective? Which candidates—challengers or incumbents, Democrats or Republicans, winners or losers—make the most promises? What sorts of promises do they make, and how reasonable (or preposterous) are they? We found over six hundred such promises in the Campaign Mapping Project database and examined them for positive or negative tone, breadth of detail, relative practicality, and policy focus (domestic or foreign). Republicans, as it turns out, were more taken with promises than Democrats, a finding that flies in the face of popular stereotypes. In addition, promises were used by candidates to put pressure on the frontrunner, to cope with especially stressful campaign events, to draw attention to the nonincumbent candidate, and to inject a note of optimism into the campaign. Promises have a special ability to break through the campaign noise. In what ways and to what ends is the story of chapter 11.

Chapter 12 focuses on an unusual, but increasingly ubiquitous, facet of the modern campaign—the campaign *consultant*. The assumption here is that media descriptions of the political worker eerily parallel people's overall feelings about the political system. By analyzing a large body of contemporary press coverage, we show how the consultant has become a receptacle for the nation's fears and hopes as well as its ambivalence about campaign politics. People's feelings about the consultant affect their reactions to political events and their notions of who is running the campaign and, ultimately, of who controls power in the United States. We find that references to consultants have increased five-fold in the last fifty years, which may explain why so many voters now feel politically dispossessed. Also, news coverage blends strategic discussions with policy discussions, thereby making politics seem less innocent than in times past. The *consultant* token also gives campaign reporting an intimate, personal feeling, thereby contributing to the drama (but also the psychic distance) of the campaign. In a variety of ways, then, the consultant has become the synecdoche for all of politics.

Political Keywords covers a lot of ground, but it has a single purpose: to show how language tracks broader political and cultural developments. Although linguistic analyses have their limitations (they can be too impressionistic, too contorted, too ideological), they feature data that are too often ignored. For that reason alone they are valuable. We will argue here that to disregard words, even political words, is unwise because people take their cues from one another and because those cues are often fashioned from language. Keywords are with us from dawn to dusk, from cradle to grave. We ignore them at our peril.

CONCLUSION

Political Keywords attempts to go broad and deep simultaneously to make sense of what Americans say. We track only a few of the available keywords but enough to show that language is inextricably bound up with the democratic enterprise. Our root assumption is that political language is both a watch and a compass. It tells us what time it is (i.e., what forces are operating at a given moment, what makes today different from yesterday) as well as where we are (i.e., how our society differs from that of others). Tracking political keywords is therefore a kind of cultural anthropology, but it is a practical business as well. Candidates sometimes win or lose campaigns because of how they speak. If that were not so, $50 million would not be spent on the crafting of words during presidential elections. Candidates make visual images, too, but it is the words—the words—that often trip them up or raise them to the heights.

Tracking a polity's words can be revealing. Raymond Gozzi reports, for example, that over 45 percent of the new words introduced into the American lexicon in the last twenty-five years were technological in nature, a fact that has clear implications for political affairs. Words produce "memories" in us, says Gozzi, and these memories affect how we process each day's events.[37] When words become more technological—words like *environmental degradation, Treasury benchmark,* and *broadband connection*—our political discussions change (as do the relevant lobbyists). But politics continues to be politics because its traditional words—the words focused on in this book—also have their day in the sun. We will try not to overstate their influence here, but we will also not shy away from the questions they prompt and the answers they provide. Politics depends on many things, one of which is language. And so this book is a paean to political words.

NOTES

1. R. Weaver, *The Ethics of Rhetoric* (Chicago: H. Regnery Co., 1953).

2. "Fighting the War of Words," *Time,* April 28, 3003, 24.

3. J. Scanlon, "Douglass Women Then and Now," *Rutgers Focus,* http://uc. rutgers.edu/focus/index.phtml?Article-ID=830 (May 12, 2003). This essay reports the research of Rutgers sociologist Roberta Sigel and her colleagues.

4. J. Brainard, "Some NIH Officials Advise Researchers to Avoid Certain Words in Applications for AIDS Projects, Reports Say," *Chronicle of Higher Education,* http://chronicle.com.daily/2003/04/2003042101n.htm (April 21, 2003).

5. R. W. Emerson, "Essay Eight: Nominalist and Realist," in *Ralph Waldo Emerson: Essays, Second Series* (New York: Vintage Books, 1844, 1990), 105.

6. W. E. Connolly, *The Terms of Political Discourse* (Lexington, MA: D. C. Heath, 1974), 186.

7. Ibid., 197.

8. R. Hanson, *The Democratic Imagination in America: Conversations with Our Past* (Princeton, NJ: Princeton University Press, 1985), 15.

9. Ibid., 59.

10. J. Farr, "Understanding Conceptual Change Politically," in *Political Innovation and Conceptual Change*, ed. T. Ball, J. Farr, and R. L. Hanson (Cambridge: Cambridge University Press, 1989), 38.

11. R. Lakoff, *The Language War* (Berkeley: University of California Press, 2000), 40.

12. F. A. Beer, *Meanings of War and Peace* (College Station: Texas A&M University Press, 2001), 24, 46, 57.

13. R. Merritt, *Symbols of American Community, 1735–1775* (New Haven, CT: Yale University Press, 1966).

14. J. B. White, *When Words Lose Their Meaning: Constitutions and Reconstitutions of Language, Character, and Community* (Chicago: University of Chicago Press, 1984), 4.

15. Q. Skinner, "Language and Political Change," in *Political Innovation and Conceptual Change*, ed. T. Ball, J. Farr, and R. L. Hanson (Cambridge: Cambridge University Press, 1989), 8.

16. R. Anderson, " 'Look at All Those Nouns in a Row': Authoritarianism, Democracy, and the Iconicity of Political Russian," *Political Communication*, 13 (1996): 145–64.

17. N. Fraser and L. Gordon, "A Genealogy of *Dependency:* Tracing a Keyword of the U.S. Welfare State," *Signs: A Journal of Women in Culture and Society*, 19 (1994): 309–36.

18. D. Rodgers, *Contested Truths: Keywords in American Politics Since Independence* (New York: Basic Books, 1987), 181.

19. C. M. Condit and J. L. Lucaites, *Crafting Equality: America's Anglo-African Word* (Chicago: University of Chicago Press, 1993).

20. Rodgers, *Contested Truths*, 42–43.

21. D. Noyes, "Group," in "Common Ground: Keywords for the Study of Expressive Culture," special issue, *Journal of American Folklore*, 108 (1995): 449–78.

22. Farr, "Understanding Conceptual Change," 38.

23. T. McLaughlin, "Introduction," in *Critical Terms for Literary Study*, ed. F. Lentricchia and T. McLaughlin (Chicago: University of Chicago Press, 1990), 4.

24. U. Poerksen, *Plastic Words: The Tyranny of Modular Language* (University Park: Penn State University Press, 1995), 39.

25. M. Emmison, "'The Economy': Its Emergence in Media Discourse," in *Language, Image, and Media*, ed. H. Davis and P. Walton (New York: St. Martin's, 1983), 154.

26. R. Williams, *Keywords: A Vocabulary of Culture and Society* (New York: Oxford University Press, 1985), 21.

27. K. Burke, *A Grammar of Motives* (Cleveland: World Publishing Co., 1962), 393.

28. Connolly, *Terms of Political Discourse*, 39.

29. E. T. Lim, "Five Trends in Presidential Rhetoric: An Analysis of Rhetoric from George Washington to Bill Clinton," *Presidential Studies Quarterly*, 32 (2002): 328–67.

30. P. H. Zernicke, "Presidential Roles and Rhetoric," *Presidential Studies Quarterly*, 7 (1990): 231–45.

31. A. J. Pierce, "The People Have Spoken: The Rhetoric of Mandates in Twentieth Century Presidential Victory Speeches," paper presented at the annual convention of the International Communication Association, Washington, DC, May 2001.

32. For further information see the American Freedom Library's website, http://www.nccs.net/afl.html (May 21, 2003).

33. For further information, see R. P. Hart, *Campaign Talk: Why Elections Are Good for Us* (Princeton, NJ: Princeton University Press, 2000), 30–34.

34. Specifically, content analysis is a technique that allows researchers to classify items objectively and systematically according to explicit rules and criteria. This method of research ranks high on external validity (i.e., the findings are generalizable to other populations or social settings) but is low on internal validity since it does not result in strong causal links being established among the variables tested. For more on this matter, see K. Krippendorff, *Content Analysis: An Introduction to Its Methodology* (Newbury Park, CA: Sage, 1980).

Key considerations in any content analysis are the sample, unit of analysis, and the reliability and validity of the coding scheme (see K. Neuendorf, *The Content Analysis Guidebook* [Newbury Park, CA: Sage, 2001]). There are strengths and weaknesses to all samples, and our project is no exception. We used a number of different datasets here, and while that creates problems of comparability it also permits triangulation among different sorts of public discourse, thereby leading to broad, cultural insights. Using multiple datasets also allowed us to (1) overcome the potential weaknesses of any one of them, (2) use the findings about one corpus (e.g., speeches) to prompt questions about another (e.g, news coverage), and (3) situate the meanings of keywords in a richer political context.

To accommodate the unique nature of each keyword and the specialized genre studied, the units of analysis and coding schema also shift from chapter to chapter. For additional information on the content analytic schemas used, please see the referring footnotes in each chapter.

35. T. Patterson, *Out of Order* (New York: Alfred A. Knopf, 1993).

36. M. P. Wattenberg, *The Decline of American Political Parties: 1952–1994* (Cambridge, MA: Harvard University Press, 1996).

37. R. Gozzi, *New Words and a Changing American Culture* (Columbia: University of South Carolina Press, 1990); see especially 1–7.

UNIT 1

THE LANGUAGE OF POLITICS

There was no shortage of **politics** during the presidential campaign of 2004. Even before the fall election, the year was marked by a raft of best-sellers. Ron Suskind's *The Price of Loyalty* told the story of former Treasury Secretary Paul O'Neill's sad experience in George W. Bush's administration; another former Bushie, counter-terrorism advisor Richard Clarke, wrote a tell-all book (*Against All Enemies*) that also attacked his old boss. As if to balance things, Bush's on-again, off-again advisor, Karen Hughes, penned *Ten Minutes from Normal,* a book that praised both Bush and suburban country kitchens.

Politics consumed everything in 2004: The press covered electoral politics, of course, but it also described student politics, literary politics, family politics, protest politics, voodoo politics, and even hip-hop politics. The first American political reality show debuted in 2004: *American Candidate* featured ordinary citizens "competing" for the highest office in the land. The show, originally scheduled to air on Rupert Murdoch's Fx network in January 2004, was almost undone by pesky campaign finance laws, but a watered-down version ran on Showtime in the summer of 2004.

Americans become consumed with politics every four years, but few stop to consider what the term means. As we will see in this unit, politics often resides in the eye of the beholder. For the ancient Greeks, it was seen as the science of the city—how a democratic people gets its work done. Others think of politics as the field of human boundaries—how they are defined, where they are drawn, how they are enforced.[1] Some writers treat politics as a network of social hierarchies (who is in charge of whom), while others think of it as the story of human preferences (who wants what). Some describe politics as the science of information management (who knows what),[2] while others treat it as the business of human associations (who talks to whom). As if to settle the confusion, the *Urban Dictionary* declares that politics comes from the Greek root *poly,* meaning "many," and *tics,* which are, of course, bloodsucking parasites.[3]

Unit 1 takes these matters of definition seriously by reporting on how the term politics has been used in recent years. It does so by analyzing some five thousand book and article titles, focusing on how politics has acquired so many meanings. Books are a good source for such an effort because they are written for wide audiences and often become fodder for our conversations with others. We will see here that politics has become an increasingly popular concept during the last thirty years. Today, poets and artists talk as much about politics as do historians and economists, although they often refer to quite different realities when doing so. We will see that some authors hold to a "fundamentalist" understanding of politics (it means one and only one thing), while others use the term to describe practically everything—how we dress, what we buy, how we speak, where we travel. As one writer observes, politics is now like "spores in the air."[4]

We will also see, however, that even though politics has become atmospheric, it still retains certain inherent meanings no matter who uses the term or for what reason. Whether speaking of the politics of Finland or the politics of film, writers return time and again to a stable set of meanings. It is as if the term is controlling the writers who use it rather than they controlling it. These writers often do not talk to one another and rarely read each other's books, and yet they still share an understanding of what makes the world political even though they, themselves, probably could not articulate their underlying assumptions. As we will see throughout this book, keywords play the tune to which all of us dance. We begin our waltz with politics itself.

NOTES

1. R. Rieben, "The Passion of Liberty: Part One—The Soul of Politics," http://www.strike-the-root.com/4/rieben/rieben3.html (April 21, 2004).

2. P. A. Strassmann, "The Politics of Information Management: Policy Guidelines," http://www.infoeconomics.com/info-politics.php (April 21, 2004)

3. *The Urban Dictionary*, http://www.urbandictionary.com (April 21, 2004).

4. R. Tawa, "Politics Sells Books, Left and Right," *Newsday*, http://www.newsday.com (April 20, 2004).

2

Whither *Politics?*
An Evolving Construct

This book focuses on the words we make and the words that make us. One of those words is *politics* itself. When everyday people use that term, they typically do so unconsciously, confidently expecting others to conjure up similar images—of the mayor and the city council, of incessant campaign commercials, of the chief executive giving a speech from the Oval Office. Little seems complicated here. A moment's reflection, though, opens up politics to a kaleidoscope of meanings, especially when we focus on its function. Samuel Johnson, for example, has said that "Politics are now nothing more than a means of rising in the world," while Ambrose Bierce was more acidic when declaring politics "a strife of interests masquerading as a contest of principles." Former Canadian Prime Minister Lester Pearson provided a world-weary definition—"Politics is the skilled use of blunt objects"—while the French essayist Paul Valéry turned ideological: "Politics is the art of preventing people from taking part in affairs which properly concern them." For anyone who has studied politics carefully, who has observed both its possibilities and its difficulties, Max Weber provides the most trenchant definition: "Politics is a strong and slow boring of hard boards."[1]

As we see here, to describe politics is to take a position on it. Johnson connects politics with personal ambition, Valéry to class warfare. Pearson and Weber are entirely functional while Bierce denounces politics even when defining it. As with all words, people bring their entire beings to *politics* when discussing it. Lately, however, that term has become even more complicated, and therein lies an interesting story. We trace that story here by studying, in essence, the politics of politics. This is no mere semantic exercise. Our definitions of politics determine who gets power and who does not, who is included in the public dialogue and who remains silent. When the nonvoter declares "I'm not interested in that; it's only politics," he or she seals off an enormous part of the world. It takes little reflection to determine, for example, that politics determines where our children go to school, what textbooks they read, the lunch they will have (or be denied), and the quality of the teachers who teach them. Even in the pristine sanctity of the grade-school schoolroom, politics abides, which is why PTA meetings often get stormy and why superintendents of schools are sometimes handed their heads when test scores go down. To define politics too narrowly is to let other people—people we do not know, people whose motives may be malignant—determine what happens to us.

Because of such fears, the domain of politics has expanded considerably over the years. As Maurizio Viroli notes, thinkers in the thirteenth century viewed politics as "the art of ruling a republic or a kingdom according to justice and reason." By the end of the sixteenth century, however, politics came to be understood as "knowledge of the means of preserving and enlarging a state."[2] This was a profound change for these pre-Enlightenment Europeans, the kind of reconceptualization that created social, political, and psychological changes as well. No longer were kings and courtiers seen as the sole sources of political power. When nation-states began replacing duchies, communication was suddenly bidirectional; "public opinion" became a potent social force; printed documents began to be archived for legal and institutional reasons; state expenditures came under greater scrutiny; taxpayers gained a voice. This did not happen all at once, and none of it happened without turmoil. But slowly, irresistibly, politics became visible. That visibility made clear who did what to whom and why. It also made leaders accountable. Even today, no matter whether a State is ruled by democrats or socialists, clerics or tribalists, uneasy lies the head that wears the crown.

To think of the modern state, then, is to think of a place besotted with politics. Even being born is a proto-political act: We are named and footprinted and then registered in City Hall. Eating is a political act, and so we have the Department of Agriculture to feed us and the Food and Drug Administration to feed us safely. Breathing is a political act, and so the Environmental Protection Agency watches over us. Dying is a political act, and so our town mortuaries are inspected annually. Politics envelops us from cradle to grave.

Because "everything we do is rooted in a contestable point of origin," says Stanley Fish, "and since the realm of the contestable is the realm of politics, everything is political" in a certain sense.[3] So, for example, some feminists now declare the family rather than the state to be the "primary site of power relations."[4] "Definitions of politics are themselves political," says Vicky Randall, and so we must examine power wherever we find it lest it be left to its own, clandestine devices.[5]

But wait! says Russell Jacoby. To have too broad a definition of politics is to fail to sort the wheat from the chaff, the powerful from the marginal. In modern writings, says Jacoby, "The traditional arena of politics—affairs of government and the state—has grown to include all of life and culture." Not only is the personal political, says Jacoby, but now everything is. What is wrong with that? "The difficulty," Jacoby warns, "is that when everything is political, nothing is."[6] To overpoliticize the world, Jacoby fears, is to depoliticize it. To look for politics everywhere is to make it so atmospheric that it can no longer be seen at all. Jacoby is concerned that too broad a definition of politics will turn political analysts into armchair activists and nothing more. "This notion of bottomless intellectual dismantling of oppressive structures can stultify political action," says Leslie Wahl Rabine, turning attention away from the real forces affecting real people in the real world.[7]

This chapter tracks this story of definitions. It does so by focusing on book titles, a curious project indeed. Book titles, after all, cause no social movements to be launched or legislation to be written. Books are sedentary. As Eric Hoffer observes, men-of-words (authors, clerics, academics, visionaries) inevitably give way to men-of-action in the social world.[8] It is these latter individuals who mount the barricades and lead the battalions. But books do force us to think new thoughts and make new assumptions. The Gutenberg Revolution was indeed a revolution, a way of doing politics powerfully but insidiously.

Admittedly, books are written by what sociologists call society's "elites," persons who are smarter and more literate, often richer and more powerful, than the average individual. But books are also written for large audiences and that, too, was part of Gutenberg's Revolution; it succeeded in democratizing knowledge. And so the conversations begun in books now continue in restaurant conversations and television sitcoms. Books contain both tentative thoughts and fully declarative ones; they record what we imagine as well as what we fear. Sometimes, books are written half-consciously, its authors trying to understand a world that resists understanding. Some books give answers, some only questions.

We focus here on books dealing with politics. But which ones? If politics is omnipresent, after all, should we not examine the holdings of the entire Library of Congress? We could, of course, focus only on books featuring state relations, but that would bias our study from the beginning. And so we let the authors themselves tell us what is political by focusing on titles containing the phrase *the politics of*, a curious phrase but an increasingly popular one. Lest this choice seem unnaturally restrictive, consider these book titles from 1998 alone:

- *Blaming Children: Youth Crime, Moral Panics and the Politics of Hate*
- *Big Bill Thompson, Chicago and the Politics of Image*
- *Hidden Politics of the Crucifixion*
- *The Politics of Performance in Early Renaissance Drama*
- *Politics of Illusion: The Bay of Pigs Invasion Reexamined*
- *Beyond Sex and Romance? The Politics of Contemporary Lesbian Fiction*
- *Medicine Stories: History, Culture and the Politics of Integrity*
- *Presence of Mind: Education and the Politics of Deception*
- *The Oklahoma City Bombing and the Politics of Terror*

These titles range across the social and academic landscape, finding politics in all its cracks and crannies. There were still more books published in 1998: *The Politics of Unfunded Mandates, The Politics of Australian Child Care, The Politics of Fishing, The Politics of Cyberspace, The Politics of Breastfeeding, The Politics of Religious Apostasy.* With all these books in print, surely politics has no place to hide.

We will track these titles across time and topic to see what larger story they might tell. In doing so we make these assumptions: (1) Authors trade on certain political understandings when they write and often do so unconsciously; (2) in publishing such books—and by titling them in creative ways—publishers recirculate these understandings; (3) the ideas contained in these books not only affect how ordinary citizens conceive of politics but what they will do about it as a result.

MAPPING POLITICS

According to the electronic card catalog at the University of Texas at Austin (one of the ten largest university libraries in the United States), some 4,504 books were published between 1954 and 1998 containing the phrase *the politics of*, with 92 percent of these titles being published after 1967. A Lexis/Nexis search of scholarly journals discovered another 1,261 titles containing this phrase between 1983 and 1998, although subsequent analysis found no appreciable difference between the books and articles on the dimensions studied here. As a result, they were dropped from subsequent analysis, as were some 471 article titles in popular magazines.

As we see in Figure 2.1, there was a steady rise in the production of all English-language books between 1967 and 1998, but political titles increased sharply during the 1980s. This was true across the academic disciplines but, as we see in Figure 2.2, it was especially true in the humanities, where Marxist, feminist, and postmodern essays opened up a new set of problems. As sociologist Orville Lee observes, this was a time when the political was seen as circulating "vertically" through state mechanisms but also "horizontally" throughout civil society.[9] Patrice McDermott detailed the logical result of these practices: "[A]ll arenas of female experience—whether located in the boardroom, the factory, the kitchen, or the bedroom" were now eligible for analysis.[10] Jane Mansbridge explains why the text-centered disciplines (English, history, American studies) had a special stake in these new formulations: "[T]here are no deliberative spaces in which power does not enter. And because traditional deliberative arenas are the most likely to draw on symbols that support the dominant order, democracies cannot rely on these arenas to produce the ongoing critique of power they need."[11]

University presses produced 42 percent of the political books during the last three decades, with commercial publishers issuing the remainder. Eighty percent of these books were written by lone authors (the rest by authorial teams), with women producing more and more books over time. In part this can be attributed to women's growing strength in the academy, but it also results from their increasing interest in "vertical" politics—abortion, job equity, legal rights, healthcare—as well as "horizontal" politics—political identity, multiculturalism, and the literary canon.

Table 2.1 shows important shifts in the focus of these publications, with government officials, nation-states, and transnational entities being de-

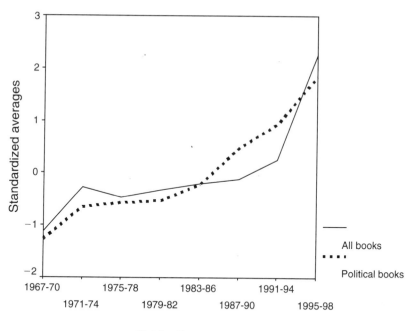

Figure 2.1 Political Titles Versus All Books, 1967–1998.

emphasized over time and political activists and members of marginal social classes taking up the slack. But there has also been an increasing focus on the political lives of individuals. Often, these titles reflect a concern for aesthetics, as we see in *Antonio Canova and the Politics of Patronage in Revolutionary and Napoleonic Europe* or *Simone Weil and the Politics of Self-Denial.* Too, books like *Pistol Packin' Mama: Aunt Molly Jackson and the Politics of Folksong* and *Radical Heroes: Gramsci, Freire and the Politics of Adult Education* show how authors have de-emphasized the politics of City Hall in recent years.

A detailed examination of the topics discussed in these publications presents a more layered view. Table 2.2 contains the coding scheme used to capture the books' subjects. In many cases, the topics were made clear in the title itself; in about a third of the cases we had to either inspect the book directly or rely on published abstracts to properly code them. To ensure precision, the titles were originally coded into 135 discrete topics and subsequently collapsed into 63 mediate categories. We eventually settled on the 15 master categories listed in Table 2.2.

Figure 2.3 presents the results of our coding. The picture is stark: While there has been a leveling off of interest in the topics of Infrastructure Politics (education, economics, etc.) and a rise and then a fall in State Politics (gov-

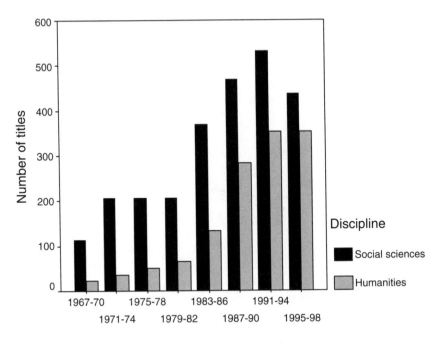

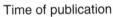

Time of publication

Figure 2.2 Disciplinary Orientation of Book Titles.

TABLE 2.1 Main Protagonists Across Time (in Percent)

		TIME OF PUBLICATION				
Political actor	Number of cases	1967–1974	1975–1982	1983–1990	1991–1998	Total
Individual	310	9.8	9.5	14.0	17.8	13.5
Social class	319	7.9	12.1	16.5	15.7	13.9
Formal organization	298	9.8	14.0	16.0	10.9	13.0
Political activists	226	10.1	7.7	8.9	12.2	9.8
Government officials	234	13.1	13.4	10.3	6.3	10.2
Nation-state	611	33.0	29.6	20.8	27.0	26.6
Transnational	297	16.3	13.6	13.4	10.2	12.9

TABLE 2.2 Topical Codes for Published Titles

State Politics	Infrastructure Politics	Cultural Politics
Political practices (legislative affairs; election activities; political realignment; political crime or scandal; executive politics)	*Communication practices* (media industries; mass persuasion; public opinion; language behaviors)	*Aesthetics* (arts and architecture; literature and poetry; performance arts)
Governmental services (bureaucratic affairs; state finance; urban policy; government assistance; national defense)	*Economic relations* (economic development; business practices; monetary policy; labor practices)	*Entertainment* (sports and leisure; popular culture; social rituals)
Law and justice (law enforcement; legal institutions; individual rights)	*Educational practices* (educational policy; research practices; academic disciplines)	*Interpersonal affairs* (family relations; gender relations; social relations; personal identity)
International affairs (diplomatic relations; war and terrorism; Third World development; trade and science policy; national identity)	*Health and medicine* (medical institutions; patient services; sexual health; mental health)	*Minority affairs* (race; ethnicity; class; gender; other)
	Science and technology (agriculture and land policy; energy and environmental policy; science policy; transportation policy; modernization)	*Political philosophy* (liberalism; Marxism; postmodernism; conservatism; authoritarianism; feminism; political theory)
		Religion and ethics (ethics and morality; denominational practices; Church-State relations)

ernmental services, etc.), there has been a consistent increase in all dimensions of Cultural Politics. These shifts have been both broad and deep. Despite the extraordinary progress during the latter twentieth century in science, health, and new technologies, publishers' interest in those matters has become anemic recently. Even though the nation's economy surged impressively during the Clinton administration, publishing in that area declined as well.

State Politics fared no better: International affairs, governmental services, and legal matters have prompted little interest, and even concern for practical politics began to wane. These drops are even more remarkable when one reflects on the last three decades of the twentieth century, which saw two major wars (Vietnam and the Persian Gulf), unprecedented political scandal (Watergate, Iran-Contra), burgeoning federal programs (school lunch, NASA, victims assistance), complex legal affairs (the Rodney King and O. J. Simpson trials, the Robert Bork and Clarence Thomas hearings), and dramatic new international developments (a reconstructed South Africa, a deconstructed Berlin Wall). In publishing, however, these events hardly produced a flood tide.

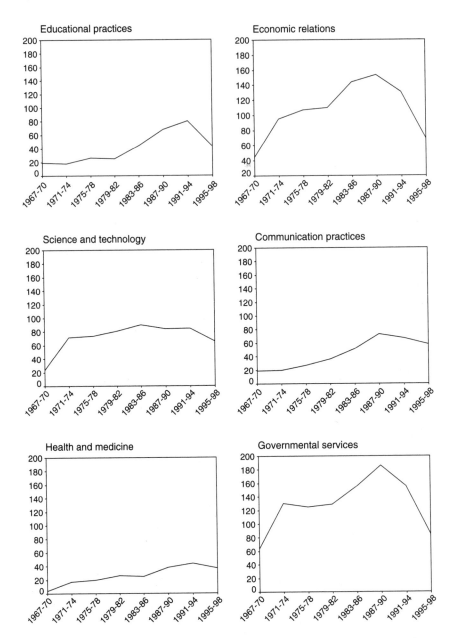

Figure 2.3 Topical Shifts Across Time.

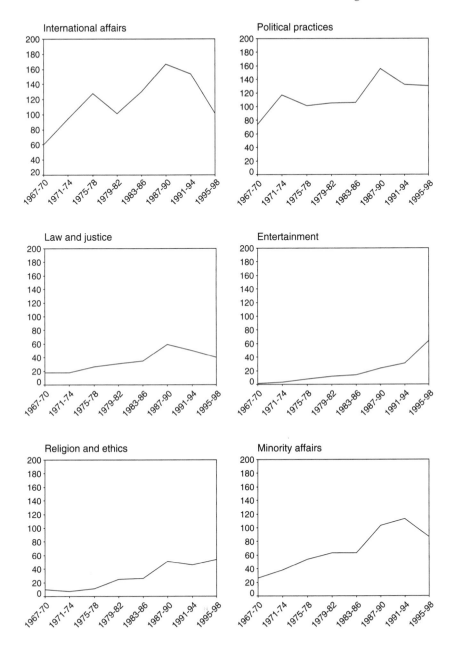

Figure 2.3 (Continued)

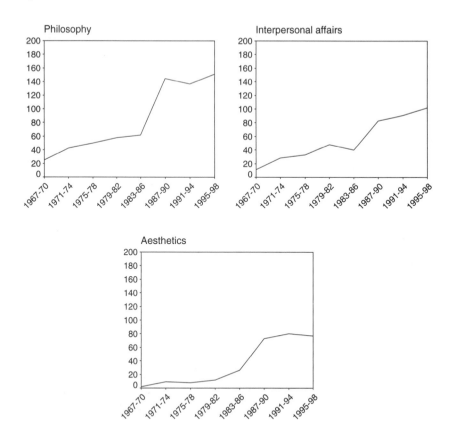

Figure 2.3 (Continued)

The picture is different for Cultural Politics. As we see in Figure 2.3, all of its subcategories enjoyed a steady rise in popularity between 1967 and 1998, and several showed dramatic increases. It is tempting to chalk all this up to mere literary fashion. The publishers were clearly responding to new demands, but why were these demands being made? What was going on in the United States, in the world at large, that made a book like *Masterpiece Theater and the Politics of Quality* more desirable than *The Politics of Downtown Development*? Did prurient interest alone ensure a publishing contract for *Hard Bargains: The Politics of Sex* while books like *The Politics of Central Banks* had to struggle for sales? Admittedly, as we saw in Figure 2.1, the 1970s through 1990s saw a raft of publishing in all fields, but Cultural Politics was especially on the ascendency.

What does all of this mean? Why has political interest migrated into formerly cloistered areas like literary criticism and Continental philosophy? How did interpersonal affairs—getting married, raising children—suddenly turn political? Why would a book like *Lords of Misrule: Mardi Gras and the Politics of Race in New Orleans* seem like a good bet to acquisition editors? What is it about contemporary life that makes a book like *The Politics of Fandom* or *Malaysia: Politics of Golf* a good read? While cultural historians have always taken on obscure topics, does the existence of a book like *The Politics of Courtly Dancing in Early Modern England* signal something special?

It is not surprising that issues of race, sexuality, and ethnicity have been dissected in recent years. New laws have ensured gender equity on the job, affirmative action in schools, and open housing in all communities. But *identity*, not law, is now the watchword in these domains, and that signals an important shift in the locus of political action. Figure 2.3 reveals true intellectual migration, with the State now seeming old and withered and MTV young and relentless. Judging by book titles, at least, something portentous is happening in the United States. But what? And why?

WRESTLING WITH POLITICS

The publishing trends described here track a number of contentious arguments being waged in the scholarly community. Over the years, two political camps have emerged, and they frame the world differently. *Fundamentalists* see politics where it has always been seen—in the legislatures, in the courtrooms, in the diplomatic circles—and regard all attempts to apply the concept too liberally as dangerous. According to political scientist Iris Young, fundamentalists have a "distributive" bias featuring how money, land, power, and capacity shift from one group to another.[12] These distributions are undeniably important, says Young, but they are inevitably guided by something deeper—what people think about their lot in life, their social station, their marital status, their sexual identity, their intellectual capacity. Getting ahead in life requires food, clothing, tools, land, and machines to make a living, but it also requires mastering the rules of the workplace, learning how to make useful social contacts, and figuring out how to maintain one's self-respect. Political forces can grind down the latter, which is why pouring more money into failed school systems rarely equalizes educational opportunity. Children can learn only when they think they can learn. As a result, says Young, social relations have become a quintessential kind of politics.

Echoing Young, *pluralists* focus on the kind of power that spreads throughout society in places both grand and humble. "What has been exploded," say Laclau and Mouffe, is the idea of "a unique space of constitution of the political."[13] In previous times, says Agnes Heller,

> even cultures with the strongest political awareness, for example, the Greek and the Roman, shared the quasi-naturalistic and therefore unproblematic view that only acts which have been decided upon and performed by the members of the political class(es) can be termed political. . . . Slaves cannot engage in politics, nor can women, unless very highly placed in the hierar-

chy of the political class. Institutions established and run by the members of political classes are political; other institutions are non-political.[14]

These assumptions have been clearly attacked in recent years.

One way of capturing the differences between the fundamentalists and the pluralists is to focus on the concepts they deem pivotal. Fundamentalists, for example, focus on these terms:

1. *Authority.* The State is the incarnation of politics for the fundamentalists because it causes individuals to cede their rights—voluntarily or by force—to some larger entity in exchange for goods, services, and protection. The State becomes the embodiment of the people, doing their bidding but also constraining them. Driving a car is pleasurable, for example, but stealing someone else's car to experience that pleasure is unacceptable. The State makes people regulate their impulses on behalf of some larger principle—a safe society, a healthy business environment, and so on. When voluntary restraints fail as, for example, when looting occurs during a hurricane, the State enters the picture.

2. *Reason.* Mention of politics conjures up an image of weighty arguments and long-winded declarations, of jury deliberations and congressional hearings. The promise of democratic politics has been the promise of rational decision-making guided by concepts of universal truth and disinterested objectivity. Lately, however, says Thomas Pangle, pluralists have described politics as a "pure contest of Nietzchean wills . . . in which the notion of a common ground of reasoned and imaginative or sympathetic dialogue is dismissed as superficial and deceptive, necessarily exploitative, a clear sign of bad faith, where it is not a sign of culpable simplemindedness."[15] In such a world, says Pangle, a fundamentalist defense of politics is needed as never before.

3. *Action.* Politics is not philosophy. Its distinction, says Hannah Arendt, is that it *performs* the people. It uses reason for a reason—to build roads and make wars. Political power is measured, says Arendt, by our ability to "act in concert," to harness our collective energies and leave a mark on the world.[16] For Arendt, a revolution becomes the ultimate political act because it constitutes action-for-the-ages, action that cannot be undone. During such moments, revolutionaries step from the shadows to exert their wills on the world and thereby change it. History is marked off by such moments, which makes all history a kind of political history.

4. *Economy.* Nation-states preserve themselves only when they create viable lives for their citizens. The Russian, French, and American Revolutions were inspired by many things—culture, history, and religion, among others—but they were essentially economic in nature. It was the genius of Karl Marx, says Kirstie McClure, that showed how forces of production contribute to State power and how the State protects its industries in return. Marx examined the economies of the nineteenth century, teasing out the agencies, practices, and forms of knowledge that kept certain economic relations in force

(often exploitatively, according to Marx). It is hard today to think of politics without also thinking of economic matters. It was Marx who helped us do so.

5. *Institutions.* Authority, reason, action, and the economy cannot exist in hyperspace. Formal institutions inevitably develop to make authority visible, reason social, action controlled, and economics purposeful. Societies are now distinguished by their institutions—monarchies, the papacy, the FBI, the United Nations, Congress. Political institutions are like any collectivity in that they have distinct histories, practices, and hierarchies; the older the institution, the more seriously they take them. As a result, institutions develop regulatory mechanisms to protect their interests. The concept of a "political crime," for example, is really an institutional concept. Committing an act of terrorism (as opposed to simply going mad and detonating a bomb) is treated harshly because it undermines institutional legitimacy. No society can remain illegitimate for very long, which is not to say that all societies measure legitimacy in the same way.

6. *Conflict.* The foregoing components are certainly part of politics, but conflict lies at its center. As the noted philosopher Carl Schmidt once said, "A world in which the possibility of war is eliminated, a completely pacified globe, would be a world without the distinction of friend and enemy and hence a world without politics."[17] Politics is politics, says Schmidt, because the State retains "the possibility of waging war and thereby publicly disposing of the lives of men."[18] The concept of cultural politics would make little sense to Schmidt since only the State can exact the ultimate sacrifice. When a group cannot distinguish its enemies, says Schmidt, whether that group be a foreign nation or the National Trial Lawyers Association, it ceases to be a political group. Societies die when they cannot identify those who oppose them. So, for example, when the aristocracy in France began sentimentalizing the nation and stopped paying attention to the desperate conditions of the masses, the old regime was doomed.[19] The enemy lived among the aristocrats, but they discovered them too late.

Fundamentalists know where politics is located. It resides in the State and in the infrastructure the State superintends. Politics is actional, not contemplative. Institutions work hard to sustain themselves, and it takes money to do so. Money inevitably begets conflict, and resolving conflict requires authority, the more stable the better. In its best moments, politics is guided by human reason since dialogue is less costly than savaging one another. But because balancing all these forces is difficult, politics is often unpretty.

Politics is no handsomer for the pluralists, but it is more subtle. They argue that not all politics begins and ends in the State and that some of the most powerful forces are invisible. All too often, they argue, political effects are mistakenly attributed to "fate," "chance," or "nature." Women get paid less for their work and African Americans cannot find proper housing not because of fate or chance, they stress, but because some group has decided that these conditions are acceptable. When fundamentalists respond that laws have been written to banish such practices, pluralists tell them to look deeper. Examine people's latent *cultural assumptions,* they suggest, because assumptions perpetuate such conditions. Fixing a culture is far harder than fixing a law.

Operating on such notions, pluralists identify a different set of forces for study. These forces do not emanate from the State although the State colludes with them to keep certain persons privileged and others marginalized. To offset these conditions, an entirely new set of forces must be identified, but identifying them will not be easy. When power and culture become intertwined, distinctions between them becomes blurred. Here is why.

1. *Routine.* Pluralists note that people's expectations usually determine what they will do. So, for example, if one thinks that getting a proper education will lead to a better job, one will pursue the former to ensure the latter. But what if one assumes differently? What if one assumes that only a certain *type* of education at a certain *type* of school attended by a certain *type* of student spells success? And what if one is not one of those types? One might well avoid college. That which is assumed and unquestioned—that women stay at home, that blacks are the best athletes—determine people's possibilities. Michel Foucault saw "the modern world as one in which power is insinuating itself into our lives in ways that we are not able to grasp very well with the traditional cognitive machinery of political reflection."[20] Given Foucault's assumptions, we need to question the unquestioned. It may be true, for example, that blondes are prettier than brunettes. But it may be even truer that Clairol and Hollywood have created these perceptions via their advertising practices, thereby turning the normal (brunettes) into the abnormal and filling their coffers simultaneously.

2. *Privacy.* Fundamentalists study politics on a grand stage. Biographies of great leaders sell well because they have become familiar to us. With billions of dollars to propel them, political campaigns sear our eyes for nine months at a time, which is why traditionalists distinguish sharply between the public and the private, locating politics in the former domain. The pluralists see things differently, arguing that everyday practices constrain people even more. We spend our lives in private, they note, working at modest jobs, living in modest homes, raising modest families. But our privacy is not sealed off. For centuries, says Kurt Bach, monarchial forces perpetuated the patriarchial family, making it seem God-given and natural.[21] There has always been a "policing of families" as a result, says Jacques Donzelot, a superimposition of public expectations on our private lives.[22] So, for example, "private" issues like abortion, euthanasia, child-rearing, and even gardening are now declared matters of public concern. One cannot hide from politics by avoiding City Hall, say the pluralists. City Hall continually seeks us out.

3. *Relationships.* "Politics," says Patrice McDermott, "refers to the distribution and functions of power as it is manifested in social institutions, codes, and relationships."[23] It is these relationships, these intertwinings, that expand and contract our influence. In taking a job or getting married, for example, we voluntarily curtail our personal freedoms. We expect a return on investment, of course—the corner office, the loving spouse—but signing

the nondisclosure agreement or the marriage certificate also opens the door to the State. Marriages are economic in character (e.g., the two-income family; palimony disputes); they often pivot on questions of authority (e.g., child-visitation rights); they can be conflict-ridden (marital counseling, spousal abuse); and they are beset by institutional arrangements (the PTA, the Church, the neighborhood association). Pluralists tell us that power "reticulates" through society, forming weblike ties among all persons. To ask why some relationships (e.g., that of student and teacher) are compensated so poorly compared to other relationships (e.g., that of physician and patient) is thus to ask a thoroughly political question.

4. *Freedom.* The political watchword for the fundamentalists is *constraint.* Because they focus on institutional arrangements (which often result in the creation of laws) and on economic realities (which are ultimately limited and limiting), they see politics as a place for settling distributive disputes. To emphasize *freedom* is to make an entirely different move. Things become political, says Agnes Heller, when we begin arguing about how freedom should be concretized.[24] For example, having the freedom to own a dog is prized by many Americans. But so too is the freedom to get a good night's rest. Neighborhood disputes erupt because freedoms easily and widely apportioned beforehand are suddenly brought to the fore—when barking enters the picture. On a more serious note, the ranks of the pluralists are filled with those whose freedoms have been curtailed by traditional forces and who have, as a result, sought out political remedies for their personal circumstances. To ask questions about freedom rather than constraint, then, is to ask a different set of questions and to get a different set of answers.

5. *Identity.* Issues of identity lie at the heart of cultural politics, and it is this concept that most unnerves the fundamentalists. For the latter, identity has no economic or actional character and hence is irrelevant to political life. No laws are made about "identity," they argue, and conflicts about it largely center on matters of personal taste. Because a psychological concept like identity does not admit to rational deliberation, they continue, it cannot be addressed politically. The pluralists disagree with all of the foregoing, arguing that a person's identity is highly tangible, at times even a commodity (as we see with celebrities, for example). How people are perceived (homosexuals, for example) can affect the jobs they are offered, the bars they frequent, and the legal rights they obtain (partner medical benefits, for example). Even worse, how a group perceives itself—women, for example—can affect the rights it has (equal pay for equal work) as well as the rights it demands (relief from spousal abuse, for example). Reflecting on issues of identity, Martin Duberman has said, "You cannot link arms under a universalist banner when you can't find your own name on it. A minority identity may be contingent or incomplete, but that does not make it fabricated or needless. And cultural unity cannot be purchased at the cost of cultural erasure."[25]

6. *Discourse.* Although fundamentalists examine discursive activity (e.g., presidential addresses, congressional testimony), pluralists radically expand the kinds of texts studied. Cultural messages bombard us constantly, they

observe, and these un-self-conscious texts are far more powerful than the easily ignored remarks of politicians. Novels, plays, television, the Internet, music videos, advertising, sports, the tabloids, and much else tell us how to think and act and what we are worth. Says Linda Alcoff, "Who is speaking, who is spoken to, and who listens is a result, as well as an act, of political struggle. Simply put, the discursive context is a political arena."[26] Popular culture tells us what is possible for us and what is out of our reach—the very essence of political work. The popularity of popular culture constantly "disciplines" us. By doing the bidding of society's most entrenched sources of power (that is, its monied interests), popular culture becomes a perfect delivery system for making us docile. Ironically, because society's most marginal citizens consume popular culture in great gobs, they seal their political fates even while feeling hip and contemporary.

Judging from the dramatic shifts in publishing mentioned previously, it is clear that pluralists have worked feverishly to expand the political. Focusing on life's shadowy spots, they find power where it is not supposed to be found, where it does not want to be found. Guided by such aims, feminists, postmodernists, Marxists, and race and gender scholars have filled the book bins in recent years, causing a "sense of the political" to envelop us all. Their work puts us on guard, calling our attention to rights ignored or denied. Because fundamentalists and pluralists are housed in different disciplines, however—the social sciences for the former, the humanities for the latter— these camps rarely speak to one another. But which is right and which wrong? Does it matter how widely the arc of politics is drawn? Can't we all get along? These questions are worth considering.

FINDING A PLACE TO STAND

While some may argue that extending political analysis to popular culture "is nothing more than the self-indulgent and narcissistic impulse resulting from the embourgeoisment of the Left,"[27] that is too dismissive a posture because very real issues are at stake. Restricting the study of politics to State affairs might even be the result of a masculinist bias, according to some scholars. Jodi Dean, for example, says that sharply dividing the public from the private "prevents issues of sexuality, child care, and domestic violence from entering the public debate." When private life is "interpreted as 'free from state intervention or public concern,' most of the activities and needs of women could not be understood as political issues."[28]

The pluralists argue that expanding the political increases our range of vision. If one assumes, for example, that child care is strictly a family matter, one would hardly imagine fostering federally funded daycare programs or putting pressure on private corporations to adopt family-friendly policies for their employees. When Hillary Clinton says that it take a village to raise a child she is therefore politicizing a previously unpoliticized issue. According to sociologist Doug McAdam, there has always been a dynamic relationship between the political system and the family, as, for example, when federal tax policies advantage some family units over others (e.g., two-parent versus one-parent families) and when legislation affecting aid to dependent children languishes in the nation's legislatures.[29] According to Laura Balbo, it is women who typically must do the "consumption work" needed to keep a household running. "It is women who keep in touch with teachers and school staff," says Balbo, "who take children to clinics and hospitals, who visit agencies to obtain what the family is entitled to."[30] In performing these functions, women are not just doing family work but also societal work since these activities limit "the time and energy women have to devote to other pursuits, including careers."[31] Moreover, says McAdam, the willingness of women to do such work "minimizes the pressures on men and on major social institutions to promote changes which would . . . promote gender equality."[32]

There is an even deeper "masculinist" bias to traditional understandings of politics, says McAdam. For example, solutions to family-related issues are usually first espoused by movement organizations rather than governmental agencies. Because institutional politics is "synonymous with rational political action" and because social movements are "relegated to the status of expressive coping mechanisms," women's absence from State politics "merely 'confirms' her nonpolitical [read: irrational] 'nature.' " Women are every bit as political as men, says McAdam, even though they typically discover politics in different locales. According to political scientist Jane Mansbridge, we need to begin examining "sequestered spaces," places like churches, community groups, work teams, and neighborhood associations. Women's awareness of their political possibilities (and political repressions) often emerges in such locales. These private spaces are typically less adversarial than State-based forums and hence produce a different kind of politics. "The battle against domination cannot be restricted to the formal institutions of government," Mansbridge warns. "It must be waged on all fronts, including within the self."[33]

Oddly enough, it is often difficult to convince a group that it is, in fact, a group. With women being dispersed among so many different ethnic, racial, linguistic, and age-based and class-based entities, for example, erecting the banner of universal womanhood takes massive political work. Cultural traditions, religious predilections, and rank sexism often keep such groups, apart, causing them to believe "that their sufferings are natural or merely personal."[34] "Feminist politics evaporates," says Iris Young, "without some conception of women as a social collective."[35] Thinking of women as black women, young women, Brazilian women, or Jewish women focuses on their differences rather than their similarities and thus forestalls concerted action. If women are not part of the same group, says Young, they are at least part of the same *series.* So, for example, when a female candidate for the local school committee says she wants to "represent all minorities" if elected, says Young, she sends out a complex political signal but a needed one. Feminist politics must always be coalitional in nature, says Young, for in such complexity lies a new and powerful civic vision.

Those who champion cultural politics want to expand the scope of politics so that new kinds of social change can be advanced. Their calls to action have been met with resistance from the fundamentalists, however, who argue that pluralizing politics by de-emphasizing institutions ensures that traditional power will remain in traditional hands. "The specialists in difference may do their best to deny the fact," says Todd Gitlin, "that for a quarter of a century they have been fighting over the English department while the Right held the White House as its private fiefdom"[36] during the Reagan years. In other words, it is not just conservatives who criticize the pluralists but an angry group of *liberal* fundamentalists as well. Cultural studies trivializes politics, they argue. The more pluralists confine themselves to the library, says Gitlin, the more aggressive their language becomes.[37] And the more irrelevant, too, he might add.

Fundamentalists launch a number of specific charges against the pluralists:

1. *Cultural politics is effete.* In a scathing essay entitled "The Idiocy of American Studies," Steven Watts argues that the pluralists' expanded political agenda has given "radical intellectuals something to do politically: unlocking codes, exposing linguistic repressions, subverting accepted meanings as a path-clearing for liberation."[38] But what is really going on, says Watts, is that "an emphasis on texts and language as the focus of cultural authority . . . provides a way for tenured, prosperous scholars to persist in a radical reading of American life."[39] Watts accuses the pluralists (or the "linguistic Left," as he dubs them) of being dilettantes, of producing a critique that has no impact beyond the ivory tower. "If you can't deconstruct American social structures, the current hope seems to be that you can deconstruct *Moby Dick* and pretend it's the same thing," says Watts.[40] Then he really gets angry:

> For small farmers holding a notice of a loan foreclosure, for desperate members of the urban underclass facing the deterioration of the nation's cities, for working-class families struggling with the burden of jobs and mortgages and education for their children, the glib liberationist proposition of poststructuralism—a decentered discourse will set you free—must seem puzzling indeed.[41]

2. *Cultural politics is naive.* The fundamentalists are fundamentalists because they believe that State politics is inevitable and that avoiding it is to be dominated by it. Television talk shows like *Oprah* and *Sally Jesse* can be involving, says communication scholar Janice Peck, and their personalization strategies compelling.[42] But these shows largely lead to "therapeutic" effects for viewers while the problems they dramatize—abusive relationships, child endangerment, unfair divorcement settlements—are matters only the State can solve. To address any really important problem, says Christopher Beem, traditional

political agencies must be enlisted. "The inexhaustible quest for numbers and dollars," says Beem, "renders coalition politics inescapable. The need for power, the need for numbers, requires that groups join forces with other more or less like-minded groups."[43] While popular culture can be entrancing, real politics is rooted not in a "covert and semiconscious . . . Nietzchean struggle for power"[44] but in real nations situated in real space and time.

3. *Cultural politics is inert.* Anything that is effete and naive is likely not to take action. "How much more edifying, rigorous, hip, virtuous, it is to discuss the constitution of the self, the nature of community, the proper way to read an old book,"[45] says Jeffrey Isaac, than to solve an international border dispute or fund a domestic poverty program. Cultural politics, says Terry Eagleton, largely reduces to a "suburban moral ideology, limited in practice to largely interpersonal matters. It is stronger on adultery than on armaments."[46] In the eyes of pluralists, says columnist Russell Jacoby, "Reinterpreting pop culture becomes as political as running for office, organizing labor unions, or working on the local school board."[47] The great tragedy of pluralism, says Todd Gitlin, is that it leads to nothing—no legislation passed, no institutions reinvigorated, no arms linked in unison. Because the pluralists specialize in identity politics they get a feeling of change without its attendant empirical benefits. The very questions they focus on—"Who am I? Who is like me? Whom can I trust? Where do I belong?"—lead to self-enlightenment but little else, especially not to coalition-formation, which lies at the very heart of politics.[48]

On the other hand, because identity politics televizes well, says one scholar, people often get a sense of change even when doing nothing.[49] Figure 2.4 seems to confirm this, suggesting that the tendencies to *read* about politics and to *do* something about it are moving in opposite directions. A society that is content to have political feelings but loathe to act upon them is a society surely headed for trouble.

CONCLUSION

This chapter has featured a debate about a word. Debates about words can be petty, but a debate about a word like *politics* is hardly that. According to James Boyd White, any significant alternation in language "is not merely a lexical event, and it is not reversible by insistence upon a set of proper definitions. It is a change in the world and the self, in manners and conduct and sentiment."[50] Here, we have seen prodigious changes in how politics has been conceived in the last thirty years; those changes have pointed to a widening chasm in the intellectual landscape. For many reasons, more and more authors have written about politics, and that is good. To ignore power, to ignore how authority is used, is to ignore life itself. At the same time, to ignore what the pluralists are telling us—that much social influence occurs behind closed doors, that the mass media and other forms of popular culture

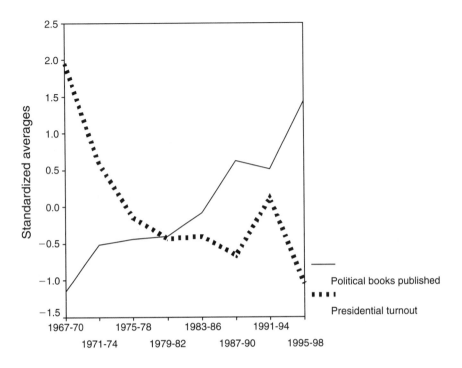

Figure 2.4 Book Publishing Versus Presidential Turnout, 1967–1998.

shape our conceptions, that what people feel about themselves affects what they will do for themselves—is to ignore important forces that will eventually enter the political mainstream.

But emphasizing cultural politics should come with a warning: To ignore the State is to be determined by it. If concentrating on culture blinds us to who is doing what to whom we will be poorly served indeed. The State is powerful and invasive and reticulated. It affects us from birth to death and determines what happens in between. As of this writing, for example, it takes $2 trillion to run the United States of America for one year. Miraculously, the funds needed to make this happen are collected from the nation's citizens willingly—through payroll deductions and through Schedule C for the self-employed. The people's willingness to help in this way is admittedly augmented by the (occasionally armed) members of the Internal Revenue Service. Every four years, the nation's politicians run about the country promising that the IRS will become kinder and gentler, but the national budget never gets smaller. All of this is politics—money, power, compulsion, government services, institutions. We can ignore these matters but that will not make them vanish.

Pluralists and fundamentalists. Horizontal power and vertical power. We must study it all. Many important issues have been placed on the State's agenda in recent decades—open housing, affirmative action, the rights of the unborn, local control of schools. All these issues were originally the concerns of small groups of people who chose to act on their beliefs. As Christopher Beem notes, "political leaders rarely start anything, and when they do pick up a cause, it is rarely for reasons that do not involve their own self-interest."[51] At the same time, says Beem, "while a moral dialogue rarely begins in government, its processes and institutions can, in a unique and indispensable way, move that discussion to a national level. Government is the means by which we citizens express our considered judgment about our identity, our values, and our purposes back to ourselves."[52]

We need to know more about this dialogue. We need increased discussion between the pluralists and fundamentalists. We need the humanists and the social scientists to really listen to one another. Right now, they are publishing their books but doing so separately, engaging in a kind of intellectual arms race. We need a detente. And then we need to know what they have to say to one another.

NOTES

1. For these and other aphorisms about *politics,* see D. B. Baker (ed.), *Political Quotations: A Collection of Notable Sayings on Politics from Antiquity Through 1989* (Detroit, MI: Gale Research, 1990), 162–70.

2. M. Viroli, "The Revolution in the Concept of Politics," *Political Theory,* 20 (1992): 476.

3. S. Fish, "Is Everything Political?" *Chronicle of Higher Education,* March 29, 2002, http://chronicle.com/search (November 4, 2002).

4. D. H. Coole, *Women in Political Theory: From Ancient Misogyny to Contemporary Feminism* (Sussex: Wheatsheaf Books, 1988), 257.

5. V. Randall, *Women and Politics: An International Perspective,* 2d ed. (Chicago: University of Chicago Press, 1987), 10.

6. R. Jacoby, "America's Professoriate: Politicized, Yet Apolitical," *Chronicle of Higher Education,* April 2, 1996: B1–2.

7. L. W. Rabine, "A Feminist Politics of Non-identity," *Feminist Studies,* 14 (1988): 14.

8. E. Hoffer, *The True Believer: Thoughts on the Nature of Mass Movements* (New York: Harper, 1951).

9. O. Lee, "Is the Public Sphere a Political Field?," paper presented at the annual meeting of the American Political Science Association, San Francisco, September 1996, 22.

10. P. McDermott, *Politics and Scholarship: Feminist Academic Journals and the Production of Knowledge* (Urbana: University of Illinois Press, 1994), 111.

11. J. Mansbridge, "Reconstructing Democracy," in *Revisioning the Political: Feminist Reconstructions of Traditional Concepts in Western Political Theory,* ed. N. J. Hirschmann and C. Di Stefano (New York: Westview, 1996): p. 131.

12. I. M. Young, *Justice and the Politics of Difference* (Princeton, NJ: Princeton University Press, 1990), 21.

13. E. Laclau and C. Mouffe, *Hegemony and Socialist Strategy* (London: Verso, 1985), 181.

14. A. Heller, "The Concept of the Political Revisited," in *Political Theory Today*, ed. D. Held (Cambridge: Polity Press, 1991), 330–31.

15. T. Pangle, *The Ennobling of Democracy: The Challenge of the Postmodern Age* (Baltimore: Johns Hopkins University Press, 1992), 78–79.

16. For more on Arendt's understanding of political action, see A. Heywood, *Key Concepts in Politics* (New York: St. Martins, 2000), 33.

17. C. Schmidt, *The Concept of the Political*, trans. G. Schwab (Chicago: University of Chicago Press, 1996), 35.

18. Ibid., 46.

19. Ibid., 68.

20. S. K. White, "Poststructuralism and Political Reflection," *Political Theory*, 16 (1988): 190.

21. K. W. Bach, "Why Is Abortion a Public Issue? The Role of Professional Control," *Politics and Society*, 15 (1986–87): 201.

22. Quoted in ibid., 201.

23. McDermott, *Politics and Scholarship*, 5.

24. Heller, "The Concept of the Political," 342.

25. M. Duberman, "In Defense of Identity Politics," In These Times.Com, July 9, 2001, http://www.inthesetimes.com/issue/25/16/duberman2516.html (November 8, 2002).

26. L. Alcoff, "The Problem of Speaking for Others," *Cultural Critique* (Winter 1991–2): 15.

27. This is a view attributed to Steven Watts by Nancy Isenberg in "The Personal Is Political: Gender, Feminism, and the Politics of Discourse Theory," *American Quarterly*, 44 (1992): 453. Isenberg's reference is to an article by Watts entitled, "The Idiocy of American Studies: Poststructuralism, Language, and Politics in the Age of Self-Fulfillment," *American Quarterly*, 43 (1991): 625–60.

28. J. Dean, "Including Women: The Consequences and Side Effects of Feminist Critiques of Civil Society," *Philosophy and Social Criticism*, 18 (1992): 384.

29. D. McAdam, "Genre Implication of the Traditional Academic Conception of the Political," in *Changing Our Minds: Feminist Transformations of Knowledge*, ed. S. H. Aiken et al. (Albany: SUNY Press, 1998), 65.

30. Quoted in ibid., 68.

31. Ibid.

32. Ibid.

33. Mansbridge, "Reconstructing Democracy," 131.

34. I. M. Young, "Gender as Seriality: Thinking About Women as a Social Collective," in *Rethinking the Political: Gender, Resistance, and the State*, ed. B. Laslett, J. Brenr, and Y. Arat (Chicago: University of Chicago Press, 1995), 105.

35. Ibid., 105.

36. T. Gitlin, "The Rise of Identity Politics," *Dissent* (Spring 1993): 173.

37. Ibid., 173.

38. Watts, "Idiocy of American Studies," 631.

39. Ibid., 631.

40. Ibid., 650.

41. Ibid., 650.

42. J. Peck, "TV Talk Shows as Therapeutic Discourse: The Ideological Labor of the Televisual Talking Cure," *Communication Theory,* 5 (1995): 75.

43. C. Beem, *The Necessity of Politics: Reclaiming American Public Life* (Chicago: University of Chicago Press, 1999), 202.

44. T. Pangle, *The Ennobling of Democracy: The Challenge of the Postmodern Age* (Baltimore: Johns Hopkins University Press, 1992), 78.

45. J. C. Isaac, "The Strange Silence of Political Theory," *Political Theory,* 23 (1995): 643.

46. T. Eagleton, "Political Criticism," in *Rhetoric: Concept, Definitions, Boundaries,* ed. W. A. Covino and D. A. Jolliffe (Boston: Allyn and Bacon, 1995), 510.

47. Jacoby, "America's Professoriate," B2.

48. Gitlin, "Rise of Identity Politics," 172.

49. R. P. Hart, *Seducing America: How Television Charms the Modern Voter* (New York: Oxford University Press, 1994).

50. J. B. White, *"When Words Lose Their Meaning: Constitutions and Reconstitutions of Language, Character, and Community* (Chicago: University of Chicago Press, 1984), 4.

51. Beem, *Necessity of Politics,* 256.

52. Ibid.

3

What Is *Politics?*
An Inventory of Meanings

With D. Joel Wiggins and John Pauley

Chapter 2 told a story of change. The migration of ***politics*** from one realm to many realms has been bold and sweeping, stirring up new conversations and new confrontations in the academic and social worlds. Today, writers talk easily about the politics of marriage, as if Congress were somehow positioned at the foot of our very beds. Writers also talk about the politics of identity, treating identity as something that can be captured, processed, quantified, legislated, and adjudicated. Today's authors treat us all as political animals roaming through the jungle of a common life. But their books also treat us as sinners, leviathans, managers, literateurs, resisters, liars, laborers, judges, insurgents, reformers, globalists, and even gods. At the turn of the millennium, each individual has a politics, each a story to tell.

The books written during the last fifty years do not tell us everything, but they tell us much. For example, when their book *The Politics of Representation* was published in 1974, Denis Sullivan and his colleagues hoped to clarify how the Democratic party was changed by the so-called McGovern Reforms, which brought new voices into the party when it convened in 1972 in Miami Beach.[1] Fourteen years later, another book called *The Politics of Representation* was published but, this time, its author had no interest at all in partisan skirmishes.[2] Michael Shapiro was after bigger game—how the nation's biographers and photographers inscribed a comfortable hegemony into their works and, hence, into the lives of their patrons. Two books, two political scientists, vastly different stories. Sullivan and Shapiro serve as bookends to the evolution of political thought during the last thirty years.

No author, of course, willingly shares a book title. But it happens from time to time, in part because even a capacious language like English has its limitations. Consider, for example, these titles:

- *The Politics of Space: Regional Development and Planning in Mexico*
- *The Politics of Space: A History of U.S.–Soviet/Russian Competition and Cooperation in Space*
- *The Politics of Space: Architecture, Painting, and Theatre in Postmodern Germany*

These books bear a certain lexical similarity but contain entirely different epistemologies and worldviews.

But that was the story of chapter 2. This chapter tells a different story, one of continuity. Much has changed during the last fifty years, but much has also stayed the same. Consider, for example, some of the titles that have been repeated over the years: Five books on the *politics of oil,* an equal number on the *politics of food,* another five on the *politics of poverty.* Five titles have treated the *politics of justice*—its constituents, reform, deployments, and problems—and another five the *politics of motherhood.* The eight books on *the politics of education* cover a bewildering set of subtopics (state reforms, Capitol Hill legislation, French colonialism), while the eight on the *politics of women* treat their rights, biology, work, liberation, health, and spirituality. The *politics of development* has also been popular, focusing on Pakistan, Peru, Colombia, Nepal, Botswana, Kenya, Muharashtra, and Brazil, as well as twentieth-century Asia. The *politics of international* sport, air transport, credit, telecommunications, debt, banking, crisis, shipping, and, again, health and economics serve to emphasize that certain cross-national pressures are never abated.

Some authors pay no attention to how their books are titled, while others weigh each word carefully. In still other cases publishers make the decisions themselves. Nevertheless, a book's title often reveals the author's political assumptions. This chapter traces those assumptions. We will again look at titles containing the phrase *the politics of,* but, this time, we examine the authors' presuppositions, not their subject matters, concentrating on how the authors use metaphors to explain politics "in terms of something else."[3] Operationally, we will assume that mothers can have a politics (they are people, are they not?) but that motherhood cannot, nor, for that matter, can food, poverty, oil, or justice. Naturally, we get the author's "drift" when she titles her book *The Politics of Health,* but that does not make the endocrine system a legislature. The human body does what it does—churns blood, secretes urine. When it performs those functions adequately health results. When it perform them poorly we die, a decidedly unmetaphorical state. As if in protest, Gary Ebersole titled his book *Ritual Poetry and the Politics of Death in Early Japan.*[4]

As numerous authors have observed, metaphors have a way of becoming conventionalized, "lexicalized," when they are used so often that their figural qualities are overlooked. So, for example, the construction *crane* seen in so many American cities is no such thing at all. It is made of steel, not bones; although it stands tall, it cannot fly. Too, for most of us a *red herring* is a deficiency in logic, not an malodorous fish used by prisoners to throw pursuing bloodhounds off the scent.[5] Such metaphors may now be "dead," but that is not to deny their rhetorical impact. We use these devices because they give our ideas power and currency. For Gary Ebersole, for example, it was not enough to recount the ancient Japanese's lacrimations; he saw more than religious rituals operating in the cultures he studied. He also sensed a certain power dynamics, a kind of ideological work being done. Professor Ebersole found a *politics of death,* which is to say, he invented a politics of death, just as construction cranes and red herrings were once invented. Such metaphors "move on an ocean of convention, conformity, majority usage, habit and opinion until they are called out."[6] Here, we shall call them out.

APPRECIATING METAPHORS

Almost by their nature, metaphors resist empirical study. A book title like *Small Wars: The Cultural Politics of Childhood,* for example, is a complex locution, containing diminutive, martial, and cultural components, each of which vies for our attention.[7] Which element did the authors wish to emphasize? Which did readers themselves feature? Equally important, what sort of *additive effect* is produced when these diminutive/martial/cultural features are combined? For example, are "small wars" trivial compared to major conflicts, or are they more heinous because children are the casualties? Is a "cultural politics" more polite (more "cultured") than a legislative floor-fight, or is it longer-lasting, more insidious, and hence more toxic? In short, even a simple metaphor has worlds of meaning, which is to say, there are no simple metaphors.

Trying to capture the essential nature of a metaphor is not a fool's errand, but it is demanding. Using multiple coders and formal content analytic procedures helps, but even then there can be slippage given the complexity of the English language and the way a metaphor can become "sedimented" in a given culture. Demanding though such study is, we cannot abandon it, for metaphors are influential. As scholars have shown, it makes a real difference whether we think of politics as an occupation or a contest,[8] ethnicity as a heritage or an infestation,[9] war as an infirmity or a chess match,[10] Europe as a polyglot or a unity,[11] the world as a lifeboat or a spaceship.[12] These different framings describe different realities, and, more important, they *argue for* different sorts of politics. Only an Adolf Hitler could find a disease in Jewishness.

Metaphors are more than just colorful; they also structure thought. One who thinks of politics as a game, for example, is likely to engage in gamelike behavior: scoring *points* on the opposition rather than reasoning cooly or crying *foul* to the press when one's opponent has violated some trivial convention. Metaphors are therefore "disciplinary," superintending what thoughts can be thought and which pathways taken. As David Bromwick points out, for example, when higher learning came to be thought of as an *institution* it took on certain encrustations and that led to a deadly academic conformity. While "we are used to regarding the academy as the freest part of a society remarkable for its freedom," says Bromwick, "nothing . . . in the nature of an academy makes it so."[13] That is because our metaphors so often lead us by the nose, driving our emotions one way, our thoughts another way. As Andrew Goatly notes, Catholics and Protestants have always split over the notion of the body and blood of Christ, with the former treating them literally and the latter metaphorically.[14] Wars have been fought and families anguished over such notions.

The important thing to remember, then, is that *metaphors have entailments.* To use a metaphor repeatedly is to open up certain policy options and to close off others. In his discussion of international relations, for example, Keith Shimko asks how U.S. policy toward Latin America may have been affected by the region's treatment as America's *backyard* versus a network of sovereign polities.[15] And what happened when certain Southeast Asian nations came to be seen as *dominoes,* unstable ones at that? Did it make a difference that China came to be viewed as a *market* for U.S. goods rather than a *rapacious* and *backward* nation?

The metaphors used most frequently often go unquestioned, however. Such images become comforting to us, simplifying the world and clarifying our options. Only the hardy dare question them. To think of Latin America or China or Vietnam as part of a *brotherhood of nations,* for example, demanded considerable temerity on the parts of certain U.S. politicians in recent history. But defamiliarizing things in this way can be critical to changing foreign policy because the world often turns when metaphors turn.

In short, paying attention to metaphors is important for several reasons:

- *Metaphors signal cultural change.* Michael Osborn notes, for example, that the shift from metaphors of the *sea* to metaphors of *space* dramatically altered American political discourse, allowing the nation to think in more cosmic and less insular ways.[16] Metaphors can be, in that sense, subversive devices, making it hard to think in old ways.[17]

- *Metaphors signal intellectual change.* Adam Smith thought of politics as a machine, notes Yaron Ezrahi, and that caused him to focus on the *balancing* and *self-regulating* processes that produced *equilibrium* within political *systems.* But the postmodern era has increasingly treated politics as *theater,* thereby trivializing it in some people's eyes (e.g, by turning citizens into bystanders) but throwing a spotlight on those who are good with symbols (e.g., Jesse Jackson and Martin Sheen).[18]

- *Metaphors signal authorial assumptions.* Few of us consciously track the metaphors we use, which is why they can help shed light on an author's underlying point of view.[19] Lyndon Johnson, for example, was probably unaware that he used an almost equal number of male and female metaphors in his political conversations, but he did just that, showing that he was equal parts *temptress* and *warrior,* a duality that made him infinitely colorful and infinitely difficult to corral, countermand, outstrategize, or ignore.[20]

- *Metaphors signal ideological commitments.* One author notes that Martin Luther King, Jr., uniquely combined premodern understandings (e.g., "justice rolls down like waters," "the flames of withering injustice") with high modernism ("we have come to . . . cash a check," "the architects of our republic") in his famous "I Have a Dream" speech, thereby giving his talk a biblical tincture even as it promised new, concrete bounties to its auditors.[21] Reverend King was, in that sense, both a preacher and an entrepreneur.

- *Metaphors signal latent values.* Sometimes, metaphors expose beliefs hidden within us, beliefs that can sometimes be embarrassing. In an imaginative study, Otto Santa Ana followed the tropes used to describe Mexican migration to the United States and found a preponderance of animalistic metaphors (e.g., *"ferreting out* illegal immigrants") and images of natural disasters (*"uncontrolled tides* of dark-skinned people").[22] It is one thing to protest U.S. immigration policy, Santa Ana notes, another thing entirely to dehumanize an entire people, even worse to do so actively and consistently.

Metaphors, then, are workhorses. They extend our intellectual reach, allowing us to describe hard-to-describe feelings. Metaphors give us cognitive shortcuts, making it easier to access our ideas and share them with another. Metaphors are, as well, the language of the emotions. Hallmark Cards has made a fortune giving its customers the imagery needed for the special occasions in their lives. Metaphors are also hortatory, pushing us forcefully in certain directions. Above all, metaphors have cumulative impact. When used repeatedly they do our thinking for us.

CHASING METAPHORS

Because metaphors access both the mind and the feelings they are particularly useful for studying politics, which also blends those two elements. Using the same three thousand books (and fifteen hundred articles) published between 1954 and the present, each of which contained the phrase *the politics of,* we analyzed the titles for their root "metaphorical family," following Lakoff and Johnson's lead that a concept gets its meaning from the images that "nest" around it.[23] As before, we excluded titles featuring a literal person or nation-state (because they functioned referentially rather than metaphorically), but that eliminated fewer than 10 percent of the books. We analyzed the primary and secondary metaphors in each title, applying sixty-three elementary "tags" when first coding the data. Eventually, these categories were recoded into twenty-eight more manageable groupings and, finally, into the nine master categories represented in Figure 3.1.

Coding tropes is a demanding task. Metaphors, almost by their nature, are multi-meaningful. To call politics *bewitching,* for example, is to humanize, exoticize, and demean it even while casting gender-, age-, and class-based aspersions on it. To apply a single code to this collection of sentiments is obviously difficult. Nonetheless we persevered, eventually settling on an imperfect but workable set of coding conventions:

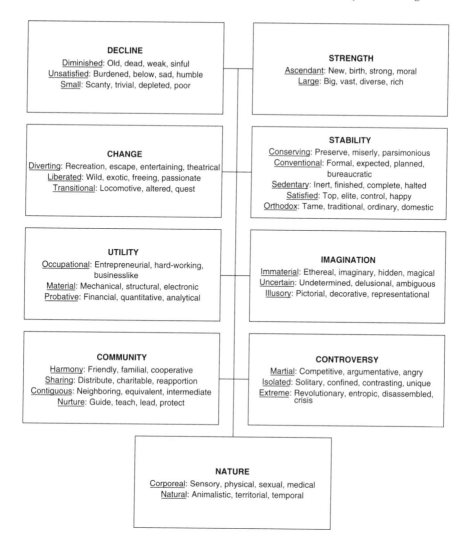

Figure 3.1 Major Metaphorical Families.

1. We used multiple analysts and frequent reliability checks to minimize idiosyncratic codings.

2. We adopted the perspective of the average reader rather than that of the specialist.

3. We opted for the simplest interpretation rather than the most provocative.

4. We coded a large number of titles to reduce the possibilities of systematic error.

5. We used early codings to anchor later codings, thereby assuring consistency across the dataset.

6. We hyperspecified first-order tags to capture the nuances of a title.

7. If a title's initial metaphor was unclear, we used the rest of the title to clarify its meaning.

8. When intercoder agreement could not be achieved, the title was discarded.

These conventions did not ensure perfection, but they proved functional. So, for example, a title like *The Politics of Greeting* was first tagged "Friendly" (viz., Figure 3.1), then "Harmonious," and finally assigned to the "Communal" category. Most of the codings were unproblematic, but some were not. For example, a book like *The Politics of Housework* could be judged Familial/Harmonious/Communal (our coding) if a coder featured its domestic qualities. Just as easily, a coder with Marxist leanings could justify an Entrepreneurial/Occupational/Utility tag while a feminist could make an Inert/Sedentary/Stable assignment.

We resisted such grand theorizing, choosing the most pedestrian categorical assignment in all cases. Procedurally, we coded both the primary and secondary metaphor in each title (61 percent of the books had at least two pieces of imagery). When a title had multiple metaphors (e.g., *Battered Women's Justice: The Movement for Clemency and the Politics of Self-Defense*), we used this convention: Code the first metaphor first. So, for example, we assigned the *battering* token to the Angry/Martial category and labeled it the title's primary metaphor. Then we assigned the *movement* metaphor to the Locomotive/Transitional category and called it the secondary metaphor. We ignored the Protect/Nurture metaphor (i.e., *the politics of self-defense*).[24] By way of example, Table 3.1 presents some of our coding decisions.

Our purpose in doing this coding was straightforward: to discover the implicit attributions made about politics by contemporary authors and to see if those attributions varied by time, topic, political focus, or scholarly orientation. We were comparatively unburdened by a priori philosophical assumptions when doing so, trusting that the books would tell their own stories without much prodding from us. We did not expect to find a stable, robust model of politics impervious to time and circumstance. But that was largely what we found.

DIMENSIONS OF POLITICS

Metaphors are helpful for studying politics because they are often underestimated. That is, it is part of our natural arrogance to assume that language is under our control, that it does our bidding without leaving a trace. But even a moment's reflection puts the lie to that. As of this writing, for example, it is impossible to talk about professional baseball without also address-

TABLE 3.1 Metaphorical Families: Some Examples

Decline	Utility

Decline

The Politics of Apology
The Politics of Corruption in Latin America
Fall Guys: False Confessions and the Politics of Murder
The Politics of Overfishing
Wounded Workers: The Politics of Musculoskeletal Injuries

Utility

The Politics of Architecture
The Politics of Porcelain
The Politics of Human-Embryo Research
The Politics of Whisky: Scottish Distillers, the Excise, and the Pittite State
Hard Bargains: The Politics of Sex

Strength

The Politics of Baptism
The Politics of Big Money
Declining to Decline: Cultural Combat and the Politics of Midlife
The Politics of Prison Expansion: Winning Elections by Waging War on Crime
A Politics of Enlarged Mentality: Hannah Arendt, Citizenship, Responsibility, and Feminism

Imagination

Libya's Qaddafi: The Politics of Contradiction
The Politics of Meaning: Restoring Hope and Possibility in an Age of Cynicism
Hong Kong: Culture and the Politics of Disappearance
Smoke and Mirrors: The War on Drugs and the Politics of Failure
Middle Class Dreams: The Politics and Power of the New American Majority

Change

Women, Ethnicity and Nationalism: The Politics of Transition
The Politics of Rescue
The Politics of Cultural Freedom: India in the 1950s
Transformation: The Promise and Politics of Empowerment
Senators on the Campaign Trail: The Politics of Representation

Community

The Politics of Our Own Backyard
The Politics of Parity in the Midwest
The Politics of Attachment: Toward a Secure Society
Dickens and the Politics of the Family
A Marriage Made in Heaven: The Sexual Politics of Hebrew and Yiddish

Stability

Governing the Atom: The Politics of Risk
The Unsinkable Fleet: The Politics of the U.S.'s New Expansion in World War I
The Politics of Managing the Maine Lobster Industry: 1860 to the Present
Policing Women: The Sexual Politics of Law Enforcement and the LAPD
Governing the Tongue: The Politics of Speech in Early New England

Controversy

Bad Mothers: The Politics of Blame in Twentieth Century America
Perfect Enemies: The Religious Right, the Gay Movement, and the Politics of the 1990s
Out of Bounds: Sports, Media, and the Politics of Identity
Fighting Words: The Politics of Hateful Speech
Green Backlash: The History and Politics of Environmental Opposition in the U.S.

Nature

Politics of the Visible: Writing Women, Culture, and Fascism
Listening to the Sea: The Politics of Improving Environmental Protection
The Cultural Politics of Fur
Greening the Millennium? The New Politics of the Environment
Creating Boundaries: The Politics of Race

ing the players' salaries, their drug habits, and their flamboyant girlfriends. These topics are thrust upon us each day by a torrent of media discourse, obliterating all discussion of curve balls being hit and second bases stolen. Our personal language habits, the way others talk to us on the job, and the topics the media make salient to us affect what we hear and what we say. As the poststructuralists are fond of saying, we write, yes, but we are also written.

When we began this study, we were confident that studying metaphorical patterns would be helpful, but we were largely agnostic about what we might find. We did assume, however, that the changing academic fashions detailed in chapter 2—the migration of *politics* from State to culture—would be accompanied by *textural* changes. Following the lead of William Connolly, we assumed that because politics is a "cluster concept" composed of a wide range of subconstructs (e.g., policing as politics, corporate payoffs as a politics, writing poetry as a politics), its meaning would dance wildly from topic to topic.[25] We were wrong.

Figure 3.2 tells a remarkable story: No matter what sort of politics is discussed, the same metaphorical families appear again and again. While each political domain has its preferred metaphorical grouping (e.g., Stability for state politics, Utility for infrastructure politics), all nine families are tapped

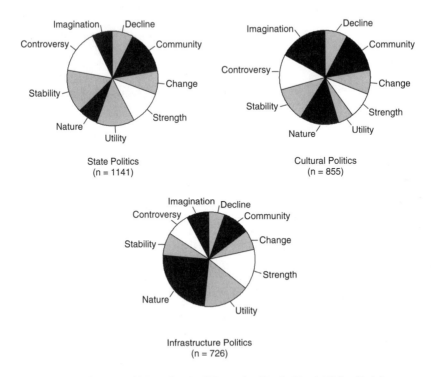

Figure 3.2 Distribution of Metaphorical Types by Topic (Book Titles Only).

continually across all three topical domains. In the almost five thousand titles examined here, each set of tropes was drawn on 11 percent of the time (slightly lower for Change and Decline, slightly higher for Utility and Community). This redundancy is remarkable since the books dealt with such different matters and were written by so many different authors.

What explains this consistency? What is it about politics that drives authors to the same stable of images time and time again? Do the patterns revealed in Figure 3.2 point up a sad deficiency in the human imagination, or do they show that the construct of politics has a distinct theoretical integrity? Is it possible, as Eva Kittay has suggested, that because metaphors give us "epistemic access" to ideas, once that access is granted we become caught in a spider web that traps our imaginations?[26] Is it also possible, as Richard Boyd has offered, that metaphors become "constitutive" of thought itself, thereby becoming "an irreplaceable part of the linguistic machinery" needed to describe a given object or construct?[27] While scholars are right to note that metaphors "change with time, need, desire and whim . . . [and] are rarely as tidy as we might like," what does it mean when they *are* tidy, when they do *not* change?[28] Is it possible, in other words, that Figure 3.2 does not reflect the vagaries of our particular coding scheme but the very essence of politics?

We feel that the answer to this latter question is "yes." Consider Figure 3.3, which tracks metaphorical usage across time. The steadfastness we see here is impressive, especially when remembering that there have been significant topical shifts in the book titles over the years. Not only do the bars remain roughly equivalent in height, but the *ratios* among the bars stay steady as well. Generally speaking, Strength trumps Decline and Stability trumps Change, reflecting what could be seen as an underlying conservatism on the authors' parts. Community and Controversy, alternatively, maintain a delicate balance, as if some sort of principle of equilibrium were guiding political affairs. There is some waxing and waning among these two metaphors, but they never lose sight of one another.

Utility and Imagination present a somewhat different story, with the former dominating the latter from 1967 through 1986. But the ratios began shifting in the late 1980s, and, by 1995–1998, roughly a quarter of all book titles—regardless of topic—used Imaginative metaphors. Interestingly, such metaphors were actually highest for State Politics (29.5 percent) versus Infrastructure Politics (22.6 percent) and Cultural Politics (25.5 percent), perhaps suggesting that constructivism, or what Jean-François Lyotard has called an "incredulity toward metanarratives," has gained the ascendency in the postmodern age.[29] The titles increasingly reflect these feelings of skepticism. One would expect to find such sentiments in the area of Cultural Politics, and we do: *The Politics of Uncertainty: Attachment in Private and Public Life* and *The Politics of Irony: Essays in Self-Betrayal.* But these same motifs also carried over into Infrastructure Politics: *The Mysteries of the Great City: The Politics of Urban Design, Lost Fathers: The Politics of Fatherlessness in America,* and *Mistaken Identity: The Supreme Court and the Politics of Minority Representation.*

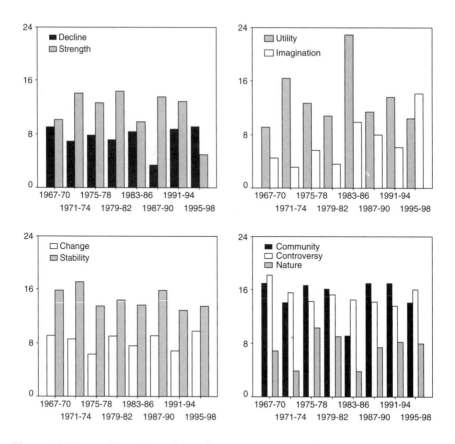

Figure 3.3 Percent Use of State Metaphors over Time (Book Titles Only; n = 2,641).

Most surprisingly, Imaginative metaphors have become the dominant image for State Politics as well, where they are now twice as popular as Nature, Stability, Community, and Controversy metaphors, three times more common than tropes of Utility, and *five times* more frequent than Strength metaphors. Only Change and Decline come close in popularity, and they are not that close (18.8 percent and 18.0 percent, respectively). In other words, the skepticisms of the 1970s have given birth to a full-fledged cynicism where State Politics is concerned. Television has always abetted such feelings, but publishers now lend a hand as well:

- *Mr. Bush's War: Adventures in the Politics of Illusion*
- *Game Without End: State Terror and the Politics of Justice*
- *Britain in the Nineties: The Politics of Paradox*
- *The Politics of Disenchantment: Bush, Clinton, Perot and the Press*

- *The Politics of Duplicity: Controlling Reproduction in Ceausescu's Romania*
- *Man Behind the Smile: Tony Blair and the Politics of Perversion*

Despite these recent developments, however, the overall picture of politics is one of constancy. For the authors studied here, politics is politics regardless of the topic addressed or the author's intellectual orientation. Our results reveal a four-part dialectic (diagrammed in Figure 3.3) whereby Strength and Decline, Change and Stability, Utility and Imagination, and Community and Controversy compete—and compete equally—for dominance. Individual authors are probably not aware of such equivalencies, but, collectively, they keep things in alignment. For each book employing a metaphor of Decline (e.g., *Slump City: The Politics of Mass Unemployment*), our database holds one with greater brio: *Reviving the Industrial City: The Politics of Urban Renewal in Lyon and Birmingham* or *Empowerment: The Politics of Alternative Development*. This is not to imply that some books are irretrievably cheery and others mindlessly apocalyptic. The titles of book and the contents of books are entirely different matters. But some sort of scoreboard seems to be operating when book titles are chosen, a recognition that politics presents four consistent challenges: to move forward or stay still; get better or worse; fashion plans or fashion dreams; compete or make common cause. Politics is about much else, but it is never not about these things.

Nature stands alone (at least in our model), suggesting that it takes all of politics, all of human invention, to cope with the natural world. Politics is small compared to nature (hurricanes and earthquakes, for example), which makes the federal Office of Emergency Preparedness something of a small miracle, a quintessentially political way of addressing calamity through group resolve. As Kenneth Burke has said, "men build their cultures by huddling together, nervously loquacious, at the edge of an abyss."[30] We are never more loquacious than when the air we breathe or the water we drink is imperiled. As a result, Nature is always part of the political imaginary:

- *Korea: The Politics of the Vortex*
- *The Broken Eagle: The Politics of Austrian Literature from Empire to Anschluss*
- *Fire on the Prairie: Chicago's Harold Washington and the Politics of Race*
- *Thunder on the Right: The "New Right" and the Politics of Resentment*
- *Jaws of Victory: The Game-Plan Politics of 1972*

It is perhaps not surprising that our model of politics turned out to be dialectical in nature. Politics is, after all, a great impertinence: It intrudes where it is not wanted and enforces compromises between opposing forces. It makes private matters public, balances morality with expediency, and often declares a half loaf of bread sufficient. Previous definitions of politics have exposed these tensions as well:[31]

- In politics nothing is *just* save what is *honest;* nothing is *useful* except what is *just.* (Maximillien Robespierre, 1791)

- It is indeed a law of politicks as well as of physicks, that a body in *action* must overcome an equal body at *rest.* (Fisher Ames, 1805)

- In politics one must take nothing *tragically* and everything *seriously.* (Louis Adolphe Thiers, 1873)

- Politics is not an *art*, but a *means.* It is not a *product,* but a *process.* (Calvin Coolidge, 1924)

- Politics is not the art of the possible. It consists in choosing between the *disastrous* and the *unpalatable.* (John Kenneth Galbraith, 1969)

What is it about politics that makes us so double-minded? Why can we only speak of it in contrasts? One possible answer: Politics makes faded idealists of us all. In politics, that is, what looks good on paper during a planning session often ignites a furor in the subsequent committee meeting. A deal struck at eleven in the morning can melt into nothingness by five in the evening. As a result, the aforementioned definitions harbor a sense of resignation, as if accommodationist politics is the only sort of politics possible. Collectively, they echo Peter Thorneycroft's observation that "the choice in politics isn't usually between black and white. It's between two horrible shades of gray."[32]

Our findings tell the same story but a bit more pointedly. We find a certain willed enforcement of politics' dualisms, an insistence that Decline and Strength be monitored carefully and that change not become undisciplined or Stability an excuse. There is something faintly Aristotelian about all of this equanimity, something Western and American as well. One wonders if the metaphors would be balanced so perfectly in a less diverse and fractious society. In any event, our authors present us with a new definition of politics:

> Politics is a distinctively human way of reacting to the exigences of the *natural* world. To do so, it attempts to maximize group *strength* to offset the forces of *decline,* keeping things as *stable* as the winds of *change* allow. By inventing *imaginative* solutions to *utilitarian* problems, politics regulates social *controversies* to produce provisional forms of *community.*

There is nothing inspiring about this definition. It is a definition only an octopus could love: On this hand, on the other hand. But it also features politics' unique menu of choices: whom to confront? how to negotiate? when to cut one's losses? Nothing about politics reduces to a science in this model. Instead, one shuffles along, the antimonies of politics making us constantly vigilant. Political philosopher Carl Schmidt explains why: "The high points of politics are simultaneously the moments in which the enemy is, in concrete clarity, recognized as the enemy."[33] Schmidt was a dialectician to the core. He would not be surprised by our exquisitely balanced metaphors.

PERSPECTIVES ON POLITICS

The overall result, then, was a stable pattern of images. At least for book authors, *politics* is dialectical to its core. Its dualisms undergird all drama as well. Shakespeare's *King Lear* embodied those tensions, as did Edwin O'Connor's *The Last Hurrah*. Politics is often the story of great persons who can be surprisingly small. Just as often, it is the story of average people challenged to become great (Harry Truman comes to mind). This emotional back-and-forth makes politics endlessly fascinating.

As consistent as these patterns were, however, some authors struck out on their own. Figure 3.4 shows that humanists and social scientists, for example, discussed politics in similar ways with one notable exception: They diverged along the Utility/Imagination axis, perhaps revealing underlying epistemological differences. So, for example, while some social scientists drew on contractarian metaphors (e.g., *Big Deal: The Politics of the Illicit Drugs Business* and *Feminists Negotiate the State: The Politics of Domestic Violence*), others focused on temporal matters (e.g., *Borrowed Time: Artificial Organs and the Politics of Extending Lives*). Still other books (like *Automatic Government: The Politics of*

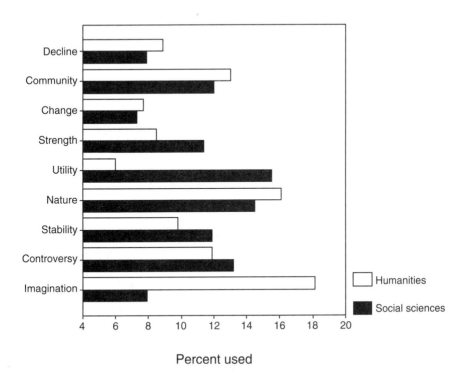

Figure 3.4 Metaphors by Disciplinary Orientation (Books and Periodicals; n = 3,938).

Indexation) reveal the structuralist underpinnings of the scientific mindset, while others (like *Democracy at Work: Municipal Reform in the Progressive Era* and *The Politics of Efficiency: Labor and Politics of New Work Organization*) reflect a long-standing American love affair with mercantilism.

The humanists' metaphors were bolder and more athletic. Some posited idealized states (*Paradise Remade: The Politics of Culture and History in Hawaii*) or essential conditions (*The Politics of Being: The Political Thought of Martin Heidegger*), titles that would be audacious to the average social scientist. Humanists were also tempted by narrative, often focusing on ontological matters (*Medicine Stories: History, Culture and the Politics of Integrity*). They also used representational images heavily (*Exhibiting Cultures: The Poetics and Politics of Museum Display*), and their titles frequently had a restless, exploratory quality (*The Quest for the Russian Soul: The Politics of Religion and Culture*).

This disciplinary divide is hardly surprising when one considers the different sorts of persons attracted to humanistic and social scientific work. But why are these the only differences reported in Figure 3.4? Why such a stability of tropes? Why did the word *reform* appear in eighty-five book titles, *public* in seventy-nine others, and *power* in eighty-nine more? Whether the subject matter was Wordsworth or stagflation, irony or iron ore, the authors returned to the same essentials again and again.

Given the results reported in chapter 2, one might have expected sharp differences in how male and female authors interpreted the political. Few such variations were found, however, although women did use Natural metaphors twice as often as men. That was true in discussions of State Politics, where male authors outnumbered female authors seven to one, as well as in Cultural Politics, where women were outnumbered only two to one (there were not enough female authors in the area of Infrastructure Politics to make a meaningful comparison). Why these differences? Is a certain gendered essentialism reflected here, a tendency by women to embrace the organic? Titles like *The Politics of Pain, The Politics of the Visible, The Politics of Water,* and *The Sexual Politics of Meat* suggest that possibility.

Some might champion that interpretation, heralding women's aversion to the abstractions (and mechanism) that men often bring to political matters. But no such notion is supported by the data collected here. Women did not emphasize Community more often than men, for example, nor were they loath to invoke images of Controversy and Change. They were just as Utilitarian as their male counterparts, and they used metaphors of Strength equally often as well. Politics, it appears, is politics—regardless of gender. Indeed, even when comparing male authors writing about State Politics (their traditional domain) to female authors writing about Cultural Politics (where they have become increasingly dominant), gender differences did not emerge. Even there politics continued to be politics.

But the picture changed considerably when titles appearing in popular magazines (e.g., *Time, Newsweek, Atlantic Monthly, Harpers,* etc.) were compared to those in a broad selection of scholarly journals (e.g., *Political Science Quarterly, Sociology, The Iowa Review, American Philosophical Quarterly*, etc.). Our database contained roughly five hundred magazine articles and over twelve hundred scholarly titles, giving us access to both popular and formal accounts of politics. Because we are especially concerned with State Politics in this book (and because the differences were particularly dramatic in that domain), we will concentrate on how governmental systems were framed by the authors. Unquestionably, the framings were different. Figure 3.5 presents the details.

Only in relationship to the popular press could the scholarly community seem establishmentarian! The patterns revealed in Figure 3.5 are distinctive: Despite their often trenchant criticisms of the State, scholars were positively salvific compared to the media. They emphasized Community more often than Controversy, Strength more frequently than Decline, and tropes of Utility more than anything else. The press was entirely different, using Change metaphors to emphasize the dynamic nature of politics ("Reinventing Government: Managing the Politics of Change," "The Politics of Peacetime Conversion") and recreational images to emphasize its excitements (e.g., "Two Ways to Play the Politics of Race," "The Hardball Politics of Trade"). These

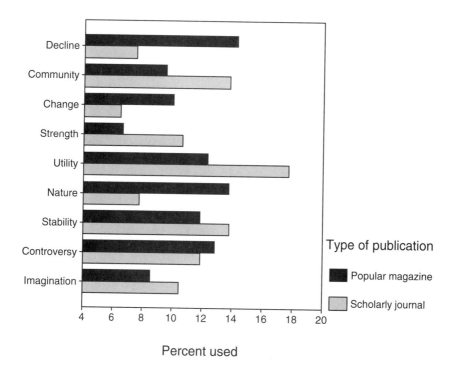

Figure 3.5 State Metaphors by Periodical Type, 1983–1998 (n = 689).

choices are not surprising given the press's need to reach an often bored audience. Popular audiences require a popular style, and that frequently causes the press to overreach. Nature provides such possibilities: "The Politics of Blood," "Bitter Politics of Fun," "The Scary Politics of Health," "The Politics of Drought."

To this point, the magazines' editorial decisions seem innocent enough: Make politics a blood sport to attract the casual reader. The downside to that approach is that the State itself finds it hard to keep pace, focused as it is on such stolid matters: building roads, curing disease, prosecuting criminals. The contrast between the excitement of magazine politics and the torpor of real politics therefore invites citizens to turn to more predictable fare: real sports rather than metaphorical sports.

The invitation to disengage is heightened by the magazines' heavy use of Decline metaphors. It is not hard to imagine what a steady diet of the following titles would do to one's civic inclinations:

- "The Politics of Embarassment in Alabama"
- "The Politics of Scarcity in Yugoslavia"
- "The Stingy Politics of Head Start"
- "The Politics of Zap: Two Bad Polls and Out"
- "The Fearful Politics of Abortion"
- "The Politics of Self-Pity"
- "The Politics of Yuck"

Each day, an avalanche of these titles descends on the average reader, making all seem dross in the world of politics. As one author suggests, these constructions help fashion a hip, misanthropic citizenry determined to feel good about feeling bad about politics.[34] The media reinforce such emotions, encouraging us to think of the State as an oaf, a conniving and witless oaf at that. While scholarly critiques of government can also sting, they are positively beneficent in contrast. Who would have imagined that?

CONCLUSION

This is not the first study to document the doleful nature of the mass media, the differences between the humanities and social sciences, or the dialectic of everyday life. But it does present surprising data about politics itself: No matter who appropriates the concept or for what purpose, they inevitably return to certain underlying choices—between what is and what can be, between the weak and the strong, between pulling together and hanging separately, between moving forward and going backward. These are not accidental dualities. They are the very stuff of politics. As J. G. A. Pocock notes, politics has always operated in the world of the contingent.[35] In this chapter, we have identified some of its contingencies.

Our route to doing so has been admittedly odd. Who would have thought that tropes and book titles would house such knowledge? For some, our enterprise may seem a scandal. Examine the mere titles of books and not their innards? Study language forms and not ideas themselves? Our defense is this: All thoughts ultimately come to be nested in language forms, so why not study them in their most native habitat? Some scholars push the matter further, arguing that human thought itself is metaphorical.[36]

In any event, there can be no doubt that language helps us think about politics, in part because that domain is so vast. As we saw in chapter 2, politics has expanded in recent years, giving us still more things to discuss. But that talk has also remained stubborn: We speak of politics today much as we did thirty years ago. We have probably always talked that way. As one author claims, "fictions and illusions are too important for maintaining good government to be left to artists like the playwright Moleiere."[37]

Eva Kittay notes that "we use metaphor when the resources of literal language are inadequate to articulate significant distinctions or unities."[38] She might also have added that using metaphor in standard ways makes the world a more comfortable place, reducing its blooming and buzzing, if not its confusion. Now, some might argue that locking into one way of talking can be dangerous, that new metaphors must be appropriated if a new politics is to be imagined. Perhaps that is true, but it is also possible that we just need to interrogate what we implicitly know—that politics is a struggle between Strength and Decline, Change and Stability, Utility and Imagination, and Community and Controversy. That observation reminds us of several things: (1) that political tensions are inevitable in any collectivity, (2) that all real growth presupposes stress and strain, and (3) that confronting the tensions of politics helps us confront Nature itself. We appear to already know such things, for they are imbedded in the way we speak about politics. It does not take a grand imagination to take solace in that realization.

NOTES

1. D. Sullivan, J. Pressman, B. Page, and J. Lyons, *The Politics of Representation: The Democratic Convention, 1972* (New York: St. Martin's Press, 1974).

2. M. Shapiro, *The Politics of Representation: Writing Practices in Biography, Photography, and Policy Analysis* (Madison: University of Wisconsin Press, 1988).

3. K. Burke, *A Grammar of Motives* (Berkeley: University of California Press, 1945), 503.

4. G. Ebersole, *Ritual Poetry and the Politics of Death in Early Japan* (Princeton, NJ: Princeton University Press, 1992).

5. A. Goatly, *The Language of Metaphor* (London: Routledge, 1997), 32.

6. F. Beer and C. DeLandtsheer, "Introduction," in *Metaphorical World Politics: Rhetorics of Democracy, Politics, and World Politics,* ed. F. Beer and C. DeLandtsheer (East Lansing: Michigan State University Press, in press), 15.

7. N. Scheper-Hughes and C. Sargent (eds.), *Small Wars: The Cultural Politics of Childhood* (Berkeley: University of California Press, 1998).

8. J. Spanier and D. Wendzel, *Games Nations Play* (Washington, DC: Congressional Quarterly Press, 1996).

9. S. Perry, "Rhetorical Functions of the Infestation Metaphor in Hitler's Rhetoric," *Central States Speech Journal*, 34 (1983): 229–35.

10. F. Beer, "The Epidemiology of Peace and War," *International Studies Quarterly*, 23 (1979): 45–86.

11. P. Chilton and I. Mikhail, "Metaphor in Political Discourse: The Case of the 'Common European House,'" *Discourse and Society*, 4 (1991): 7–31.

12. G. Hardin, "Living on a Lifeboat," in *Managing the Commons*, ed. G. Hardin and J. Baden (New York: W. H. Freeman, 1977), 261–79.

13. D. Bromwick, *Politics by Other Means: Higher Education and Group Thinking* (New Haven, CT: Yale University Press, 1992), 49.

14. A. Goatly, *The Language of Metaphor* (London: Routledge, 1997), 130.

15. K. L. Shimko, "Metaphors and Foreign Policy Decision Making," *Political Psychology*, 15 (1994): 655–71.

16. M. Osborn, "The Evolution of the Archetypal Sea in Rhetoric and Poetic," *Quarterly Journal of Speech*, 63 (1977): 347–63.

17. P. D. Nogales, *Metaphorically Speaking* (Stanford, CA: C.S.L.I. Publications, 1999), 216.

18. Y. Ezrahi, "The Theatrics and Mechanics of Action: The Theatre and the Machine as Political Metaphors," *Social Research*, 62 (1995): 299–322. For more on these same matters, see A. Coolidge, *Political Metaphors* (Iowa City: Naecenas Press, 2000).

19. S. L. Pugh, J. W. Hicks, and M. Davis, *Metaphorical Ways of Knowing: The Imaginative Nature of Thought and Expression* (Urbana, IL: N.C.T.E., 1997), 26.

20. See R. P. Hart and K. Kendall, "Lyndon Johnson and the Problem of Politics," in *The Future of the Rhetorical Presidency*, ed. M. Medhurst (College Station: Texas A&M University Press, 1996), 77–103.

21. R. P. Hart, *Modern Rhetorical Criticism* (Boston: Allyn and Bacon, 1997).

22. O. Santa Ana, *Brown Tide Rising: Metaphors of Latinos in Contemporary American Public Discourse* (Austin: University of Texas Press, 2002).

23. G. Lakoff and M. Johnson, *Metaphors We Live By* (Chicago: University of Chicago Press, 1980), 105.

24. Although we took pains to distinguish primary from secondary metaphors, subsequent analysis found virtually no differences among them. The metaphorical families, and their relative popularity, were identical for both sets of metaphors. Accordingly, we will concentrate exclusively on primary metaphors in this chapter.

25. W. E. Connolly, *The Terms of Political Discourse* (Lexington, MA: Heath, 1974), 14.

26. E. F. Kittay, *Metaphor: Its Cognitive Force and Linguistic Structure* (Oxford: Clarendon Press, 1987), 326.

27. Quoted in ibid., 325.

28. Ibid., 327.

29. J-F. Lyotard, *The Postmodern Condition: A Report on Knowledge*, trans. Geoff Bennington and Brian Massumi (Minneapolis: University of Minnesota Press, 1984), xxiv.

30. K. Burke, *Permanence and Change: An Anatomy of Purpose*, 3d ed. (Berkeley: University of California Press, 1984), 272.

31. For the following and other aphorisms about *politics,* see D. B. Baker (ed.), *Political Quotations: A Collection of Notable Sayings on Politics from Antiquity Through 1989* (Detroit: Gale Research, 1990), 162–70.

32. From ibid., 169.

33. C. Schmidt, *The Concept of the Political,* trans. G. Schwab (Chicago: University of Chicago Press, 1996), 67.

34. R. P. Hart, *Seducing America: How Television Charms the Modern Voter* (New York: Oxford University Press, 1994).

35. See K. Palonen, "Introduction: From Policy and Polity to Politicking and Politization," in *Reading the Political: Exploring the Margins of Politics,* ed. K. Palonen and T. Parkivkko (Tampere: Finnish Political Science Association, 1993), 13.

36. Lakoff and Johnson, *Metaphors We Live By,* 6.

37. This is a sentiment attributed to Rousseau by Yaron Ezrahi, "Theatrics and Mechanics of Action," 309.

38. Kittay, *Metaphor,* 125.

UNIT 2

THE LANGUAGE OF DEMOCRACY

Unit 1 of this book asked some basic questions: What is politics really about? What special problems does it present? Why are those problems so persistent? Why won't politics stay fixed? The answers to these questions come easily: We want more than we can have, and we want it now. We want it cheap, we want it plentiful, and we do not want to waste our time thinking about it. Politics would not be necessary if we were willing to live alone or if we had no ability to imagine a better life. But few of us can do either. Few of us are willing to go gently into that good night when our rights are being trampled or when our children's needs are going unmet. We need politics because we strive.

The book titles analyzed in chapters 2 and 3 remind us of these struggles. Writers from every walk of life during the last thirty years have stumbled across them time and time again. Their books remind readers why politics is a struggle but also why it is necessary. Writers from across the academic landscape could not think past nine metaphorical categories. Politics would not let them do so. Politics is demanding because it is, well, politics.

In unit 2 we turn from writers to activists, from politics writ large to politics made specific. Chapter 4 examines **government,** that large and luminous and lumbering giant that affects everyone so greatly. By looking at how politicians speak of the institution they superintend we will get a better idea of why politics is hard for some to stomach. One thing we will find is that, when soliciting our votes, politicians often ask us to reject their very occupation. Once in office, they change their tune. In chapter 4 we shall ask why this is so.

Chapter 5 focuses on the **media,** an increasingly powerful force in modern political life. Although they consume more media products than ever before, people are often unhappy with what they consume. Many of them listen to talk radio because they despise it; others queue up for bad movies because they cannot stop themselves; still others detest modern journalism even as they take it in in great gobs. Media consumption is now an addiction, and it directly affects what we feel about politics, its evil cousin. By looking at the media monitoring themselves we hope to get a fresh look at how the Fourth Estate has changed over the years and how it affects who we are as citizens.

Chapter 6 focuses on the **people** themselves or, at least, how the people are described. Our assumption here is that we are fascinated with ourselves. Many of us, for example, read every new public opinion survey in an attempt to establish our normality. Are we having as much sex as others? Is my weight correct for someone of my age, race, or gender? Are my reading habits or jogging habits or entertainment habits too idiosyncratic? We also learn about ourselves from politicians who are always ready to tell us who we are. They do so at least in part for self-interested reasons, but sometimes their search for the people is genuine. Nobody, after all, never really knows what three hundred million people believe at any given time; in describing the people, politicians try to constitute them as well. In chapter 6, we will examine the nature of these constitutions.

There is nothing automatic about any of this. Government is not wholly good or wholly bad. It is too large and too complex to be either. The media do not have one voice; they have many voices, which may be why we like them and are reviled by them simultaneously. The people, too, are never settled, never of one mind, in a nation so vast and fractious. Each of these elements—government, media, people—is part of an ongoing political struggle that will never be settled. That is why we *talk* about them. Unit 2 describes three rhetorics that will never quit.

The *Government*
A Troubling Ally

In the final days of what would turn out to be the closest presidential election in U.S. history, Republican candidate George W. Bush made a frantic series of speeches to win over undecided voters. With only five days to go before the general election, Bush tried to whip a St. Charles, Missouri, crowd into a frenzy by outlining his plans for government in general and for the Social Security Administration in particular: "This frightens some in Washington because they want the federal government controlling Social Security, like it's some kind of federal program. We understand differently though. You see, it's your money, not the government's money. You ought to be allowed to invest it the way you see fit."[1] Bush's statement is a strange one since the Social Security Program is, of course, a governmental program—always was, always will be. Predictably, an avalanche of pundits jumped on Bush's gaffe, some of them openly questioning his knowledge of how government works.[2] But in commenting on Bush's muddled facts, his critics missed a more important point—that the Governor was trading on, and fomenting, hostility toward government itself. Like many of his fellow politicians, Bush attacked the very institution he hoped to head, criticizing the government's ability to manage itself as well as the culturally out-of-touch "bureaucrats in Washington" who bedevil ordinary Americans. In making his charges, Bush tapped into emotionally salient attitudes that have been alive in the heartland since there was a heartland.

Twenty months later, the United States was a different place. With the ruins of the World Trade Center still smoldering after the September 11 attacks, and with the details of corporate malfeasance at Enron, WorldCom, ImClone, and Tyco coming to light, the times demanded something different, something inspiring. Bush complied, telling the conveners at the G8 Summit that the nation's fiscal integrity was rock solid. "People just need to know," he said, "that the SEC is on it, our government is on it."[3]

Surely this is odd—a government naysayer one day, cheerleader for the Fed the next. Government is like putty in Bush's hand, something molded and reshaped at will. Government, the bungler of two years earlier, was suddenly effective, springing to life in defense of the nation. Such is rhetoric. The facts in the case were something different: Government had not appreciably changed in the intervening months. Congress had debated laws, taxes continued to be collected, the courts dispensed justice, and the military stood ready to protect the nation. Despite the calamity of the 2000 election, the horrors of the September 11 attacks, and the plethora of corporate scandals, government continued to be government.

Bush continued to be Bush as well. Ideologically, he was still a Small Government man, easing federal regulation of businesses, supporting a strong national defense, and reducing the people's taxes. Rhetorically, however, he was ambivalent, bashing government one day and holding it up as a beacon of light the next. Was Bush uniquely schizophrenic in these ways, or was he part of a trend? If it was a trend, when did it start? Was he a bit like Groucho Marx, a person who refused to join any club that would admit him? And what did Bush's fellow Americans think of all this? Did his negative statements sap their confidence in political institutions, or did the public ignore what he said? If they were distrustful of government, did they tell their children that or did they bite their tongues? It is one thing, after all, to decry government and quite another to tell one's offspring that they live in a political system that makes no sense. Government is a problem. We are all of two minds about it.

These complex reactions will be explored in this chapter. We begin by noting that the term *government* was the fifty-third most common word spoken by elected presidents and political campaigners during the last fifty years (in a dataset containing some twenty-three thousand unique words). The word appears just as frequently as "if," "so," "he," and "been."[4] But unlike these functional terms, *government* calls up a host of feelings each time it is used. It has done so from the beginning. Like George W. Bush, Thomas Jefferson was of two minds about government, at one point recognizing that "it is error alone which needs the support of government; truth can stand by itself" but later warning that "a government that is large enough to supply everything you need is large enough to take everything you have." Today, we speak of "runaway government spending" when we are sad, "needed government subsidies" when we are happy (or covetous). "Limited government" almost always draws applause; "big government" sends people into paroxyms of anguish. "Enlightened government" is a term politicians use in their dotage; "government corruption" is the term they use to get votes. The story of government is long and complex, a story told each day in a thousand ways. We try to get a handle on that story here.

DISTRUSTING GOVERNMENT

In *A Necessary Evil*, Garry Wills describes the history of American distrust of government. He begins by reflecting on the Oklahoma City bombing, describing its perpetrator, Timothy McVeigh, as an American classic, heir to a two-centuries-long love affair with political disestablishment. Wills then sketches the family tree of mistrust, reminding us of the Constitutional Convention's debates over States' rights, John Calhoun's efforts at nullification, the seceders and insurrectionists who bracketed the Civil War, and the vigilantes who followed them—the Klan, the McCarthyites, the Montana Militia, the clinic bombers. The United States has also been home to withdrawers, transcendentalists like Henry David Thoreau, iconoclasts like H. L. Mencken, and experimentalists like the hippie communalists of the 1960s. The 1960s also gave birth to disobeyers like Martin Luther King, Jr., and the Students for a Democratic Society (SDS), persons who protested the hegemony of their nation's government.

Wills sees such pot-boiling as the price one pays for living a democratic life. But the "snobbish withdrawal from politics," says Wills, has never lasted. "There is ample reason to fear and distrust government, to probe it, make it come clean, demand access," Wills opines, but "most of the forms of fear and resistance traced in this book were futile." "Some of them tried to meet force with force and were outnumbered," while others "tried to deny the power of government to do harm by denying it the power to do much of anything." In almost all cases, Wills observes, "the cures were worse than the ills they addressed."[5] Wills concludes that a governless world can be imagined but that that is an antisocial use of the imagination.

Americans imagine it nonetheless, as research on political distrust continually shows. Political scientist Eric Ulsaner reports that in the 1950s and 1960s, about 80 percent of the American people professed confidence in government. By the 1990s, that number had dropped to about 25 percent.[6] It was not just the government in Washington that people had come to dislike, remarks Ulsaner, it was the very concept of government, state and local branches included.[7] John Alford shows this to be true across the board. Scores on trust in government from national surveys have declined for whites as well as blacks, men as well as women, rich as well as poor, Southerners as well as Midwesterners, old as well as young, educated as well as uneducated.[8] Although social science surveys were not run in the 1700s, it is likely that trust in government has never been lower than on the very day this chapter is being written.

Why? Virginia Chanley and her colleagues offer a complex answer, suggesting that economic factors affect confidence in the president and that confidence, in turn, predicts trust in government writ large.[9] Lilliard Richardson and his associates identify other causal links: People's partisan feelings predict how they feel about Congress, the economy affects how they judge the president, and their level of education determines what they think of the judiciary (the more education they have the more they like the Court).[10] Other scholars offer a directly empirical explanation—politicians' own dishonesty and self-interestedness discourage voters. If politicians would operate more forthrightly, the authors say, they would get on better with the American people.[11]

All of these explanations emphasize organic forces. But we must also consider contrivances. Political scientists Amy Fried and Douglas Harris take note of the various groups in the United States that promote governmental distrust. Political action committees, social movements, corporate lobbying organizations, and a variety of home-grown anarchists constantly decry governmental action (or inaction). According to Fried and Harris, such groups attack government in order to build their own memberships, change how citizens vote, and put pressure on Congress to pass group-friendly legislation. "Elites not only react to the public's distrustful mood," say Fried and Harris, they "also seek to shape it, frame it, and employ it."[12]

In addition, suggest Jack Citrin and Samantha Luks, the mass media denounce government—either actively or passively—and that makes viewers cynical. "From talk shows to *Saturday Night Live*," they say, "no one hesitates to mock and denigrate the nation's top leaders."[13] In addition, report David Brady and Sean Theriault, the everyday work of Congress—making laws, solving the people's problems—is rarely shown on television, so the electorate sees very little government in action.[14] As we will see in chapter 5, the media have numerous reasons for fostering cynicism, not the least of which is that it conforms to certain journalistic traditions and popular culture themes. The great danger of widespread suspicion, say Citrin and Luks, is that the very things a government depends upon for survival—voluntary compliance of its citizens, the ability to shape imaginative legislation, and the capacity to speak to other nations with one voice—are diminished. These are not small matters.

In this chapter we conduct a kind of "institutional introspection" to see what politicians themselves say about government. We locate our analysis in the most obvious of places, in the presidential election speeches, inaugural addresses, and State of the Union messages delivered between 1946 and 2001 (a total of 564 messages overall).[15] This collection provides a rich sampling of both Democratic and Republican administrations, younger and older presidents, and Cold War and post–Cold War tones.

In inspecting these messages, we focused on the *government* token exclusively, noting the fifteen words preceding and following it in the passage as well. Whenever an allusion was found we noted its tone (e.g., positive, negative, or neutral) and any accompanying adjectival phrases (e.g., "big government" or "compassionate government"). In addition, we calculated an Optimism score for each speaker, campaign, and genre, a simple ratio of positive characterizations minus negative characterizations divided by the number of tokens used. We derived a Dynamism score similarly (active characterizations minus passive characterizations divided by the number of tokens used). This was hardly a complex coding scheme, but it afforded surprisingly powerful understandings of how *government* works in modern political discourse. These data not only tell us what political actors feel about government but also what they encourage voters to feel. As it turns out, their invitations are not altogether cheery ones.

FEATURING GOVERNMENT

According to sociologist Pierre Bordieu, political leaders get their strength from the ability to translate things, from their capacity "to speak or act on behalf of a group."[16] In doing so they act as "a medium between the group and the social world" and thereby help establish its range of meanings.[17] These meanings, in turn, determine what people know, what they value, and what they take for granted. People also learn things elsewhere—in school, in church, from the mass media—but politicians affect them in subterranean ways. They do so with special impact when framing the *assumption* voters use to make decisions.

Political campaigners work especially hard at such framings, traveling about the nation every four years to tell voters what government is and what it might become. Removed as they are from politics, voters often let these references fly past them. But the faster and thicker they fly the more likely they are to be noticed, so it is especially useful to look at the sheer amount of talk about government. For instance, in 1948 Thomas Dewey, a Republican governor with no elective experience in Washington, spoke about government three times more often than his rival, Harry Truman. Fifty years later, George W. Bush, an outsider with similar credentials, was six times more likely to speak of governance as his opponent, Al Gore, a person with twenty-four years of federal experience. As far as *government* is concerned, rhetorical insistence and political authority are inversely correlated.

Political scientist Murray Edelman says that political candidates have something to gain and something to lose every time they discuss a given subject. To address a topic, says Edelman, is to reach for a kind of "borrowed prestige."[18] Taking the initiative in a campaign, that is, can give an otherwise unknown candidate special claim on an audience's attention. In 1968, for example, George Wallace's brassiness let him speak for many Americans who felt they had no voice; that was true again in 2000 when Ralph Nader tilted at the windmills of Washington. In a rhetorical world, owning an issue (jobs for George Wallace, the environment for Ralph Nader) can turn into political currency.

Table 4.1 tells two stories. The first is the challenger's story. In eight of the nine incumbent elections, the challenger claimed *government* for his own. Only in 1984 did Ronald Reagan depart from that pattern. Because he enjoyed such success running as an outsider in 1980, Reagan did so again four years later, tarring his opponent, Walter Mondale, with the brush of his former boss, Jimmy Carter.[19] Why do challengers—of both parties—take on government so directly? One reason is that the challenger's job is to make distinctions "between the haves and the have-nots, between right and

TABLE 4.1 Frequency of *Government* Tokens in Campaigns, 1948–2000 (n = 1,882)

Year	Candidate	Party	Status	Frequency (Standardized)
1948	Dewey	Republican	Challenger	0.33
	Truman	Democrat	Incumbent	0.14
1952	Eisenhower	Republican	Open	0.32
	Stevenson	Democrat	Open	0.14
1956	Eisenhower	Republican	Incumbent	0.26
	Stevenson	Democrat	Challenger	0.13
1960	Nixon	Republican	Open	0.13
	Kennedy	Democrat	Open	0.06
1964	Goldwater	Republican	Challenger	0.30
	Johnson	Democrat	Incumbent	0.15
1968	Nixon	Republican	Open	0.12
	Humphrey	Democrat	Open	0.08
1972	McGovern	Democrat	Challenger	0.21
	Nixon	Republican	Incumbent	0.13
1976	Carter	Democrat	Challenger	0.33
	Ford	Republican	Incumbent	0.14
1980	Reagan	Republican	Challenger	0.22
	Anderson	Independent	Challenger	0.16
	Carter	Democrat	Incumbent	0.12
1984	Reagan	Republican	Incumbent	0.13
	Mondale	Democrat	Challenger	0.09
1988	Bush	Republican	Open	0.09
	Dukakis	Democrat	Open	0.08
1992	Clinton	Democrat	Challenger	0.20
	Bush	Republican	Incumbent	0.17
	Perot	Independent	Challenger	0.08
1996	Perot	Independent	Challenger	0.19
	Dole	Republican	Challenger	0.18
	Clinton	Democrat	Incumbent	0.09
2000	G. W. Bush	Republican	Open	0.31
	Gore	Democrat	Open	0.04

wrong, between the sensible and the impractical."[20] In such a scenario, *government* becomes shorthand for everything that has gone wrong. The predictable result: No matter who is running, government gets a drubbing.

In Erving Goffman's terms, American campaigns have become a kind of ritualistic degradation, a way for the nation to save face for having an imperfect political system.[21] Government becomes a convenient punching bag because it is everything that voters are not—removed, large, rich, smart, powerful. The challenger's rhetoric lets voters deposit all their insecurities on government's doorstep. Government, alas, cannot respond. It is gray; it is mute; it is government. Because of that, challengers "can use a bloated bureaucracy as an issue to address without saying anything substantial or risking rebuttal or opposition."[22] The *government* token evens the odds for challengers, forcing the incumbent to defend the status quo (which will be imperfect even in the best of times). As a result, the challengers speak in chorus:

- *Thomas Dewey, 1948:* "I pledge to you a government of teamwork. The executive heads of your *government* will be really qualified for their positions and they will be given full responsibility to do their job without loose talk, factional quarreling or appeals to group prejudice."[23]
- *Jimmy Carter, 1976:* "Among young people who happen to be of a minority group the unemployment rate is quite often 40 percent. This hurts our whole society, in many different ways, in crime escalation, in the breakdown of the family structure, and also in the respect of citizens for our own *government*."[24]
- *Ross Perot, 1996:* "I love the principles on which this great country was founded. . . . [T]hey are being grossly violated at this point in our country's history by the people at the highest levels in our *government*. I never thought I would live to see a major drug dealer give 20,000 bucks in Florida and then be invited to a big Democratic reception by the vice president of the United States."[25]

None of these challengers, interestingly enough, had spent even a day as an elected federal official. They had, however, the authority of emotion, the authority of lived citizenship. Any ordinary American could agree that factional quarreling was tiresome (Dewey), that good work was hard to come by (Carter), that sacred principles were being violated (Perot). From the standpoint of government itself, of course, these were drive-by shootings, wild shots ringing out in the night with no clear focus.

But there are also rational reasons for such strategies. With the party system in tatters and with the mass media able to publicize any candidacy easily, "Washington insiders" become a compelling target, the WWE wrestlers of their profession.[26] But to get the media's gratuities, the challenger cannot tell a small story. Government must be in real trouble for an incumbent to be unseated. That which is broken cannot be fixed; it must be broken some more.

What happens when challengers become presidents? Are they still as pugnacious when defending their turf? They are not. As we see in Figure 4.1, they take a higher road.[27] With the exception of George H. W. Bush, the challengers-turned-incumbents largely abandoned their attacks, focusing on values or principles or visions. Other scholars, using different approaches, have found similar patterns: Incumbents are more positive than challengers.[28] At first that seems obvious: Challengers attack and incumbents defend. But why is *government* the predictable whipping boy? Why does campaign discourse

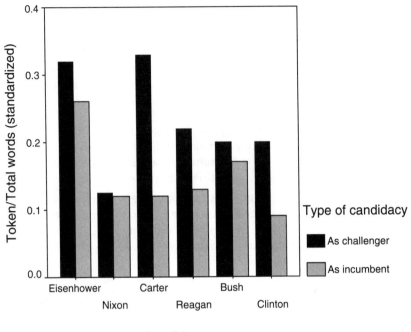

Figure 4.1 Use of *Government* Token by Campaign Type.

turn systemic rather than, say, issue-based or policy-based or even party-based? And what results from these degradation rituals, when system-bashing becomes the only game in town? Might regime support diminish? Might voting become an afterthought? Surely these are possibilities.

The easy retort is that this is "only rhetoric" and that few will notice. One wonders. The decline in civic trust comes from somewhere, after all. Why not from the campaign itself? And what makes people confident that they are insulated from such cynicism? What countervailing rhetorics encourage them to vote, to attend a rally, to send a check? Some might argue, of course, that all this is quite healthy, that the parties should debate the merits of government and do so vigorously. By and large they do. Table 4.1 shows that the Republican nominee claimed the *government* token in eleven of the past fourteen presidential campaigns. The few exceptions occurred during the tumultuous days of Vietnam (McGovern in 1972) and in the aftermath of the Watergate affair (Carter in 1976), times when governmental trust was especially low.[29] With the single exception of Bill Clinton in 1992, the Republican nominees have detailed governmental woes.

Campaign apologists might declare such rhetoric to be good for us. It is helpful, they would argue, for government to get a house-cleaning every four years. It is also helpful, they might claim, for the parties to debate the main source of their disagreements. The *government* token serves both purposes. No nation can survive, the apologists would declare, when fundamental presuppositions are ignored or poorly contested. No doubt that is true. But it is also true that these discussions can become noxious. What happens when voters hear nothing but government-bashing? Might torpor result? Might cynicism be reinforced? Might policy matters be ignored? Might the media emphasize personalities to spice up the campaign? All of these things are possible, and here is something worse: The nation could come to think that governance itself is a canard. Should that happen, it would be a consequence of some moment.

PURGING GOVERNMENT

Numerous people, fabled and forgotten, have clamored for the destruction of the State. Maximillian Robespierre, Vladimir Lenin, Nelson Mandela, and John Brown all attacked the governing structures of their times. We think of them now as revolutionaries, people who could not abide incremental change. The tools they used—guillotines, worker battalions, strikes, and armed insurrections—have also become famous. People such as this did not try to talk the world into newness.

Democracies also change, but they do so more glacially. The history of the United States, says Garry Wills, is a history of political experimentation, a restlessness born out of the nation's diversity. Americans, it might be said, are a people with comparatively little in common who live next door to one another. That condition makes them preternaturally cranky, and it affects their political campaigns as well. What do they hear about government in such moments, especially from those who would lead them?

Figure 4.2 shows that *government* has always been a topic of discussion during campaigns, although its prominence has fluctuated considerably. Harry Truman declared war on a Republican Congress in 1948, Barry Goldwater displayed Madisonian distemper in 1964, and Jimmy Carter promised to purge governance of its Watergate-related sins in 1976. These are the sounds of a churning democracy, questions about how, and how much, the people should be governed. As we see in Figure 4.2, there is also a periodicity to these cycles, and that is probably healthy as well, giving the country a chance to ask basic questions at times and quotidian questions at other times.

The rhetoric of *big government*, in contrast, has become steadily popular recently, spawning images of intrusive and inefficient systems overwhelming the citizenry. It is appropriate that this trend began in *1984*, as if Winston Smith himself had become a Reagan speechwriter. The 1992 and 2000 campaigns picked up the pace again, the former portraying a government of

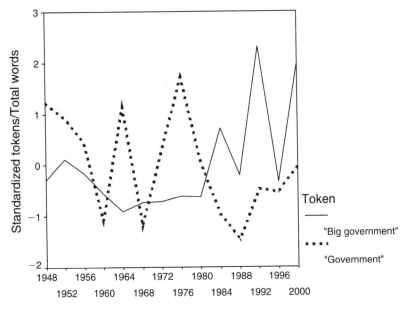

Figure 4.2 Use of *Government* Versus *Big Government* in Campaigns.

hope and the latter harking back to the sounds of the 1980s: "The nine most terrifying words in the English language are, 'I'm from the government and I'm here to help.' "[30]

The trends revealed in Figure 4.2 would warm the hearts of the federalists and the anti-federalists. We have re-engaged their quarrel. That debate, says political theorist Ernest Barker, is an argument about essence, not texture: "One of the great difficulties of democratic government may be expressed in the one word 'size.' "[31] It is curious that this issue of size has become rife in the United States, the largest democracy with the largest land mass, a democracy whose size let it fight two world wars (and win), become the world's only superpower within a generation, offer public education on a scale never before imagined, and oversee the most powerful economy in human history.

But the story of the United States is also a story of individuality—of the family farm and the small business owner, of Jimmy Stewart going to Washington and reducing the scale of its ambitions. The United States is a nation of states, one of which—Texas—still reserves the right to subdivide itself into five separate nations if the oppressions of Washington become too onerous. Popular culture also obliges: stories of the heroic cop on the beat, the batting champ born in the ghetto, the beauty queen who can sing an aria. Television shows like *American Idol*, youth groups like Junior Achievement, and network sales operations like Mary Kay Cosmetics remind us each day that the United States is a nation of individuals. The United States is a small-scale large-scale place.

Democrats, as a result, "do not believe in big government" but "in effective government—in a government which meets its appropriate responsibilities, and meets them effectively."[32] Republicans do not believe in a government "that centralizes control in Washington and makes us really the victims of absentee landlordism."[33] Nobody in the biggest government on earth believes in big government. Denunciations like these are popular because, in the words of psychologists Serge Moscovici and Marisa Zavalloni, they do not require voters to judge objective facts.[34] Instead, voters can excise a stark malignancy time and time again—a purifying ritual, an orgy of removal.

The rhetoric of big government also has an oxymoronic quality to it. Big government, a large and powerful thing, becomes weak because it is so large. Big government, a magnanimous and generous thing, becomes evil because it is rapacious. In both cases it fails because it succeeds so well.

How does myth relate to reality? Between 1948 and 1960, *big government* accounted for about 3.5 percent of all government references. During that time, federal spending averaged about 16.9 percent of the entire gross domestic product (GDP).[35] Between 1988 and 2000, government spending averaged 20.6 percent of the GDP, but *big government* references increased 445 percent. Even more intriguing, those same years saw a *steady decline in government spending* as a function of overall GDP. Government got larger rhetorically even as it shrank empirically.

For Republicans, "the private sector" becomes the foil for big government. "We will cut both debt and spending and take a whack out of the budget deficit. My feelings about big government come from my experience; I spent half my adult life in the private sector," said George H. W. Bush in 1992.[36] True, Bush had spent a few years thusly employed, but he had also spent a *lifetime* as a government worker. Bush's strategy was doubly ironic since in 1992 he ran against two individuals (Ross Perot and Bill Clinton) without a whit of federal experience. Bush thereby denied himself to advance himself. And with good reason. Studies show that Americans have becoming increasingly suspicious of governmental actions,[37] distrustful of its capacity to deliver needed services,[38] tired of its conflicts and tensions,[39] and angry at their declining sense of political efficacy.[40] The rhetoric of *big government* is therefore a classic lament, a cry for help with an illness that cannot be described but that debilitates nonetheless.

Figure 4.3 pushes the diagnosis deeper. Government is not only getting larger, but it is doing more as well (see Dynamism)—all this despite the vaunted devolutions of recent years. That is, in the 1990s the federal government asked the states to take more responsibility for food stamp programs, social services block grants, workforce investment programs, and temporary

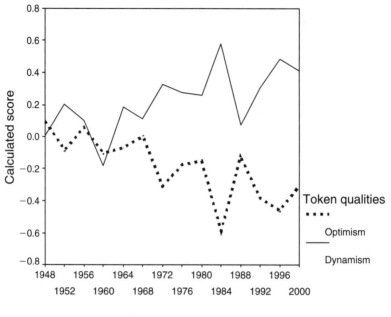

Figure 4.3 Token Qualities in Campaign Speeches.

assistance for needy families, as well as various HUD and Medicaid programs.[41] Big government got smaller, or at least that was the intention. As we
see in Figure 4.3, it got sadder as well (see Optimism).

In 1948, in contrast, one candidate declared that "the Government is
developing impressive programs in many scientific fields. Fundamental
research is being carried out,"[42] while his opponent vowed that "The Federal
Government must stand ready to lend a hand to the states to encourage programs of community development."[43] The first speaker was Harry Truman
and the second Tom Dewey, but the picture they painted was the same—
governance without embarrassment. The year 1996 was far different, with
Bob Dole declaring that "President Clinton has a million little plans for our
government to tell you how to run your life."[44] Dole's opponent, the New
Democrat, responded in kind: "Do you know when I became President, if
you wanted to buy—if a government agency wanted to buy a $4 stapler, they
had to do $50 worth of paper work."[45]

The trope of big government has now become artful: $50 staplers, costly
and abandoned defense projects, rotting food in warehouses. Stories of how
the federal government invented the Internet, encouraged small business

development through loan initiatives, built land-grant universities, constructed a national highway system, and electrified the homes of rural America are now antique. These stories may be still worth telling, but nobody is left to tell them.

Attractive though it is, the rhetoric of *big government* is not cost-free. A team of German sociologists recently studied the long-term effects of political blame on voters and concluded that constant bickering about governmental incapacity "harms the reputation of the political system, and . . . jeopardizes the parliamentary institutions—the parties, the parliament, and the government" as well.[46] Civics classrooms throughout the country tell a different story—that democratic governance is a miracle, that the State functions amidst the gloom. Presumably, the nation's parents want their children to hear such stories of uplift, even though parents themselves will not hear them, at least not if they only listen to campaign rhetoric. Fortunately, government also has its redemptive moments. They occur in January.

REDEEMING GOVERNMENT

In their classic work *The Civic Culture,* Gabriel Almond and Sidney Verba observe that a nation as complex as the United States cannot rely on a purely pragmatic discourse, that it must get beyond "a politics of opportunism" to survive.[47] Such a nation must take advantage of rituals to inspire people's allegiance to a common political system. As one researcher notes, presidents now spend over 40 percent of their time in public ceremonies to meet the nation's emotional and philosophical needs.[48] Some of these ceremonies occur in Washington and some in the nations' hinterlands; a few of them are calendrical (e.g., the State of the Union address). Others, like the inaugural address, occur episodically. Most, however, try to resuscitate government, and they therefore deserve special scrutiny.

The inaugural address, for example, brings together the outgoing and incoming administrations on the steps of the Capitol, and that speaks powerfully to the system's continuity. The State of the Union also sends a metamessage—that the three branches of government abide and, at least in part, abide one another. The State of the Union shows that work is getting done, and it celebrates that fact. The setting itself—all of government seated in the House chambers—dramatizes the possibilities of politics. If campaigns slay government, that is, rituals rehabilitate it. If campaigns are wild, rituals are settled. If campaigns ask questions, rituals offer answers. *Government* is treated far more gently in the latter settings, as we see in Figure 4.4.

Political optimism clearly varies by genre.[49] Consider the unlikely duo of Jimmy Carter and George H. W. Bush who, for their own reasons, personified the anti-government crusader when running for office. Just seconds after the chief justice administered the oath of office, however, their tone brightened. Jimmy Carter recanted his campaign rhetoric with "We know

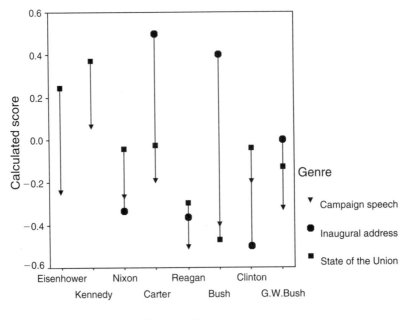

Figure 4.4 Generic Differences in Optimism by Speaker.

that if we despise our government we have no future,"[50] a sentiment that must have seemed particularly poignant in January 1977, just a few months after he had decried the persona of Richard Nixon housed in the body of Gerald Ford. During his inaugural address, George Bush made government the handmaiden of history: "Today is the concrete expression of a stunning fact: our continuity these 200 years since our government began. We meet on democracy's front porch, a good place to talk as neighbors."[51] All of this transpired just a bit after he had told a Columbus, Ohio, audience that "government has a place" in our lives but "not the central one."[52]

Such transformations continue in the State of the Union address for two reasons: (1) It would be untoward for the chief executive to decry governance in the presence of six hundred people who make it function each day; (2) it would be cruel (and suicidal) to tell a national audience that their political system is broken and their money wasted. Like the hangman's noose, the State of the Union concentrates the mind of the president. That is the negative case for being positive. The positive case is that no president really despises government or thinks it ineffectual. Their struggle is to get their arms around its vastness and find a language for rendering it whole. Because government is so complex, it daunts the rhetorical imagination.

Although Dwight Eisenhower had warned the nation about the dangers of *big government* during his campaigns ("where has this strange idea come from that government is the great provider?"),[53] he brightened up in his State of the Union addresses. In the 1954 speech, for example, he invoked *government* nearly thirty times, ticking off its benefactions serially:

- The federal government is continuing its central role in the Federal Aid Highway Program.
- The federal government will continue to construct and operate economically sound flood control, power, irrigation and water systems.
- The federal government can do many helpful things and still carefully avoid the socialization of medicine.
- A government can strive, as ours is striving, to maintain an economic system whose doors are open to enterprise and ambition.
- A government can sincerely strive for peace, as ours is striving.
- A government can try, as ours tries, to sense the deepest aspirations of the people.[54]

Eisenhower's remarks are typical of his successors—Jekylls in office, Hydes on the campaign trail. This is an odd sort of syncopation, but it conforms to primitive ritualistic patterns: a time of hope, a time of doubt, a time of conflict, a time of renewal. What is odd about this story, however, is that the same token, *government*, serves so many different purposes. "Let us destroy government in the spring," the candidates propose, "and give birth to it in the winter." The seasons of politics are therefore juxtaposed to the seasons of nature, but most Americans do not notice. They are used to these patterns and perhaps inured to them.

What does it mean when government is routinely savaged by those who oversee it? Does such a rhetoric betray an underlying distrust of democracy or its ability to establish viable political structures? Or does it signal the opposite: a supreme confidence, a willingness to question the operations of government but never its essence? Questions like these become especially important when such rhetoric becomes increasingly pessimistic (as it has) and when citizens treat that pessimism as warranted. It is one thing for a nation to believe that a government that governs least governs best, quite another to believe that governance itself is a chimera. When that distinction ceases to be a distinction, people surely will be disadvantaged.

CONCLUSION

The concept of government has proved troubling throughout human history. Almost all memorable reflections about it are dialectical in character.

Let us call the roll: *Thomas Paine:* "Even in its best state [government] is a necessary evil." *Napoleon:* "Governments only keep their word when they are forced to, or when it is to their advantage." *Andrew Jackson:* "There are no necessary evils in government. It exists only in its abuses." *Henry Ward Beecher:* "The worst thing in this world, next to anarchy, is government." *Charles de Gaulle:* "To govern is always to choose among disadvantages."

None of these is a ringing endorsement of government. This chapter reports a similar roiling. Perhaps that is how it must be in a democracy. Perhaps the constant deconstruction and reconstruction of government is a sign of national health, a dynamic that provides, in the poet Swinburne's terms, "pleasure with pain for leaven." Thomas Jefferson, the most American of Americans, saw his fellow citizens as idealists at heart, perpetually uneasy with what they created. Said Jefferson: "[E]ach generation is as independent as the one preceding. . . . It has then . . . a right to choose for itself the form of government it believes most promotive of its own happiness."[55] From the beginning, the United States has wrestled with matters of permanence and change, and the rhetoric described here is its heir.

But there are dangers in all this as well. One must ask how much pessimism a nation can handle. Numerous researchers report that hostility toward government has grown rapidly in the United States of late. Calls to "reinvent government" are now common and, as of this writing, the governor of California has just been recalled.[56] In the 1990s, Newt Gingrich's Contract with America proposed to change the political system in its entirety. He did not succeed, of course, but there will be another Newt Gingrich some day. As political scientist George Frederickson notes, the Reinvention trend closely resembled the New Public Administration movement of the 1940s and 1950s.[57] Americans have long felt that government can be fixed, and some feel it can be fixed rather easily—give it less money, hold another Constitutional Convention, establish term limits or national referenda. None of this has happened, but believing that it can happen makes life possible for many Americans.

Despite all this caterwauling, most Americans find some peace in governance as well. Each year they troop to the nation's capital by the hundreds of thousands, many of them to enter the political lists but most to see its buildings and memorials.[58] More important, they bring their children with them. The White House, the Capitol, the Washington Monument, the Lincoln Memorial. Icons of permanence, icons of democracy. Most of these Americans cannot say precisely why they have come or how their sometimes cynical attitudes square with their hushed reverence when touring the memorials. They have complex feelings, and those feelings dovetail with the rhetoric described here. Americans' willingness to embrace change after September 11 produced the Homeland Security Act, the largest bureaucratic reshuffling in the nation's history. But those same Americans rebuilt the Pentagon with limestone from the Indiana quarry used in its initial construction.[59] The

United States is a nation bothered equally by change and stability. Its politics bespeaks that legacy.

NOTES

1. G. W. Bush, "Campaign Speech," St. Charles, MO. November 2, 2000. Complete transcript available at CNN.com, accessed on June 4, 2003.

2. Associated Press, "Gore Hits Bush's Social Security," November 3, 2000.

3. Y. Dreazen, "Sorry Wrong Number—Bush Promises Tough Response," *Wall Street Journal*, June 27, 2002.

4. The sample here consisted of 564 speeches (including campaign speeches, inaugural addresses, and State of the Union speeches). Of the fifty-two more common words, forty-eight were function words—mostly articles, pronouns, prepositions, and form of the verb "to be." The only nouns used more often than *government* were *people* (which ranked twenty-sixth), *America* (forty-first) *world* (forty-second), and *years* (forty-seventh).

5. G. Wills, *A Necessary Evil: A History of American Distrust of Government* (New York: Simon and Schuster, 1999), 316.

6. E. Ulsaner, "Is Washington Really the Problem?" in *What Is It About Government That Americans Dislike?* ed. J. Hibbing and E. Theiss-Morse (New York: Cambridge, 2001), 118.

7. Ibid., 133.

8. J. R. Alford, "We're All in This Together: The Decline of Trust in Government, 1958–1996," in *What Is It About Government That Americans Dislike?* ed. J. Hibbing and E. Theiss-Morse (New York: Cambridge, 2001), 28–46.

9. V. Chanley, T. J. Rudolph, and W. M. Rahn, "Public Trust in Government in the Reagan Years and Beyond," in *What Is It About Government That Americans Dislike?* ed. J. Hibbing and E. Theiss-Morse (New York: Cambridge, 2001), 59–81.

10. L. E. Richardson, D. J. Houston, and C. S. Hadjiharalambous, "Public Confidence in the Leaders of American Governmental Institutions," in *What Is It About Government That Americans Dislike?* ed. J. Hibbing and E. Theiss-Morse (New York: Cambridge, 2001), 83–97.

11. This is but one of several explanations offered by Jack Citrin and Samantha Luks in "Political Trust Revisited: Déjà Vu All Over Again," in *What Is It About Government That Americans Dislike?* ed. J. Hibbing and E. Theiss-Morse (New York: Cambridge, 2001), 23.

12. A. Fried and D. B. Harris, "On Red Capes and Charging Bulls: How and Why Conservative Politicians and Interest Groups Promoted Public Anger," in *What Is It About Government That Americans Dislike?* ed. J. Hibbing and E. Theiss-Morse (New York: Cambridge, 2001), 172.

13. Citrin and Luks, "Political Trust Revisited," 25.

14. D. W. Brady and S. M. Theriault, "A Reassessment of Who's to Blame: A Positive Case for the Public Evaluation of Congress," in *What Is It About Government That Americans Dislike?* ed. J. Hibbing and E. Theiss-Morse (New York: Cambridge, 2001), 175–92.

15. During some years, the president did not give the State of the Union orally. This was the case with Richard Nixon (in 1973) and Jimmy Carter (in 1981) when the

message was delivered to Congress in printed form. Accordingly, these texts were excluded from the study. On the other hand, George W. Bush's "budget message" before a full Congress on February 27, 2001, was included to capture a sense of Bush's "post-inaugural" style.

16. P. Bordieu, *Language and Symbolic Power* (Cambridge, MA: Harvard University Press, 1991), 75.

17. Ibid.

18. M. Edelman, *The Symbolic Uses of Politics* (Urbana: University of Illinois Press, 1985), 117.

19. We shall see in chapter 11 that this same overall approach affected Mr. Reagan's approach to political promises as well.

20. R. Hart, *Campaign Talk: Why Elections Are Good for Us* (Princeton, NJ: Princeton University Press, 2000), 84.

21. See E. Goffman, *Stigma* (Englewood Cliffs, NJ: Prentice-Hall, 1963). See also H. Garfinkel, "Conditions of Successful Degradation Ceremonies," *American Journal of Sociology*, 61 (1956): 420–24.

22. C. Goodsell, *The Case For Bureaucracy* (Chatham, NJ: Chatham House, 1983), 145.

23. T. Dewey, "Declaring Principles," Des Moines, IA, September 20, 1948.

24. J. Carter, "Campaign Speech," Salt Lake City, UT, October 7, 1976.

25. R. Perot, "Press Club Address," National Press Club, Washington, DC, October 24, 1996.

26. S. Kernell, *Going Public,* 3d ed. (Washington, DC: CQ Press, 1997), 40.

27. Note that Harry Truman, Lyndon Johnson, and Gerald Ford were excluded from this analysis because they did not run as challengers (or in an open campaign) prior to becoming president.

28. See, for example, Hart, *Campaign Talk,* 83–90.

29. The decline of trust in government during this time has been documented by a number of scholars, including S. Lipset and W. Schneider, "The Decline of Confidence in American Institutions" *Political Science Quarterly,* 99 (1983): 379–402; M. Hetherington, "The Effect of Political Trust on the Presidential Vote, 1968–1996," *American Political Science Review,* 93 (1999): 311–26; and R. Putnam, *Bowling Alone: The Collapse and Revival of American Community* (New York: Simon and Schuster, 2000). A book that is less worried about governmental distrust is William Chaloupka's *Everybody Knows: Cynicism in America* (Minneapolis: University of Minnesota Press, 1999).

30. R. Reagan, "Press Conference on Farmers' Need for Federal Assistance," August 12, 1986, in *Public Papers of the Presidents: Ronald Reagan 1986, volume 2* (Washington, DC: United States Government Printing Office, 1989), 1081.

31. E. Barker, *Reflections on Government* (Oxford: Oxford University Press, 1945), 73.

32. J. Kennedy, "Associated Business Publications Conference," Baltimore, Maryland, October 12, 1960, *Annenberg/Pew Archive of Presidential Discourse,* CD-ROM (Philadelphia: Annenberg School for Communication, 2000).

33. D. Eisenhower, "Republican Governors Conference," New York, NY, October 28, 1952, *Annenberg/Pew Archive of Presidential Discourse,* CD-ROM (Philadelphia: Annenberg School for Communication, 2000). Our brackets.

34. S. Moscovici and M. Zavalloni, "The Group as a Polarizer of Attitudes," *Journal of Personality and Social Psychology,* 12 (1969): 134.

35. Office of Management and Budget, "Budget of the United States Government, Historical Tables, Table 1.2—Summary of Receipts, Outlays, and Surpluses or Deficits as Percentages of GDP: 1930–2008," w3.access.gpo.gov/usbudget/fy2004/sheets/hist01z2.xls (July 10, 2003).

36. G. H. W. Bush, "Remarks Accepting the Nomination of the Republican National Convention in Houston," August 20, 1992, in *Public Papers of the Presidents: George Bush 1992–93, volume 2* (Washington, DC: United States Government Printing Office, 1993), 1383.

37. E. Uslaner, "Producing and Consuming Trust," *Political Science Quarterly*, 115 (2001): 569–90.

38. S. Tolchin, *The Angry American* (Boulder, CO: Westview, 1996), 27.

39. A. Ehrenhalt, *The United States of Ambition* (New York: Random House, 1991), 48.

40. S. Lipset and W. Schneider, *The Confidence Gap: Business, Labor, and Government in the Public Mind* (New York: Free Press, 1983).

41. For more on these matters, see M. B. Sawicky (ed.), *The End of Welfare?: Consequences of Federal Devolution for the Nation* (Armonk, NY: M. E. Sharpe, 1999).

42. H. Truman, "Address Before the American Association for the Advancement of Science," September 13, 1948, in *Public Papers of the Presidents: Harry S. Truman 1948* (Washington, DC: United States Government Printing Office, 1960), 484.

43. T. Dewey, "Campaign Speech at the Ground Breaking for the Governor Alfred E. Smith Houses," New York City, October 10, 1948.

44. R. Dole, "Campaign Speech at Villanova University," September 16, 1996, *Annenberg/Pew Archive of Presidential Discourse,* CD-ROM (Philadelphia: Annenberg School for Communication, 2000).

45. W. Clinton, "Remarks on Concluding a Bus Tour in Portland, Oregon," September 9, 1996, in *Public Papers of the Presidents: William J. Clinton 1996, volume 2* (Washington, DC: United States Government Printing Office, 1998), 1631.

46. H. Kepplinger, "The Declining Image of the German Political Elite," *Harvard International Journal of Press/Politics,* 5 (2000): 79.

47. G. Almond and S. Verba, *The Civic Culture* (Newbury Park, CA: Sage, 1989), 354.

48. R. P. Hart, *The Sound of Leadership: Presidential Communication in the Modern Age* (Chicago: University of Chicago Press, 1987).

49. The data for campaign speeches in Figure 4.4 includes only those speeches in which candidates ran for office as nonincumbents. As a result, Harry Truman, Lyndon Johnson, and Gerald Ford are not included here at all (since they never ran as challengers or as candidates in an open race).

50. J. Carter, "Inaugural Address," January 20, 1977, in *Public Papers of the Presidents: Jimmy Carter 1977* (Washington, DC: United States Government Printing Office, 1977), 2.

51. G. H. W. Bush, "Inaugural Address," January 20, 1989, in *Public Papers of the Presidents: George Bush 1989, volume 1* (Washington, DC: United States Government Printing Office, 1990), 1.

52. G. H. W. Bush, "Speech to the Republican State Convention," Columbus, OH, September 27, 1988, *Annenberg/Pew Archive of Presidential Discourse,* CD-ROM (Philadelphia: Annenberg School for Communication, 2000).

53. D. Eisenhower, "Eisenhower Campaign Train Speech," Des Moines, IA, Sep-

tember 18, 1952, *Annenberg/Pew Archive of Presidential Discourse*, CD-ROM. (Philadelphia: Annenberg School for Communication, 2000).

54. D. Eisenhower, "Annual Message to the Congress on the State of the Union," July 12, 1816. In *Public Papers of the Presidents: Dwight Eisenhower 1954* (Washington, DC: United States Government Printing Office), 6–23.

55. T. Jefferson, "Letter to Samuel Kercheval," July 12, 1816, in *Thomas Jefferson: Writings* (New York: Library of America), 1402.

56. C. Fox, "Reinventing Government as Postmodern Symbolic Politics," *Public Administration Review*, 56 (1996): 256–62.

57. G. Frederickson, "Comparing the Reinventing Government Movement with the New Public Administration," *Public Administration Review*, 56 (1996): 263–70.

58. Washington DC Convention and Tourism Corporation, www.washington.org (January 15, 2003).

59. B. Rosenberg, "Indiana Legacy Set in Stone," Associated Press, October 20, 2002.

5

The *Media*
Powerful Despite Themselves

T he story is an old one. Every few years, pollsters ask the American people what they think about professionals' ethics. Most recently, for example, medical personnel scored highest (nurses, veterinarians, physicians, and
pharmacists), followed by teachers, judges, policemen, and engineers. At the
bottom of the list (in forty-fifth place) were, predictably, used car salesmen
and telemarketers. Politicians did not do well either, nor did the mass media:
TV commentators were found in twenty-fifth place, newspaper reporters
were in twenty-eighth place, entertainment industry executives came in
thirty-fourth in the rankings, and Internet publishers were nestled with insurance salesmen at fortieth place.[1]

Why the opprobrium for the mass media? After all, they allow 285 million
Americans to stay in touch with one another and to keep overweening
power in check. The media help make complex ideas clear, an especially
important function in an age featuring adjuvant Tamoxifen therapy, strained
silicon chip production, streamlined tax deduction phase-outs, and the military's force-protection battle laboratories. The media help us discuss these
imponderables with some intelligence, and they let political underdogs have
their say as well. Through television, we can visit Paris without leaving our
homes, attend a royal wedding in London or a royal Superbowl in Miami,
and weep with our fellow citizens at important cultural moments like the
Kennedy assassination, the *Challenger* disaster, and the September 11 terrorist attacks. The media let us touch the world.

But hosannas are rarely sung for them. More commonly they are decried
by citizens, politicians, and social activists. Authors critique the media for
being too liberal (e.g., *Bias: A CBS Insider Exposes How the Media Distort the
News*)[2] or too conservative (e.g., *Rich Media, Poor Democracy: Communication
Politics in Dubious Times*).[3] Watchdog groups like Fairness and Accuracy in
Reporting purport to offer "well-documented criticism of media bias and
censorship,"[4] while Media Watch challenges "abusive stereotypes and other
biased images" that disadvantage certain groups in society.[5] To buy a newspaper in the United States is to have an opinion about it.

That has always been true. Thomas Jefferson, for example, once mused
that "the man who never looks into a newspaper is better informed than he
who reads them, inasmuch as he who knows nothing is nearer the truth than
he whose mind is filled with falsehoods and errors." "It is very difficult to

have a free, fair and honest press," opined Eleanor Roosevelt, because "the papers are largely supported by advertising, and that immediately gives the advertisers a certain hold over the medium that they use." The late senator Daniel Patrick Moynihan was more layered in his observations: "When a person goes to a country and finds their newspapers filled with nothing but good news, he can bet there are good men in jail." Television fares no better than newspapers. Architect Frank Lloyd Wright once called it "chewing gum for the eyes," while writer/iconoclast Hunter S. Thompson termed the TV business "a cruel and shallow money trench" where "thieves and pimps run free, and good men die like dogs." Evangelist Jimmy Swaggert was spellbindingly succinct: "[T]he media is ruled by Satan."[6]

Journalists are frustrated by such commentaries but also by their own work conditions. Consider these data from a 2002 survey: Sixty-nine percent of journalists felt that "the distinction between reporting and commentary has seriously eroded"; 68 percent agreed that "news organizations are going too far in the direction of entertainment"; and 40 percent of them felt that economic pressures, competition, and commercialism were the most important problems facing their industry today.[7]

Citizens happily join the chorus: Fifty-one percent believe that the media get in the way of society solving its problems; 72 percent think the press has too much power in Washington; 73 percent believe the news media are biased; and a whopping 80 percent hold that journalists chase sensational stories merely to sell newspapers.[8]

This chapter focuses on a conundrum: If the mass media are the nation's best storytellers, why have they lost the confidence of their audience? One possibility, a curious one, is that the media tell their own story poorly. We examine that possibility here by tracking how the *media* and the *press* have been discussed in reportage during the last fifty years. The story they tell is fairly complicated, but, because their story is part of the nation's story, it is a story that must be told.

THE MEDIA AT THE MILLENNIUM

How central are the mass media to modern political life? Oddly enough, nobody really knows, although some believe their influence is considerable and that they are prideful as well. These observers note, for example, that public officials have been accorded increasingly smaller "sound bites" on the nightly news, with reporters filling the void with their own, omniscient voices. This results in the media framing themselves as mere referees, distanced experts about a cynical political process. James Fallows, a former reporter himself, says that political coverage has moved in these directions because of the temptations of profit, celebrity, and punditry. These forces, claims Fallows, inevitably compromise "straight news" presentations.[9] Political scientist Thomas Patterson extends the case, arguing that politicians' actions are now fitted into predetermined news narratives rather than being the raison d'être of reportage.[10] In comparative research, Holli Semetko and her colleagues have shown that these tendencies are especially pronounced in the United States (compared to Great Britain).[11] Paul D'Angelo makes the ironic point that reporters often present themselves as victims of a political establishment gone publicity-mad.[12]

As a result of these changes, getting first-order data—direct perceptions of what is happening in politics—has become harder for citizens. Why? Because media coverage of an event changes that event. For instance, Marion Just and her colleagues have found that a longer news story will inevitably be more favorable to a candidate than a shorter story. If they had their way, that is, candidates would rather be covered by PBS than by ABC or CBS.[13] In a creative experiment, Wolfgang Donsbach and his associates found that simply watching a political speech on television (versus being there live) made citizens more negative about a candidate because television's frame is so cynical.[14] Press routines have also made it harder for candidates to receive decent coverage, a process exacerbated by increased media competition (e.g., the emergence of cable channels) and by the shortening of the news cycle. These changes in the electronic media also have implications for the print press, making newspapers more inclined to offer *interpretations* of events rather than just the facts.

As media roles change, so does their coverage. Maxwell McCombs reports, for example, that the media may not be successful in telling citizens what to think but they are good at telling them what to think about.[15] The media explain what is important and who is responsible for what is happening (even when that is hard to know).[16] So, for example, research by Marc Hetherington shows that news reports on the economy greatly overestimate the impact politicians can have on our pocketbooks, thereby giving viewers a bleaker view of public affairs than is warranted.[17]

The burgeoning media industries change things, but so too do cultural forces. Michael Schudson has argued that journalism is made up of two parts, "a set of concrete social institutions" and "a repertoire of historically fashioned literary practices."[18] As a result, says Schudson, the news has us in mind even before it is written. In addition, the system "is organized by conventions of sourcing," "taken-for-granted assumptions" about "who is a legitimate source or speaker or conveyer of information."[19] This makes the media jealous guardians of their own credibility and inspires them to find new ways of demonstrating their mastery of politics, thereby giving them recursive impact on democracy and democracy on them.

Rather than being objective stewards, then, the mass media actively construe political reality. Timothy Cook sees the media as a true Fourth Estate, one that impinges each day on the other three branches of government. The media do not simply report the news, says Cook; they are insurgents, similar in many ways to political parties and special interest groups.[20] But there are important differences too. Nelson Polsby observes, for example, that while political parties recruit candidates, sponsor campaigns, mobilize voters, and coordinate the activities of leaders, the media play a far more ambiguous (and less easily monitored) role.[21] In contrast to the parties, the media are bashful suitors who constantly deny their influence even as they try to maximize it.

Robert McChesney moves the discussion in another direction, contending that "the media have become a significant anti-democratic force in the United States."[22] For McChesney, as corporate media giants have become wealthier and more powerful, opportunities for real, participatory democracy featuring citizen involvement have becomes poorer. In his words, "capitalism works best when elites make most fundamental decisions and the bulk of the population is depoliticized." As a result, says McChesney, "the media have come to be expert at generating the type of fare that suits, and perpetuates, the status quo."[23]

And so we come to the focus of this chapter. If the media are (1) constantly inserting themselves into the news narrative; (2) altering public priorities by stressing some issues (and some actors) more than others; (3) supplanting the roles of other, traditional political players; and (4) slanting things in the direction of profit-making entities, we must learn more about them. There are several ways of getting such knowledge. As we have seen, scholars have used public opinion polls, laboratory experiments, and historical and cultural analysis to better understand the mass media. They have also used content analysis, primarily concentrating on the themes, sourcing patterns, and ideational content of news reports.

We also use content analysis, but our approach is different. We will concentrate here on how the media frame themselves. We began our research by tracking uses of the *media* token in news reports, but we quickly found that that keyword had an institutional bias built into it. So we supplemented it with references to the *press* to capture its personal aspects. This dual perspective allowed us to tap both the human and the corporate features of the mass media system.

These coding decisions led us to the long-standing tension between the mass media and American politics, a tension that goes to the very heart of democratic governance: Should the press support the political system or challenge it? Should government regulate the size of media conglomerates? Should press secretaries be allowed to leave the Oval Office for the studios of CNN? Should the media report only the good news, only the bad news, or, more unsettling, should the news be determined by plebiscite, using surveys to determine what the people want to know (versus the news they need to know)? We cannot answer these far-reaching questions here, but by watching the media watch themselves we will get a unique look at these matters and more.

The data for this analysis come from the Campaign Mapping Project, a broad-based attempt to capture campaign materials produced between Labor Day and Election Day during the fourteen presidential campaigns occurring between 1948 and 2000. To date, the Project holds some eight thousand newspaper articles from the *New York Times, Washington Post, Christian Science Monitor, Atlanta Constitution, Chicago Tribune,* and *Los Angeles Times,* as well as AP and UPI syndicate stories. In focusing on print reports, we followed Michael Schudson's lead that while "television confirms, anoints, and dramatizes" the news, it rarely finds the news. That remains the task of print.[24] We analyzed campaign reporting because Americans pay so much closer attention to politics during campaigns.

As with other chapters in this book, we used a keyword-in-context program to isolate instances of *media* and *press,* paying careful attention to the language immediately surrounding these focal terms. All together, we found 1,152 references to the former and 3,286 to the latter. All instances of *media* were examined, and a stratified random sample of *press* instances was explored as well. To get a bit more nuanced look at media self-reflections, we also looked at cognate terms like *journalist, reporter, newspaper,* and *television.*

Our coding procedures were fairly straightforward. We examined the *role* ascribed to the mass media (i.e., whether they were part of the problem, part of the solution, unclear, or conflicted) as well as their *potency* (whether the media/press were treated as actors, recipient of action, or unclear). We also observed the keyword's *valence* (whether the media/press had been caught up in a positive, negative, balanced, or unclear social scene) and took note of any persons having *associations* with the media (i.e., media personnel, Republicans or Democrats, citizens, media experts, scholars, other government officials, etc.).

These codes gave us the basic information needed for each token. To get a more fine-grained look, we noted the *qualities* of the media (i.e., were they seen as a neutral technology, a corporate commodity, an ideological force, a socially omnipotent entity, or unclear/none?). Finally, we noted the keyword's *location* (i.e., was it part of a direct quotation, in the title of a quoted source, or other?). While basic, these codings produced considerable data about the perceived purposes of the mass media. Our keyword approach seems particularly useful when examining reportage since media personnel pride themselves on their verbal dexterity. But keeping track of minute, lexical choices is hard even for professional writers, thereby giving us a glimpse of the implicit assumptions they make about their craft.

THE ASCENDANT MEDIA

Our first finding will strike persons with modern sensibilities as surprising: The mass media are a fairly recent arrival in American politics. As Figure 5.1 shows, the term first appeared in news coverage in 1956 and was used only thirty-three times during the next three elections. The *media* began to be featured more prominently in the 1970s and continued to escalate from that point forward. In part these data reflect historical trends—newly developing

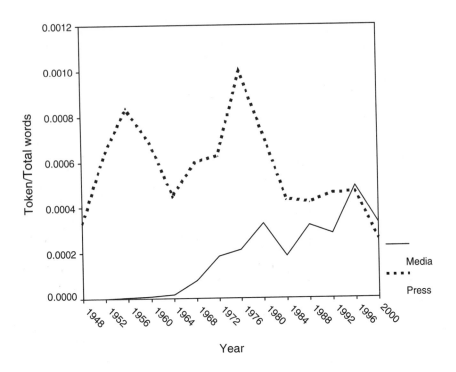

Figure 5.1 References to *Media* and *Press* in News Coverage, 1948–2000.

electronic technologies, the consolidation of individual media properties, the growth of an information society. But these data also hint at political, linguistic, and cultural changes in the United States.

Figure 5.2 features some of the media's cognates. As we see, the use of *media* is predated by workforce terms (*journalist* and *reporter*) as well as industry terms (*newspaper* and *television*). There is a simplicity to these constructions. They reflect an age when writing the news was a job and broadcasting the news a social obligation. The most traditional term of all, the *press* (see Figure 5.1), harks back to the guarantees of the First Amendment and is therefore honorific in the extreme, the term with which print personnel are still most comfortable. It is noteworthy, for example, that the term *press* peaked in usage during the 1976 campaign, just after the Watergate scandal and just after two print reporters—Bob Woodward and Carl Bernstein—broke the story (with the help of the mysterious "Deep Throat").

The term *journalist* appears sparingly over the years, perhaps because it has a faintly patrician feel to it. The term *reporter* is considerably more popular, suggesting a poorly paid but honest bloke who is not "an industry person" but who digs up the facts and dishes them out. The term *newspaper*

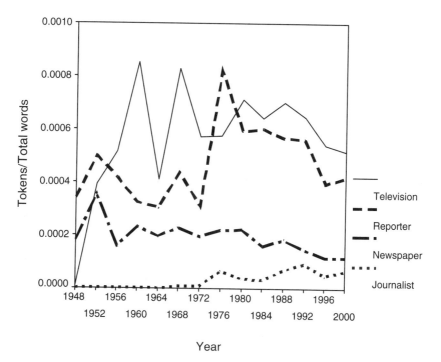

Figure 5.2 References to Media Phenomena in News Coverage, 1948–2000.

appears consistently over time but was especially prominent in 1952, a year when Democrats complained about Republican newspaper owners support-ing Dwight Eisenhower for president. (This was also a time when most major cities still had two newspapers, a morning paper that supported the Republi-can party and an afternoon paper that backed the Democrats. The economics of publishing eventually proved too much for these distinctions, which is why it is now hard to find a "two-newspaper town" in the United States).

The term *television,* quite naturally, grew prodigiously over time as more sets invaded more homes and as "TV politics" became its own colorful genre. It is worth noting, however, that the term did not overwhelm its rivals in the coverage studied here, perhaps because print reporters have always been suspicious of television's charms. The fact that the average TV anchor now makes twice as much as the average print reporter may have something to do with these sentiments as well.[25]

The purely *linguistic* facts reported in Figures 5.1 and 5.2 should be put in historical perspective. Between 1948 and 2000, newspaper subscriptions declined precipitously, even though college undergraduates continued to be attracted to that honorable profession.[26] In the case of television, just 9 percent of households had a set in 1950. Within five years, that number had increased to 64.5 percent. By 1960, television penetration had reached 87.1 percent of homes, rising to 92.6 percent in 1965, 95.3 percent in 1970, 97.1 percent in 1975, and hovering at 98 percent until 2003.[27] Today, the 2.4 television sets in the average American home are on for a total of seven and one-half hours per day.[28]

With regard to media ownership, whereas fifty corporations controlled half or more of the media business in 1982, by December 1986 that number had shrunk to twenty-nine. At that same time, 98 percent of the nation's seventeen hundred newspapers were owned by local monopolies and fewer than fifteen corporations controlled most of the country's daily circulation.[29] At the time of this writing, six companies own much of the world's media, including AOL Time Warner, Disney, Bertelsmann AG, Viacom, News Corp, and Vivendi Universal. A decision by the Federal Communications Commission to relax rules on the concentration of media ownership during the summer of 2003 may distill ownership even further (in the United States at least).

Given these trends, it should come as no surprise that print reporters have spent considerable time detailing the media's impact on political life. Media industries have gotten larger, richer, and bolder during the last fifty years and their coffers are reliably filled by proceeds from television advertising. During the *off-year* election of 2002, for example, the media garnered $900 million by running 1.4 million political spots throughout the United States. During that same year, news coverage of the political campaign was down 72 percent compared to the 1994 mid-term election.[30] In other words, what the media rake in with the left hand they obscure with the right hand.

So Figure 5.1 really tells two stories: (1) that media industries are incontrovertibly powerful in the United States but that (2) the *press* remains an important icon in political coverage. While print reporters dutifully report new kinds of political influence, they also keep their profession in the center of things. Figure 5.1 therefore shows a tension between an industry and a profession, an acknowledgment that media buzz and political substance must constantly be disentangled from one another. While such weighty matters as "Presidents and Pop Stars" have become reportorial staples in recent years because of market-based determinacies, print reporters counter those emphases with more substantive fare. This latter trend is to be applauded, but it is also possible that there has not been *enough* focus on the media titans. As one observer remarks, "Executives of large corporations who may often have more influence on the daily lives of citizens than government officials are invariably less visible in general news."[31] Put another way, the captains of media may be part of a "Silent Establishment," persons who have great influence but who are rarely seen in the news or, better, whose news presence is not proportional to their influence.[32] And so Figure 5.1 displays a contest between a sleeping giant (the *media*) and a feisty dowager (the *press*), a contest rife with political implications.

THE TROUBLESOME MEDIA

Rivals that they are, the *media* and the *press* do quite different work for the nation's print reporters. Generally, the former term does more work than the latter, which is to say, it is emphasized during campaigns. The *press* is more elliptical, weathering the occasional critique, but, because of its noble lines and First Amendment connections, it normally transcends the fray. The media are something of a pack-mule, saddled with the weight of modern politics. The press has a pedigree. The media do not.

Table 5.1 shows the differences in how the terms are treated, but it also shows a striking similarity: They appear to have no specific political function (witness, for example, the high percentages of "uncertain," "unclear," and "none" in Table 5.1). That is, while both the press and the media are mentioned quite often in news reports they are more a "presence" than an active social force. They walk through the campaign but leave no footprints, an approach that is consistent with their professional self-description—detached, objective, superrogatory.

Consider, for example, the following excerpt from a story about the Carter campaign in 1976. The narrative clearly intends to spotlight the press, but somehow the press becomes left in the shadows, an object of Jimmy Carter's scorn (or bemusement) but an object with no personal agency or coloration. The press is part of the mist surrounding the Carter campaign, but its qualities are never revealed, a strategy that directs more attention to candidate Carter himself:

> They say he has failed to understand the press in its more active, post Watergate incarnation. They say he is too secretive. They say he has turned aides loose to browbeat the press for writing critical stories. Yet the hostility seems more professional than personal, an almost natural clash between an ambitious politician and a skeptical press. Judging from reporters' comments, Carter has never been vindictive, nor tried to punish them, for their coverage.[33]

The treatment the *press* receives in news coverage is stable over time. It is consistently described as part of the action although its specific role is not detailed. This makes the press an adjunct to the political process—always doing, never done. How can an entity be present and absent at the same time? By having others speak for it. In 1948, for example, Governor Earl Warren of California warned that freedom of the press is undermined when "the press is not given all the facts on public matters no matter how freely it may write."[34] In 1952, Governor Adlai Stevenson was even more lavish in his praise: The basic job of protecting the First Amendment, said Stevenson, "can be done only within and by the free press itself, by you gentlemen. I know you can do it superbly."[35]

In 1972, the stakes got higher, as George McGovern described the Nixon administration's attempts to intimidate the press. "We are confronted . . .

with both a moral and a constitutional crisis of unprecedented dimensions," said McGovern, and "a free society might never recover from a sustained assault on its most basic institutions."[36] As if to restore partisan balance, Ronald Reagan declared twelve years later that the American press was "one of the cornerstones of society."[37] These gratuities attest to what wags have long known: It is dangerous to antagonize media magnates. It is also futile since reporters can write their own press clippings or, as we see here, can employ ghostwriters to write them.

TABLE 5.1 Rhetorical Features of *Media* and *Press* Tokens (in Percentages)

Variable	Feature	Media	Press
Role	Uncertain	85.5	87.4
	Part of the solution	1.6	1.2
	Part of the problem	11.5	11.1
	As conflicted	1.5	0.3
Potency	Unclear	40.7	67.3
	As actor	26.5	21.8
	As recipient	32.2	10.8
Valence	Unclear	82.0	89.0
	Positive	1.4	1.5
	Negative	16.5	9.5
Associations	None	4.6	0.7
	Media	23.7	1.3
	Journalist	1.9	2.3
	Republicans	27.5	34.1
	Democrats	21.2	30.6
	Independents	3.0	6.3
	Citizens	5.7	2.8
	Media expert	4.4	0.7
	Scholar	1.4	1.0
	Politician/institution	2.5	9.5
	Other	4.1	10.5
Characteristics	None	72.2	95.7
	Technology	7.7	0.4
	Commodity	11.1	0.0
	Ideology	3.4	3.5
	Omnipotent	5.6	0.4
Location	Within a quotation	19.7	15.8
	As a quoted source	14.8	16.4
	No quotation	65.4	67.7

If the *press* gets off easy, the *media* receive rougher treatment, often serving as a placeholder for the changes felt by people living in a technological, distantiated society (see Valence in Table 5.1). In the early 1960s, the phrase "electronic media" first appeared in the nation's newspapers, followed in short order by "media telecast," "mass communications," and "electronic media." This was an era that took George Orwell's warnings of an overly regulated society seriously. The wonders of the microchip were still unimagined by most people, and so the thought of something *coming between* them and their leaders—a medium—was a new and awesome thing. "I think American politics ought to be humanized, not mechanized, not computerized," Hubert Humphrey declared. "I'm perfectly willing to see us use the modern media," he continued, "but somewhere along the line you really ought to find out . . . what a fellow is really like. Look at him, feel him, touch him, smell him, hear him. That's what a campaign is about."[38]

If Americans of the 1960s were reading *Nineteen Eight-Four,* Americans of the 1970s were beginning to understand what William H. Whyte had talked about in *The Organization Man.* The political reportage of the 1970s revealed a new sensitivity to the corporate aspects of the media. It contained ominous new phrases like "all the mass media and money," "time-buying competition," "a substantial political media package," "media expenses," "outspending . . . 4 to 1 in traceable media," and "funding media advertising." Although the 1976 presidential campaign cost only $500 million, roughly one-sixth of the $3 billion spent by the candidates in 2000, the media were no longer seen as neutral overseers.[39]

And so the 1976 campaign added a fresh commonplace to political reporting—the audit statement: Gerald Ford "could come up with a media blitz," declared the *Los Angeles Times,* because his campaign "hoarded campaign funds at the start of the campaign . . . whereas Carter spent much of his money earlier."[40] The *New York Times* saw the problem this way:

> The $10 million originally budgeted for media campaigning—most of it for political commercials—had been increased to nearly $12 million and that the cost of Mr. Ford's personal media programming would be easily accommodated in the $4 million still to be spent on advertising. The purpose of the closing media blitz is to expand drastically the audience for Mr. Ford's political remarks.[41]

During this same era, politicians were beginning to think of the media—the conglomerated press—as a force in its own right. The press—the child of the First Amendment—was almost never singled out in this way, but the media were being described as (what the postmodernists would soon call) a "social construction," a force having empirical, economic, and symbolic power. Spiro Agnew was not a postmodernist, but when he lashed out at the media during the 1968 and 1972 campaigns, his comments resonated with many "Silent Americans," persons who were beginning to tire of the media hotshots.

Agnew's remarks soon became a refrain, and the press reported them. In 1988, for example, Vin Weber of Minnesota voiced concern that vice presidential candidate Dan Quayle was "being portrayed as the victim of the evil liberal media . . . and there's nothing that gets conservatives more aroused than the thought that the media might do in one of our people."[42] By 1996, Agnew's remarks were a torrent, a standard part of conservative doxology. Senator Bob Dole, never one to back away from a fight, was quoted as "blaming the news media for protecting Democrats and trying to 'steal' the presidential election for Clinton."[43] Ordinary citizens like Pat Berry also joined the chorus: "Once the media gets a hold of you, if you've never stolen a hog you might as well have, because they'll prove it somehow."[44]

A quick summary: In the 1960s the media had novelty; in the 1970s they became incorporated; in the 1980s they were powerful; by the 1990s they had the most important political characteristic of all—they had motive. The nation's reporters faithfully described these transformations, thus adding a new whipping boy to the American political scene. The scribes stood back when doing so, putting the charges in the mouths of others. At times the attacks seemed personal (charges about "the Republican papers" in the 1950s and "the liberal media" in the 1990s), but the real problem was modernity itself—fear of new scientific advances in the 1960s, worries about the economic downturn in the 1970s, concerns about multinational corporations in the 1980s. Even the *Washington Post*'s Watergate story came to be attacked by revisionists as an example of Big Media's antipathy for middle America.[45]

In contrast to the media, the *press* has gotten off lightly, perhaps because it is more removed from these shifting cultural techtonics and in part because it is connected to basic American freedoms. But reporters themselves are also ambivalent about living in a mediated age. As Theodore Gup, a professor of journalism, has opined, "That's why I am against the M word. Journalists have about as much in common with the media as I do with the ancient kingdom of Media or the convention of those mediums who speak with the spirits of the long departed."[46] Gup declares that there is no such thing as a U.S. media system:

> [The] reporter covering the war in Afghanistan has nothing in common with the rap singer who spews misogynistic lyrics, or the talk-show host who lures a pregnant teenager and her cheating boyfriend before the cameras. David Broder is not Matt Drudge. *Meet the Press* is not *Temptation Island*. And I am not Jerry Springer. I do not speak for him. He does not speak for me. Yet "the media" speaks for us all.[47]

Gup captures the views of many working journalists here. There is, after all, the issue of money. The media are businesses; reporters have jobs. The press is not universally loved, but most Americans understand that reporters, unlike Rupert Murdoch, do not own The Family Channel, *TV Guide*, Twentieth Century Fox, the Los Angeles Dodgers, and Mushroom

Records. The *press* may be snotty, but the *media* will soon own the world. Now there's something to hate.

THE RELUCTANT MEDIA

Aspiring reporters learn several maxims in journalism school, two of the most important of which are: (1) Report today's news, and (2) stay out of the story. Michael Schudson observes that these twin features—contemporaneity and detachment—have been crucial to the professionalization of the press during the last hundred years. Unlike earlier times when a publisher's politics dictated coverage (Joseph Pulitzer and William Randolph Hearst come to mind), reporters are now on a quest for objectivity that would have seemed impossible earlier in the twentieth century.[48]

We found, however, that these strictures changed when the subject matter was the mass media itself. Although reporters dutifully recounted media criticisms, they did so in an oddly detached way. They did not, for example, interview journalism experts or editors when discussing such charges nor did they bring to such stories the same empirical assessment they brought to other matters. They were not really defensive but they also did not extol the virtues of their profession. They were, instead, passive, almost nonchalant. That seems a strange response.

The data supporting these claims can be found in the Potency, Association, and Role variables in Table 5.1. Potency explores the extent to which a keyword acts upon or is acted upon by some other social force. As we see, the *media* are more likely than the *press* to be preyed upon by others. In many cases, this took the form of passive constructions in which a quoted or named source criticized the media for some overstatement or omission. Sometimes the charges made were comparatively mild. For example, in 1996 the *Washington Post* quoted aides to presidential candidate Al Gore urging the media to "hold Bush to the same standard to which Gore was held after his misstatements during the candidates' first debate last week."[49] During that same campaign, the press acknowledged its own salaciousness when discussing the media's interest in George W. Bush's drunk driving escapade: "It was an intoxicating narrative for a campaign season short on sizzle, and the news media ate it up."[50]

This tendency by the press to take a shot across its own bow gives its coverage a patina of objectivity. That effect is heightened by the Association variable in Table 5.1, which shows that the press is also reluctant to call on members of its own tribe (journalists and researchers) to defend it. Instead, it reports the opinions of political campaigners and party bosses, the very persons who question their practices. In addition, the Role variable indicates that both the press and the media are likely to be framed as part of the problem rather than part of the solution.

TABLE 5.2 Media Critiques from Left and Right

Critiques from the Left

"The President [Harry Truman] charged that the Republican Congress 'is trying to tear up the Bill of Rights.' He said his hard working campaign tour was due to the fact that he had to point up the 1948 issues 'for the simple reason that you'll never find out about them if I can't face you and tell you about them, because between 80 and 90 per cent of the press is against the Democratic Administration because it is for the people, they're for the special interests.' " ("Truman Says GOP Wants Surrender of Public's Rights," *New York Times*, September 28, 1948, A1.)

"One Truman fan shouted this hoarse admonition to reporters in the press bus: 'You Republicans write him up right.' " ("Huge Crowds Hear Truman in Camden, Philadelphia," *Washington Post*, October 7, 1948, A1.)

Critiques from the Right

"'I know of no justifiable standard which requires American media to repeat every unsubstantiated charge leveled against the Nixon Administration while simultaneously requiring the media to ignore the psychological warfare and espionage being practice by the McGovernites,' MacGregor said." ("Probe McGovern Camp, Macgregor Asks Press," AP-UPI, October 20, 1972, A29.)

"The president reserved special attention and scorn for media reports. From rally to rally, he railed against the 'talking heads' and 'network know it alls' on Sunday morning talk shows. Bush said the news media 'has been asking itself if it has been fair,' and he answered his own question to the cheers of a throng of Michigan supporters: 'They know very well they haven't, but we're going to win without them. It's not the pundits, it's the people that decide elections,' Bush said as he repeatedly cited a campaign slogan, 'Annoy the Media Re-elect Bush.' The president claimed that Clinton was constantly defended by the media, 'all his apologists out there, all these talking heads.' " ("Bush Accuses Media of Being 'Apologists' for His Opponent," *Chicago Tribune*, September 2, 1992, A5.)

All of this suggests a self-abnegating press. Can that possibly be true? After all, does not research show that journalists have increasingly inserted their own voices into news coverage, thereby pushing politicians to the sidelines? Perhaps, but when dealing with charges made against them, the press gets downright humble or, at least, downright cagey.[51] As we see in Table 5.2, these patterns become especially clear when the press discusses media bias. In none of these examples does one find contrasting testimony from a media apologist or an irate city editor. Instead, the bias charge is woven into the campaign report and then left hanging. Often, these charges-without-response are given prominent status in the news report.

Sometimes the newspapers take a kind of perverse glee in sharing the views of their detractors. Consider the *New York Times* story about Senator Bob Dole during the 1996 presidential race:

> "When do the American people rise up and say, 'Forget the media in America! We're going to make up our minds! You're not going to make up our minds!' This is about saving our country!" Singling out *The New York Times* for the second straight day, Mr. Dole went on: "We are not going to let the media steal this election. We're going to win this election. The country belongs to the people, not *The New York Times*."[52]

Charges by candidates like Dole create something of a rhetorical dilemma for the press: (1) Report the objection and thereby give it more attention than it deserves, or (2) overlook the criticism and thereby feed the campaign rumor mill. As we see here, the *Times* sees yet another possibility: (3) Report the charge to show that the press is consequential.[53]

We also find that the press frequently quotes industry sources in their bias stories, thereby adding to their self-flagellation. Notice in the following report, for example, how the *Los Angeles Times* calls the roll of media darlings:

> Al Hunt, the Washington bureau chief of the *Wall Street Journal,* called the networks "video nymphomaniacs," unable to resist airing the pretty pictures that candidates arranged, even if they knew the pictures contradicted the facts. In 1990, the Washington bureau chief of NBC, Timothy J. Russert, called on the networks to use the daily stump appearances as an introduction to examine a candidate's record. David Broder, the veteran political correspondent for the *Washington Post,* urged the media to press candidates on the issues voters cared most about.[54]

Again, it is worth noting that no counterattack is launched here: The charges are made by high-profile individuals and the discussion is then abandoned. The fact that *media* references have increased exponentially over the years makes such stories a standard part of recent campaigns.

If journalists do not (or cannot) rise to their own defense, can they depend on academics to champion their cause? Alas, no. We examined news reports that quoted academic researchers and found that they only added to the media's burden. In 1984, for instance, Professor Kathleen Hall Jamieson was quoted as saying, "'We learned some things from the debates . . . but the news media never picked up on them, focusing instead on the bags under Mondale's eyes and the style of the candidates.'"[55] Twelve years later, responding to another debate, she declared: "[T]he media's insistence on declaring 'winners' and 'losers' misreads the process. . . . You can't count the number of touchdowns scored or the number of runs scored."[56]

Mark Levy discusses a process he calls "disdaining the news," a trope used by journalists to distance themselves from troublesome phenomena.[57]

Levy contends that reporters use such devices to build trust with readers, to signal that they can be depended upon. That is the approach we find here. Reporters not only disdain the news, but they sometimes disdain *their own* news as well.

This discussion has focused on how journalists discuss anti-press sentiment. But a recent survey of three hundred journalists and news executives commissioned by the Pew Research Center and the *Columbia Journalism Review* concludes that reporters often try to keep their industry out of the news in the first place. Specifically, the pollsters found that 25 percent of local and national journalists have "purposely avoided newsworthy stories," that a similar number "softened the tone of the stories to benefit the interests of their news organization," and that 41 percent had done so "to benefit their workplace and industry."[58] Journalist Geneva Overholser has called attention to how these strategies-of-suppression ultimately compromise the press.[59] Here, we have found another tendency—strategies-of-silence—but they, too, seem counterproductive. If the media allow themselves to be attacked without responding, after all, they will become complicit in their own demise. An one press defender puts it:

> Clearly, those of us in the press are not blameless. We have, through our docility and our arrogant belief that such media mumbo jumbo is irrelevant, been complicit. Out of sloth, we sometimes even use the term "media" to describe ourselves. But we remain very much a distinct breed despite the mongrelization implicit in the word "media." By failing to assert and maintain that distinction we run the risk of becoming what is already said of us—that we are merely an appendage to something much larger and less noble.[60]

Although it is ungracious to do so, another point must be made: Reporters sometimes tell the media bias story out of convenience. This sort of coverage is what Neil Hickey calls a "talker story," material that will gain attention and that does not require much work from the reporter.[61] In modern politics, that is, Republican campaign managers can always be counted on to provide fresh meat for the liberal-bias story. It is easy to see how a harried journalist could be attracted to that. Once written, however, these criticisms become etched in the national mind, especially when not counterbalanced by an industry defense. That seems an odd approach for an already ailing profession.[62]

The data reported here are not so dramatic as to leave one speechless. But they do point out the media's tendency to offer self-criticism without self-defense. These data contradict the image of an imperious press with only its own interests in mind. We have discovered something different here: a press without a counterpunch. Whether this approach emerges from a new journalistic norm, from a long-repressed humility on the press's part, or from corporate decisions to turn the other cheek for economic or political reasons, it results in discussion without dialogue. That a free press would encourage same is at least a curiosity.

CONCLUSION

The story told here is that the media succeed despite themselves. Over the past fifty years they have become a dominant (sometimes dominating) player in American politics. Until now, very little research has been done on how they look at themselves. We have opened up those questions here, finding that the media have played an increasingly larger role over the years and that they often play the heavy, re-presenting the charges that politicians lob at them. What's more, they are passive in their own defense. Admittedly, we have looked only at print reporters here. Perhaps they are an especially genteel lot (although most politicians would blanche at that description). In any event, we find that the media tell their story in surprisingly deferential ways.

Right now, the media serve as convenient targets for many in the United States who are frustrated with politics. Some would argue, for example, that the negative reportage studied here is more than offset by the return on investment that media industries enjoy. Others might note that print journalism has become a bit player in a political world now dominated by TV spots and direct mail. Still others might argue that a reviled media is a democratically useful thing, bread-and-circuses for the great unwashed. "The people need to hate something," the cynics might say, "let them hate the media. It cannot hurt." But it can, of course. A nation that finds it easy to disparage its messengers of truth can easily become unimpressed with truth itself. That is a consequence of some magnitude.

As we have seen here, the press is not the media. One is a profession and the other a business. Businesses come and businesses go. They begins as start-ups and end as mergers. But professions are designed to last because they stand for something grander. It would be dangerous if the *press* went the way of the *media*. The former is designed to tell us the unvarnished truth; the latter is designed to do many things—make a profit, entertain us. The corporate scandals that hit the United States in the early 2000s dealt with industries—oil, finance, computer networking—that are vital to the nation. Fortunately, the media industries were not caught up in those scandals, but that could happen; if it did, journalism would be the loser as would a nation that needs to stay informed. The *media*, the *press*. Two keywords. Two worldviews. May they ever remain separate.

NOTES

1. L. McAneny, "Nurses Displace Pharmacists at Top of Expanded Honesty and Ethics Poll," Gallup News Service, http://www.calnurse.org/cna/new2/glp111899.html (June 21, 2003).

2. B. Goldberg, *Bias: A CBS Insider Exposes How the Media Distort the News* (New York: Harper Perennial, 2003).

3. R. W. McChesney, *Rich Media, Poor Democracy: Communication Politics in Dubious Times* (Urbana: University of Illinois Press, 1999).

4. Fairness and Accuracy in Reporting (FAIR) is located online at http://www.fair.org/.

5. Media Watch is located online at http://www.mediawatch.com/.

6. For these and other commentaries on the press, see D. B. Baker (ed.), *Political Quotations: A Collection of Notable Sayings on Politics from Antiquity Through 1989* (Detroit: Gale Research, 1990), 70–73.

7. "This Just In," *Public Perspective* (July/August 2002): 24–25.

8. Ibid, 25.

9. J. Fallows, *Breaking the News: How the Media Undermine American Democracy*, 2d ed. (New York: Vintage, 1997).

10. T. Patterson, *Out of Order* (New York: Vintage Books, Random House, 1994).

11. H. A. Semetko, J. G. Blumer, M. Gurevitch, and D. H. Weaver, *The Formation of Campaign Agendas: A Comparative Analysis of Party and Media Roles in Recent American and British Elections* (Hillsdale, NJ: Lawrence Erlbaum Associates, 1991).

12. P. D'Angelo, "Framing the Press: A New Approach to Assessing the Cynical Nature of Press Self-Coverage and Its Implications for Information Processing in the Political Campaign Context," paper presented to the Mass Communication Division at the 49th Annual Conference of the International Communication Association, San Francisco, May 27–31, 1999.

13. M. R. Just, A. N. Crigler, D. E. Alger, T. C. Cook, M. Kern, and D. M. West, *Crosstalk: Citizens, Candidates, and the Media in a Presidential Campaign* (Chicago: University of Chicago Press, 1996).

14. W. Donsbach, H-B. Brosius, and A. Mattenklott, "How Unique Is the Perspective of Television: A Field Experiment on the Perception of a Campaign Event by Participants and Television Viewers," *Political Communication*, 10 (1993): 37–53.

15. See M. McCombs and D. Shaw, "The Agenda-Setting Function of Mass Media," *Public Opinion Quarterly*, 36 (1972): 176–85; and M. McCombs and D. Shaw, "The Evolution of Agenda-Setting Research: Twenty-five Years in the Marketplace of Ideas," *Journal of Communication*, 43 (1993): 58–67.

16. S. Iyengar, *Is Anyone Responsible? How Television Frames Political Issues* (Chicago: The University of Chicago Press, 1991); S. Iyengar and D. Kinder, *News That Matters* (Chicago: University of Chicago Press, 1987); and S. Iyengar, M. D. Peters, and D. R. Kinder, "Experimental Demonstrations of the 'Not So Minimal' Consequences of Television News Programs," *American Political Science Review*, 76 (1982): 848–58.

17. M. Hetherington, "The Media's Role in Forming Voters' National Economic Evaluations in 1992," *American Journal of Political Science*, 40.2 (1996): 372–95.

18. M. Schudson, *The Power of News* (Cambridge, MA: Harvard University Press, 1995), 2.

19. Ibid., 14.

20. T. E. Cook, *Governing with the News: The News Media as a Political Institution* (Chicago: University of Chicago Press, 1998).

21. N. Polsby, *Consequences of Party Reform* (Oxford: Oxford University Press, 1983), 183.

22. McChesney, *Rich Media*, 2.

23. Ibid., 3.

24. M. Schudson, *The Good Citizen: A History of American Civic Life* (New York: Free Press, 1998), 287. Schudson continues: "Newspapers retain more authority than people often realize. Newspapers are no longer the primary source for most people directly, but they remain the primary source indirectly because they supply news to television. Television news, even the national network news programs, are parasites of print. Rarely does a broadcast journalist pick up a story that newspapers and newsmagazines are not already on top of."

25. See for example, the data displayed on the Journalism.Com website, http://www.journalismjobs.com/salaries.cfm (June 23, 2003).

26. While references to newspapers, reporters, journalists have been modest over the years, newspaper readership has declined and journalism school admissions have risen. Reports published by *Public Perspective* suggest that the average weekday readership of newspapers dropped from 79 million in 1998 to 76.4 million in 2001 (according to the Newspaper Association of America), while the adult population rose from 134.9 million to 140.6 million. That continues a trend dating back to at least 1964. See E. Witt, "Necessary Embrace," *Public Perspective* (July/August 2002): 27. Additionally, the number of college students earning journalism degrees rose steadily and peaked in the early nineties, then declined slightly (although exact numbers are difficult to calculate given differing accounting methods and changes in college department titles). Thus, there is still a desire to join the journalistic profession among college students despite the negative connotations the word *media* has acquired in some quarters. "The Annual Survey of Journalism & and Mass Communication Graduates," http://www.grady.uga.edu/annualsurveys/ (June 25, 2003).

27. Nielsen Media Research-NTI, recorded in January of each year.

28. These data are included in *Consumer Reports'* description of "The 21st Century Consumer," June 23, 2003, http://www.consumerreports.org. Accessed on June 15, 2003.

29. B. Bagdikian, "The 50, 26, 20... Corporations That Own Our Media," June 1987, http://www.fair.org (June 25, 2003, via Fairness and Accuracy in Reporting).

30. For more on these data, see the Alliance for Better Campaigns, a watchdog group committed to changing how political campaigns are financed in the United States, http://www.bettercampaigns.org/press/release.php?ReleaseID = 39 (June 23, 2003).

31. Schudson, *The Power of News*, 14.

32. R. P. Hart, *Seducing America: How Television Charms the Modern Voter* (New York: Oxford University Press, 1994), 123–49.

33. "Boys on Carter Bus Say He's a Tough Nut," *Chicago Tribune*, October 25, 1976, A05.

34. "Warren Raps Secrecy in Government; 12,000 Applaud Plea for Unity," *Chicago Tribune*, October 7, 1948, A1.

35. "Stevenson Urges Wider Developing of U.S. Resources," *New York Times*, September 9, 1952, A1.

36. "McGovern Asserts Nixon Puts U.S. In 'Moral Crisis'; Charges Abuse of Power," *New York Times*, October 26, 1972, A1.

37. "2 Candidates Vow to Meet with Press," AP-UPI Wire, October 7, 1984.

38. "Humphrey: 'Find Out What a Fellow's Really Like,'" *Christian Science Monitor*, October 5, 1968, A1.

39. For more on these matters, see the Cato Institute's report on campaign financing, http://www.cato.org/pubs/briefs/bp64.pdf (June 24, 2003).

40. "Ford Campaigns in Dixie, Plans $4 Million Media Blitz," *Los Angeles Times,* October 24, 1976, A4.

41. "Ford Sets TV Radio Blitz; Carter Renews Vote Plea," *New York Times,* October 24, 1976, A1.

42. "Bush's Bows to the Right; Having Won Trust Among Conservatives, the Candidate Is Free to Test the Middle," *New York Times,* September 11, 1988, A1.

43. "A Seething Dole Intensifies Attack; Candidate Lobs FBI Files Accusations," *Washington Post,* October 26, 1996, A1.

44. "Voters Say Quayle Fails to Measure Up," *Chicago Tribune,* September 5, 1988, A1.

45. As Schudson details: "The aim of the Nixon administration was not only to make the president look good but to make the press as an institution look bad. In early 1970, H. R. Haldeman wrote Herb Klein a memo urging him to get the story out in the media that Nixon had overcome the 'great handicaps under which he came into office,' namely, 'the hostile press' epitomized by the *New York Times, Washington Post, Time, Newsweek,* etc., the hostile network commentators, the generally hostile White House press corps, the hostile Congress, etc. The outcome of the Nixon administration's calculated attacks on the press was just what *Chicago Daily News* reporter Peter Lisagor suggested at the time—that the administration successfully promoted for the news media an identity separate from that of the public. The very term 'the media' was promoted by the Nixon White House because it sounded unpleasant, manipulative, a much less favorable term than 'the press.' The administration claimed that the media were not, as they often claimed to be, the voice of the people. Nor were they, as many had traditionally understood them, the voice of wealthy publishers, on the one hand, or organs of political parties, on the other. Instead, they were an independent and dangerously irresponsible source of power." See M. Schudson, "Watergate: A Study in Mythology," *Columbia Journalism Review,* May/June 1992, http://www.cjr.org/year/92/3/watergate.asp. (April 8, 2004).

46. T. Gup, "'Media' Means So Much, It Means Nothing," *Chronicle of Higher Education,* 48 (November 23, 2001): B12.

47. Ibid.

48. Schudson, *The Power of News,* 9.

49. D. Balz, "Tests Passed, but Questions Remain," *Washington Post,* October 12, 2000, A01.

50. "'BUSH DROVE DRUNK!!' vs. 'Old Arrest,'" *New York Times,* November 4, 2000, 19.

51. Frank Esser's research suggests that journalists now frequently discuss their own reportage. This tendency is so common, says Esser, that a "meta-style" is now crowding out other news frames. Our research shows that while this may be true, the resulting commentary is surprisingly self-effacing. See F. Esser, "Spin Doctors in the United States, Great Britain, and Germany: Metacommunication About Media Manipulation," *Harvard Journal of Press Politics,* 61 (2001): 16–45.

52. "Politics: The Republican; Dole Is Imploring Voters to 'Rise Up' Against the Press," *New York Times,* October 26, 1996, A01.

53. We were only able to find one instance in our database where the press launched a clear counterstrike to charges of media bias, an interesting news story about the 1948 campaign of Harry Truman detailing the president's charge that he

was being unfairly disadvantaged because of "Republican ownership" of the press. See "Truman Says Ike Supports 'Isolationists,' " *Washington Post,* September 12, 1952, A01.

54. "Struggle for TV Time Forces Candidates to Switch Tactics," *Los Angeles Times,* September 29, 1992, A01.

55. "Candidates' Skillful Use of the Media," *Christian Science Monitor,* November 6, 1984, A3.

56. "The Debaters Argue over Expectations," *Washington Post,* September 28, 1996, A1.

57. M. R. Levy, "Disdaining the News," *Journal of Communication,* 31 (1981): 24–31.

58. "Self Censorship: How Often and Why; Journalists Avoiding the News," Pew Research Center for the People & Press, http://people-press.org/reports/ (June 25, 2003).

59. Overholser writes: "Editors don't want to make life miserable for the publisher. Publishers don't want to tick off corporate. What editor wants to send out word on a decrease in her training budget, or the fact that all the news hole is going to subjects tied to classified ads? And perhaps we let ourselves off the hook by telling each other we don't have any credibility when reporting on ourselves anyway. Why then should we be doing it? Because the public is affected by what we do. Because informing others keeps us (and our owners) honest, and befits a trade that prides itself on truth-telling. Because it would be consistent with the way we treat others." See G. Overholser, "Voices: Newspapers—There's No Business Like Your Own Newspaper's Business," *Columbia Journalism Review,* May/June 2003, http://www.cjr.org/year/01/2/overholser.asp (June 25, 2003).

60. Gup, "Media Means So Much," B12.

61. N. Hickey, "Money Lust: How Pressure for Profit Is Perverting Journalism," *Columbia Journalism Review,* July/August (1998): 28.

62. There is also a dangerous by-product to undue emphasis on the question of Left-Right bias: crowding-out other, deeper stories about media realities. For example, Robert McChesney argues that the conflation of the entertainment and information industries is ultimately a far greater problem for a democratic society. Says McChesney: "The clear trajectory of our media and communication world tends toward ever-greater corporate concentration, media conglomeration and hypercommercialism. The notion of public service—that there should be some motive for media other than profit—is in rapid retreat if not total collapse. [The result is] a system set up to serve the needs of a handful of wealthy investors, corporate managers, and corporate advisors." See McChesney, *Rich Media,* 77.

6

The *People*
Constructing an Electorate

With Elvin Lim

In December 1999, professional baseball player John Rocker declared that taking a trip on the 7 train in New York City required contact with "some kid with purple hair . . . some queer with AIDS . . . some 20-year-old mom with four kids. . . . How the hell did they get in this country?" asked Rocker plaintively. As if in reply, anthropologist Benedict Anderson observed that "members of even the smallest nation will never know most of their fellow members, meet them, or even hear of them, yet in the minds of each lives the image of their communion."[1] Because people can never know all of their fellow citizens, says Anderson, they must imagine them. Often, these imaginings prove artificial or contradictory and, just as often, false. The Rocker incident provoked the controversy it did because Americans, the most diverse people on earth, have never really known what a "real American" looks like. At the same time, they have stoutly clung to the notion that their fellow citizens are much like themselves even though they cannot say how. John Rocker saw through this contradiction and got in trouble for it.

But why? Who are the American people, really? What do they do? believe? know? Are they unique? How do they function politically? For some social scientists, the answers to these questions are already known. For anthropologists, the American people are an amalgam fashioned from the villages of Europe, the dynasties of Asia, and the tribes of Africa that have produced unique cultural folkways. For historians, the American people are haunted by Old World hegemonies and hence committed to individualism and modernism for philosophical and practical reasons. For psychologists, the American people are a restless and contentious lot producing a kaleidoscope of attitudes about most social issues.

Our assumptions here are different from the foregoing because we take a symbolic view of identity. We assume that (1) an electorate is not a stable, ontological entity but one "summoned up" periodically by political actors who define it in order to control it; (2) the American electorate has been an especially contested political site, in part because of its mottled demography but also because of its unique geography, history, and cultural mores; (3) American politics, as a result, rarely reduces to issues of simple expediency—how often? how much?—because the nation has never settled deeper questions: Who are we? Where are we going? What is fundamentally right and wrong? (4) during moments of political turbulence, these crises of meaning can become especially acute.

The work we report here tracks the use of collective tokens, words referring to a group (e.g., *Latinos*), a nation (e.g., *Russians*), or a cross-national entity (e.g., *Europeans*). The specific token we track—variations of the phrase *the American people*—has allowed us in previous studies to compare discourse produced by ordinary citizens during discussion groups, by professional politicians when speaking on the campaign trail, and by reporters writing for the mass media.[2] We expand on these concerns here by asking how constructions of **the American people** change during periods of national crisis. We do so by looking at speeches made in the U.S. House after the September 11, 2001, attacks in New York City and Washington, DC, and comparing them to remarks made in similar surroundings during the impeachment of President Bill Clinton. By contrasting these times of great stress to more conventional political moments, we examine who the American people are or, better, who they have been invited to become. Our underlying premise is that the way a society defines itself affects how its members reason, how they react to new policy proposals, and how they bond with one another during moments of turbulence.

TRACKING THE PEOPLE

The questions asked in this chapter—how is an electorate invited to understand itself, and what results from those understandings?—could be asked of any nation. But there is something uniquely American about these questions as well. As political scientist Richard Merelman has argued, Americans have always been "loosely bounded" and that made it difficult to fashion working political coalitions.[3] But they have had no choice but to do so, says Roger Scruton, since "no society can survive if it cannot generate the 'we' of affirmation: the assertion of itself as entitled to its land and institutions."[4] That the American people have been able to develop such affirmations is remarkable when one considers the social and geographic factors aligned against them. How have they done so?

Public opinion polls have helped. Arguably no nation has spent more time or money on polling than the United States in part because of its positivistic and mercantile roots but also because public opinion has been highly volatile in a nation so large and diverse. As Pierre Bourdieu observed, public opinion polls constantly reify the nation-state, creating the idea "that a unanimous public opinion exists in order to legitimate a policy and strengthen the relations of force upon which it is based."[5] For these reasons, says communication scholar Michael McGee, "'the people' are more *process* than *phenomenon*," an entity brought forth for political purposes that cannot be measured precisely.[6] From this vantage point, a national electorate does not really exist in some sort of primordial state but is brought into being during elections (and during crises), with "issue publics," "demographic sectors," and "media markets" substituting for hardier forms of identity.

The mass media have helped as well. Communication scholar Geoffrey Baym, for example, studied broadcast news coverage following the Oklahoma City bombing in 1995 and found two very different tropes being used. The "Institutional We" referred to the news station itself (as in *"we've* received a report that . . ."), while the "Representative We" linked the reporter to the nation as a whole. This latter "we," says Baym, often marginalized right-wing groups, as when one militia member was asked "should *we* be afraid of you guys?"[7] But Stephanie Greco Larson's work with "person on the street" interviews argues differently. She finds that the ordinary folks who testify for the American people on the nightly news decently resemble the electorate-at-large (when matched against public opinion data).[8] Professor Kathy Cramer's study of habitués of a corner restaurant found them frequently conceptualizing politics in terms of "us" and "them" despite their vaunted forms of individualism.[9] While Cramer's work shows that voters constantly seek out (and sometimes assume) a sense of the group, how and why they do so are not yet known.

Literary scholar Carolyn Miller argues that these rhetorically based communities are rarely unidimensional (especially in the United States); a careful analysis of what is said within them often reveals political fractures.[10] These cleavages, however, have not prevented American presidents from referring to *the people* in their annual addresses more and more over time. Political scientist Elvin Lim finds, for example, a steady rise in the number of such references between 1789 and 2000.[11] But why? Is it because a sense of the whole has actually increased over the years, thus making it easy for politicians to warrant their arguments? Or has there been an actual decline in such feelings (perhaps because of the nation's increased pluralism and democratization), thus forcing presidents to compensate rhetorically?[12] In an interesting book on political manifestoes, for example, Janet Lyon has written that "the use of 'we' in forms that claim to speak for a constituency is perhaps more controversial now than ever before" because of the rise of identity politics.[13] That is, says Charles Willard, "to define a people is to define a nonpeople," thereby running the risk, as did John Rocker, of thinking and acting monolithically.[14]

In previous research, we have found some evidence to support Willard's concerns. When examining small-group transcripts from the 1996 National Issues Convention, an event that brought together some five hundred ordinary Americans to discuss the issues of the day, we found that use of collective self-references ("we," "our," and "us") increased *sevenfold* when foreign policy (versus domestic matters) were being discussed. Moreover, 61 percent of the citizens' foreign policy claims contained policy recommendations (e.g., "we should tell Saddam Hussein that . . .") versus only 43 percent when they discussed economic matters, ostensibly an echo of the State's long-standing foreign policy rhetoric.[15] We also found the discussants to be *nine times* more likely to use active references ("we") than passive references ("us"), also a signal of political confidence. In other words, the language used by political officials has sunk deep roots in the United States, as we see when ordinary Americans talk about themselves.

To track these patterns further, we searched a large database of political stump speeches and campaign addresses produced during U.S. presidential campaigns between 1948 and 2000. Keying on the phrase *the American people,* we found some nine hundred uses of that expression. Subsequent analysis showed that the 1968–1984 elections contained the heaviest use of such tokens, ostensibly because that was a time of when the nation's traditional policies were being sharply debated (civil rights, Vietnam, Watergate, etc.). Not surprisingly, the American people were almost always described by the candidates in presentistic (versus historical) terms, a finding also echoed in the lay rhetoric we had examined previously. Impressively, though, candidates who described the people optimistically almost always won their races, a finding that flies in the face of the slash-and-burn advice campaign consultants often provide.[16] In the eyes of most leaders, that is, the American people are an indomitable lot, patently incapable of being vanquished. Ronald Reagan was particularly good at sounding these themes:

> I will not stand by and watch this great country destroy itself under mediocre leadership that drifts from one crisis to the next, eroding our national will and purpose. We have come together here because the American people deserve better from those to whom they entrust our nation's highest offices, and we stand united in our resolve to do something about it.[17]

To get some perspective on these matters, we compared how politicians and the mass media described the American citizenry between 1948 and 2000. We found that, compared to politicians, the press was far more negative when describing the people. Even when quoting candidates directly, for example, the media featured their more pessimistic ruminations. Table 6.1 shows how persistent this practice was for reporters. In short, then, a great many people make it their business to tell the people who they are. The press and the politicians often disagree about the electorate, the former seizing on their uncertainties and irritations, the latter emphasizing their cohesion and sense of possibility. Descriptions of the people are hardly neutral, as a result. They are part of a competitive environment designed to change the people being described.

TRACKING THE PEOPLE IN CRISIS

The logic of our approach should be clear by now: We believe that examining how a nation's people are described gives us unique insight into what

TABLE 6.1 References to the *People* in Speeches Versus Press Reports

Speaker	Characteristic Assertion	Characteristic Selection
Dewey	"No one who has come here over the years could fail to be impressed by the virility and generosity of the American people." (Santa Fe, NM, September 22, 1948)	"Gov. Dewey tonight tackled what he termed two fundamental problems facing the American people." (*Chicago Tribune*, September 23, 1948)
Kennedy	"We say, 'yes' to the next decade. The Republicans say 'no,' and I think on November 8, the American people are going to say 'yes' with us." (New York, September 14, 1960)	"'My campaign,' he said in St. Louis, 'is founded on a single assumption: the assumption that the American people are tired of the drift in our national course, . . . our steady decline.'" (*Christian Science Monitor*, September 15, 1960)
Johnson	"Our great political parties have always represented varied interests and the broad, common soul of the American people." (Jacksonville, FL, October 26, 1964)	"He called the Goldwater domestic policies 'the most radical' that have ever been made to the American people." (*Washington Post*, October 27, 1964)
Carter	"And let us put our faith in the American people, for as long as we do, no power on earth can ever prevail against us." (Ann Arbor, MI, September 15, 1976)	"Declaring that 'there has never been an American election quite like this one,' Carter said of the American people: 'We feel that we have lost control of our government, that it has become our master.'" (*Washington Post*, September 16, 1976)
Reagan	"The American people believe in freedom and the faith it takes to protect it." (Kansas City, MO, October 16, 1984)	"'I think my opponent's tax plan will be a hardship for the American people and I believe it will bring our recovery to a roaring stop,' Reagan said." (AP-UPI, October 17, 1984)

makes that nation tick, what holds it together, and what worries it. A phrase like *the American people* is therefore something of a Rorschach test. Alone, the phrase is either empty or vague. But when used by real people in real settings, it becomes filled with meaning. Because that token is so popular, it should provoke special insight when the nation is under stress. Accordingly, we will compare how that phrase is used in "normal" speech (i.e., during political campaigns) versus crisis conditions.

One of these crises occurred when the United States was attacked on September 11, 2001, an event that inspired a period of intense, national self-examination. The terrorist incidents called into question the U.S. myths—a nation more generous than all other nations, the supreme military force in the world—and brought up questions the American people had not asked in a very long time: Do we have the resolve to see this through? Can Western technologies overwhelm religious fanaticism? Has the economy been dealt a death blow? Will flying ever be safe again? Is the United States one nation or a micronesia of subnations?

These questions are different from those raised during the impeachment of President Bill Clinton, a scenario that had all the requisites of a classic political scandal—overweening power, unbridled lust, partisan warfare, massive press coverage. But it also had something else: a clear empirical record of how people actually felt about Bill Clinton. Public opinion experts agree that (1) most Americans never wanted Clinton removed from office and (2) they resented the intense partisanship surrounding the scandal.[18] But the nation's political leaders inevitably argued that they knew the people better than the polls did as, for example, when Representative Steve Buyer declared that "the American people want their elected officials to honor their oath, defend the Constitution in accordance with the laws of this Nation."[19] Arguing far more pragmatically, Representative Jim McGovern declared that "the American people want Congress to act on the real issues that face our country. A Patients' Bill of Rights, school construction, saving Social Security."[20]

One can dismiss all of this as "mere rhetoric," but that hardly stops its issuance or causes it to go unheard. In the preceding quotations, for example, the Republican brushes away the pollsters' numbers as mere silliness while the Democrat reads public opinion more deeply than the available evidence allows. As a result, the combatants become locked in both a rhetorical and an epistemological struggle, the kind of struggles that almost always surface during moments of turmoil. Table 6.2 shows that the two crises that ended one century and began another prompted a kind of national introspection (i.e., heavy use of collective tokens), making campaigns seem starkly unreflective in contrast.

But why? What is it about political crises that require such self-examination? When the people are described during such times, what are their special strengths and weaknesses said to be? Why don't political campaigns make us similarly reflective? And what different things do we learn about ourselves during an external (military) threat and an internal (partisan) cri-

TABLE 6.2 General References to the *People*

Source	Total Texts	Texts with Token	% Texts with Token
Campaigns speeches	2,357	322	13.7
September 11 speeches	449	188	41.8
Impeachment speeches	350	138	39.4

sis? While our answers to such questions cannot be definitive, they can tell us things about ourselves that are hard to know otherwise.

To pursue such questions, we conducted systematic content analysis of several different databases. For the September 11 texts, we searched for the phrase *the American people* on the House of Representatives portion of the www.congress.gov website. For the terrorist incident, House remarks delivered between September 11 and November 11, 2001, were gathered, thereby allowing us to track both immediate and delayed reactions to the calamity. That search produced 188 eligible texts (from a corpus of 449 sets of remarks) containing 280 eligible tokens. For the impeachment situation, speeches given by House members on December 18 and 19, 1998 (i.e., during that chamber's formal debate), and on January 14–16, 1999 (i.e., during the Senate trial), were searched, producing 138 eligible texts (from a population of 350 sets of formal remarks) containing 310 collective tokens. In all cases, the texts selected consisted of complete speech acts (an introduction, a body, and a conclusion). Interruptive comments made from the floor, as well as introductory prayers and ceremonial remarks, were excluded. Republicans and Democrats were represented in equal proportions.

The campaign speeches were somewhat different, having derived from both formal and informal, mediated and unmediated, and local and national addresses delivered by major party presidential candidates between 1948 and 2000.[21] These criteria produced 2,357 speeches, 14 percent of which (n = 322) contained the requisite phrase, resulting in an additional 953 tokens for study. Naturally, presidential campaign speeches are not an exact match for formal House remarks, but they did have the practical advantage of being both available and searchable, as well as the conceptual advantage of having been delivered across many years in many contexts, thus providing a broad background against which the crisis speeches could be viewed.

Two additional sets of texts were also gathered. To track how the political candidates' remarks were translated by the press, a collection of print news stories written about the terrorism incidents were extracted from such sources as the *New York Times, Washington Post, Chicago Tribune,* and the *Los Angeles Times,* as well as from a number of regional newspapers;[22] 138 references to *the American people* made by House members resulted from these searches. No analogous press coverage was generated for the impeachment period since the congressional debate's two-day news window was so limited.

All uses of the phrase *the American people* were identified by a keyword-in-context program that isolated the twenty words preceding and following our target phrase, thereby giving us needed contextual information for coding.[23] For the content analytic categories, we restricted ourselves to six clear and simple political markers. Our coding scheme included the following:

1. *The people's time:* Is the token's focus a contemporary one, a historical one, or a projected vision? Does the speaker make all-inclusive and transtemporal statements? A future orientation, for example, can easily be seen in such statements as "This country is on the right track. We are moving back

to our roots and forward into future in the best way together. The question before the American people now is, what path will we take to the 21st century?" (Bill Clinton, October 7, 1996, campaign rally, Portland, Oregon).

2. *The people's situation:* Generally speaking, what forces now confront the American people? Is the overall situation facing the nation hopeful (e.g., "the real winners will be the American people"), dire (e.g., "either way the American people lose"), or neutral ("I have offered clear alternatives to the American people").

3. *The people's role:* What stated or implied task is projected onto the American people? Are they active in the affairs of the nation (as voters, taxpayers, local volunteers, citizens), interested onlookers, or simply living their day-to-day lives (as workers, family members, or consumers, for example)?

4. *The people's actions:* Judging by the verbs immediately adjacent to the targeted phrase, what are the American people doing? Are they cognitive (e.g., hearing, thinking, appreciating, etc.) or reflective (trusting, believing, worshipping)? Are they acting on behalf of their friends and neighbors (caring, uniting, sacrificing, etc.)? Or are they unleashing their competitive (prevailing, fighting, rallying) or productive (achieving, moving, developing) energies?

5. *The people's qualities:* On the basis of the adjectives and adverbs used to describe the American people, what are their strengths and weaknesses? Is their orientation ethical or unethical (e.g., loyal, good, dishonorable, unpatriotic), intellectual or nonintellectual (wise, disillusioned, naive), or are they best characterized in psychological terms (e.g., strong, passionate, intimidated, dispirited)?

6. *The people's opponents:* What persons, groups, or agencies advertently or inadvertently thwart the will of the people? Are these forces endemic to government itself (the federal government or specific politicians), or are they external activists vying for a share of the political spoils (foreign governments, political parties, pressure groups, campaign specialists)? Or are potential opponents removed from discussion altogether?

In addition, the statement's *Scope* was measured by calculating how many of the preceding markers could be found in the same target statement (e.g., did it mention both the people's roles and qualities or their qualities alone?).[24] To better calibrate how reactions to September 11 changed over time, another variable (*Cycle*) was created, which broke the initial reaction to the terrorism incidents into three equal periods: (1) *Reaction:* September 11 through October 2; (2) *Recovery:* October 3 through October 23; (3) *Resolve:* October 24 through November 13.

THE PEOPLE AND TERRORISM

Table 6.3 reviews how collective tokens were used across the three political scenes. It includes an especially important fact: During both international and domestic crises, citizens were framed as State Agents, persons directly

TABLE **6.3** References to the *People* Across Scene

Rhetorical Features		POLITICAL SCENE		
		Campaign	September 11	Impeachment
People's time	Past	17.6%	7.9%	14.4%
	Present	60.4%	71.6%	65.9%
	Future	16.8%	3.6%	2.6%
	Across time	5.2%	16.9%	17.0%
People's situation	Advantageous	36.2%	17.9%	2.4%
	Adverse	32.5%	37.7%	59.5%
	Neutral	31.3%	44.3%	38.2%
People's role	State agent	64.9%	90.7%	97.1%
	Private person	13.2%	2.5%	1.3%
	Observer	21.9%	6.8%	1.6%
People's actions	Communal	7.2%	27.4%	2.2%
	Productive	22.5%	11.0%	2.7%
	Competitive	8.6%	15.2%	25.3%
	Cognitive	51.5%	37.2%	62.7%
	Axiological	10.2%	9.1%	7.1%
People's qualities	Ethical	33.1%	38.9%	38.3%
	Intellectual	33.7%	36.3%	55.1%
	Psychological	33.1%	24.8%	6.6%
People's opponents	None designated	45.0%	47.5%	20.2%
	Professional activists	41.1%	43.6%	27.7%
	Government officials	13.9%	8.9%	52.1%

responsible for the nation. This contrasts sharply to campaigns, where politicians appealed to voters' practical needs (as Private Persons) or describe them as mere observers. So, for example, when campaigning in 2000, George W. Bush declared he would "return about one fourth of the surplus to the American people who earned it, paid it and deserve part of it back,"[25] but that appeal would have seemed heartless during a time of national turmoil. Such moments, says Roger Scruton, require the "metropolitan power" needed to turn individual citizens into a functioning collective.[26]

A unique aspect of the September 11 speeches was their emphasis on the people's communal responsibilities (27.4 percent for the terrorism incident versus 7.2 percent for campaigns and 2.2 percent for impeachment) and considerably less emphasis on the cognitive (62.7 percent during impeachment, 51.5 percent during campaigns, but only 37.2 percent for September 11). Clearly, an attack on cultural essentials—a capitalist monument in New York City, an icon of defense in Washington, DC—required the people to look inside for strength, which they did in candle-lighting ceremonies throughout the nation. These patriotic displays made some progressives worry that militarism or ethnocentrism would erupt, but such worries did not stop the rhetoric in Washington after September 11:

> One of the beautiful things about this period in American history is we have gone beyond our State flags, beyond our corporate banners, beyond where we work, where we were elected, where we are from, and the tragedy of September 11 for this moment in American history has forced all of us to seek security in that which makes us one, the ideals that we believe in fundamentally as Americans. We have turned to our national flag. We have turned to our national government, and even our President is experiencing unparalleled approval ratings because the American people are rallying behind the concept that we can defend ourselves as a Nation from these attacks.[27]

As we see in Table 6.3, House members were four times more likely to focus on the emotional strengths of the citizenry (see People's Qualities) after September 11 than during impeachment and were less pessimistic as well, describing the People's Situation as both more advantaged (17.9 percent versus 2.4 percent) and less adverse (37.7 percent versus 59.5 percent) than during impeachment. These data rehearse the classic therapeutic encounter, where the client articulates his or her (1) felt anxieties and (2) inner strengths so that (3) self-authorized healing can result: "[E]vil stole the lives and safety of our citizens [but] it can never steal our resolve, our ideals, and our love of freedom."[28] In the House, there was frank acknowledgment that "the goal of the terrorist [is] to instill fear in the American people"[29] and that routing out the terrorists was "going to take sacrifices and, unfortunately, it is going to cost lives."[30] But there was also talk of the "tough fiber of the New Yorkers"[31] and hymns to the resilience and solidarity of the American people. And there were hymns of a more traditional sort: "[B]e encouraged; do not be terrified. Be strong and courageous, for now, as always, throughout our history, the Lord, your God, will be with you wherever you go."[32]

As rhetorical scholar Carroll Arnold has observed, there has always been a waltz between the practical and the transcendent in American life, between the high-minded and the hard-headed. Ultimately, says Arnold, the United States is distinguished by its ability to blend these elements or, at least, to require that they take turns.[33] Too much of the technocratic creates a society incapable of finding a center that holds; too much philosophizing spawns a glut of mass movements that substitutes passion for reason.[34] Because choosing between these options has been hard for most Americans, they have typically chosen both, placing their faith in the Lord even while agreeing with Calvin Coolidge that "the chief business of the American people is business."

Figures 6.1 and 6.2 show the rather remarkable shifts along these lines between September 11 and November 11. As we see in Figure 6.1, the early value-laden emphases dropped off as the House got back to the business of national defense. The technocratic kicked in and the psychological receded or, better, the psychological was asked to serve instrumental functions. Figure 6.2 shows that these behavioral shifts were attended by character-

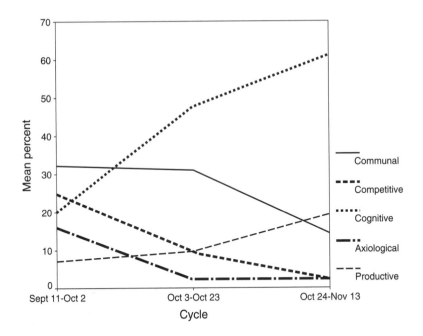

Figure 6.1 Descriptions of People's Actions Across Cycle.

centered shifts as well. These changes occurred rather quickly (our time frame here is only twelve weeks), but they unmistakably changed the tenor of the discussions, as we see when Congressman Gene Green of Texas denounced the emotionality of the early period:

> The so-called stimulus package that we have on the floor today is being presented wrapped in red, white and blue, but it is a charade. It is a Trojan horse for every special interest package that has come around for the last 10 years. The American people are not and will not be fooled. This so-called stimulus package is a wish list of every special interest tax rebate and tax cut that will not stimulate our economy and does nothing to help us from the September 11 tragedy. The wrapping of special interest legislation in our patriotic feelings is wrong, and it is not in the spirit of our bipartisan war effort.[35]

Green's remarks also illustrate the partisan differences found in the September 11 texts. Generally speaking, the Democrats were more businesslike (emphasizing the people's intellectual rather than moral/psychological qualities), while the Republicans were preachier (three times more axiological references).[36] Curiously, as we will see, this is the *inverse* of the pattern found in the impeachment debates, where the Republicans adopted a more

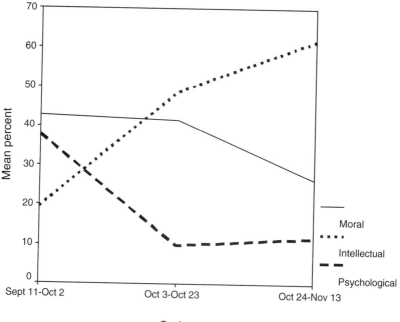

Figure 6.2 Descriptions of People's Qualities Across Cycle.

factual, legalistic, style. Why the difference? Here is one possibility: The pragmatic and transcendent are available to all politicians regardless of party, with deployment being best predicted by the peculiar circumstances being faced. Subsequent to September 11, that is, the Republicans may have felt a need to align their tone with that of the chief executive (a member of their own party). The Democrats clearly took the opposite tack, perhaps to ensure that the emotions of the moment did not overwhelm policy discussions. A more general possibility is that an attack mode encourages a legalistic style, while defense encourages the moralistic.

Even during moments of national crisis, however, not all political remarks become sound bites. Our studies show that the media featured present-day quotations most of the time (92.2 percent versus 71.6 percent for the House), while the politicians emphasized historic truths and commitments (24.8 percent versus only 5.2 percent for the press). Along these same lines, House members were four times more likely to feature the people's communal obligations, with the press stressing their cognitive skills. News norms help explain these differences: The press sees itself as the nation's watchdog, not its pastor. So, for example, while Congressman Bill Young could speak floridly right after the terrorist attack ("the world will know that our people and we as their representatives in Congress are more united behind our President as he leads this great Nation under God than most Americans alive today have ever witnessed"),[37] the media selected his most pedestrian remarks for reportage: "'If we don't act swiftly, we are going to let down the American people. . . . They want action and they want it now.' "[38] In the media's hands, that is, rationality, not blind emotion, must carry the day.

Raised on a diet of political supremacy and technocratic invincibility, the American people were shaken to the core on September 11, 2001. Shortly thereafter, a number of bromides caught the national ear: "America has lost its innocence forever"; "this is the first war of the twenty-first century"; "the U.S. just joined the world of nations." At some point, history may prove these claims true. But the events of September 11 showed something more important: the vitality of a long-standing discourse in which the people look *to themselves* for guidance. Admittedly, their talk on such occasions is shot through with contradictions and overstatements. But their attempts to discover who they are—especially during perilous times—is a curious, and curiously American, trait.

THE PEOPLE AND IMPEACHMENT

Perhaps the most famous presidential quotation in recent memory is this: "But I want to say one thing to *the American people*. I want you to listen to me. I'm going to say this again: I did not have sexual relations with that woman, Miss Lewinsky. I never told anybody to lie, not a single time—never. These allegations are false. And I need to go back to work for *the American people*."[39] Heretofore, most commentators have focused on the essence of Bill Clinton's statement and ignored its form. But note that he bracketed his remarks with collective tokens, references to the very people he governed. In his first usage Clinton lied (by most people's standards), but his second usage saved him. That is, the American people (the real ones, not the rhetorical ones) genuinely liked this president's work. Indeed, two remarkable things happened during the Lewinsky scandal: Over time, people became increasingly convinced of the president's guilt but increasingly disinclined to remove him from office.[40]

While Judge Richard Posner is probably right that the American people never had monolithic feelings about the Lewinsky affair, that did not prevent monolithic rhetorics from developing.[41] As we saw in Table 6.3, House members spent much of their time during the scandal intuiting public opinion, but they also made active use of collective tokens, providing layered and rich descriptions of the American people. The impeachment statements were broader in Scope than the September 11 remarks, while the campaign rhetoric was positively anemic in contrast.[42] In other words, at the very moment when House members were more divided than ever in recent memory, they described an electorate that was both unified and had a sense of direction. Republicans and Democrats, of course, disagreed about the source of that unity and the nature of that direction.

Indeed, one of the most distinctive aspects of the impeachment rhetoric was its hortatoriness. As we see in Table 6.3, both the impeachment debates and the September 11 texts focused on historical rights and responsibilities. The political campaigners, in contrast, expended most of their efforts imagining a brighter future. Perhaps because crisis so often obscures the future, people are naturally thrown back on their essential beliefs and commitments during such moments. It therefore must have been difficult for voters to think about sexual transgressions in the Oval Office when listening to the House's elevated rhetoric, with Republicans declaring, "We are saying that the American people who have, as the gentleman from Illinois so eloquently put it this morning, believed, fought and sacrificed this past 227 years for the rule of law,"[43] and with Democrats being equally fundamentalistic: "[I]n their fervor to punish this President they [the Republicans] will violate a sacred covenant with the American People: this government is still the people's government."[44]

Also contributing to the rich tenor of the debate was its focus on the people's enemies. Table 6.3 reports that almost 80 percent of the impeachment tokens were juxtaposed to some negative force. Strangely, the September 11 rhetoric was less antagonistic, perhaps because evil did not have to be *imagined* on that occasion. But because the impeachment process was political to the core—which is to say, because it dealt with values rather than imploded buildings—the debaters gave themselves free reign. For Republicans, Bill Clinton was the obvious enemy: "Instead of following the law, respecting the American people's values and honoring his office, [Clinton] chose to lie, cover up and evade the truth. His actions have made a mockery of the people who fought for this country, the Constitution and the laws we live under."[45] The Democrats, not surprisingly, made the Republican caucus the hobgoblin of the people: "Today they seek to substitute, in my opinion, their judgment for the will of the American people and remove their nemesis from the position to which the American people, over their objection, elected him."[46]

It is ironic that the people's situation was deemed graver during impeachment than during the September 11 incident (see Table 6.3). Again, this finding dramatizes the Republicans' challenge: They somehow had to get people's eyes off their retirement portfolios and onto the "rights and responsibilities of citizenship." As political scientist Gary Jacobson observed, it was hard to accomplish such tasks when the Misery Index was at an all-time low for most Americans.[47] But because the House members were a contentious lot, with fewer than 10 percent of them being moderates,[48] they rose to the challenge. The main reason for the impeachment's negativity, however, was probably the personal animus felt toward Bill Clinton. As Paul Quirk notes, Clinton's dazzling strengths and weaknesses virtually assured that the debates would be contentious.[49]

But they were not uncontrolled. There were comparatively few dramatic indulgences, with speakers usually asking that their cases be judged on their merits. To accomplish that, they described the electorate as eminently logical (see People's Qualities in Table 6.3): "The American People have heard the allegations against the President, and they overwhelmingly oppose impeaching him."[50] The data on People's Actions in Table 6.3 also describe a people who ostensibly wanted unambiguous answers to the questions at hand.

Republicans emphasized the people's cognitive skills (79.7 percent versus 57.9 percent for the Democrats) because they did not want the proceedings to seem a witch hunt. The Democrats were more combative, invoking the competitive aspects of the American people twice as often as the Republicans. Launching into the fray on one occasion, Congresswoman Anna Eshoo declared "a day of infamy in the House of Representatives," when the majority party, "through searing, brutal partisanship, disallowed the right of each Member, and this Member, to express their own conscience." "It is a day," continued Eshoo, "when the overwhelming voices of the American people are turned away."[51] This same approach saw the Democrats framing the people's opponents not as governmental actors (the Republicans's favorite strategy—71 percent versus 39.3 percent for the Democrats), but as political operatives (i.e., the political parties and the lobbies: 44.6 percent for the Democrats versus 8.6 percent for the Republicans).

While the Republicans were businesslike during the House proceedings, things changed in the Senate trial. There, House managers used almost twice as many collective references, perhaps a signal that they and not the Senators hailed from "the people's House." This difference in magnitude is attended by tonal differences. When all House speakers were compared to those taking the case to the Senate, the latter were preachier—less fact-based and more transcendent in tone. A number of factors may explain why: (1) Increased media coverage could have prompted a dramatic approach; (2) the impeachment facts were well known by then, leaving only interpretations to be made and implications drawn; or (3) as scholar Thomas Kazee has suggested, the remoteness of winning in the Senate may have caused the managers to throw caution to the wind.[52] Whatever the reason, the Senate speeches were often pure Americana:

> People of all nationalities, faiths, creeds, and values have come to our shores, shed their allegiances to their old countries and achieved their dreams to become Americans. . . . They fled countries where the rulers ruled at the expense of the people, to America, where the leaders are expected to govern for the benefit of the people. And, throughout the years, America's leaders have tried to earn the trust of the American people, not by their words, but by their actions.[53]

Given the evidence amassed against Bill Clinton, it is something of a small miracle he escaped with his presidency intact. A strong economy, a satisfied electorate, and political malaise may explain his good fortune. But the rhetoric of *the American people* adds to that explanation as well. During impeachment, it seemed, everyone knew what the people wanted. The Democrats sensed that voters wanted to live in the present, that they resented an overweening Republican party, and that they were pragmatic to the core. The Republicans knew that voters were proud of their history, wanted decency in the White House, and felt that facts should guide decision-making. The American people themselves probably believed all these things, and that is the problem: On most public matters, most of the time, Americans differ with one another. But even as they do, the promise of unanimity serves as a siren call for them.

CONCLUSION

Almost all nations go to great lengths to enshrine their historic documents, the grandest articulations of their people's most basic beliefs and values. Statements about the *people,* on the other hand, are rarely preserved. Ordinary folks make such statements unthinkingly (*"we've* got to do something about this pollution problem") and elites use them strategically (*"voters* simply demand the adoption of House Bill 211"). When doing so, both are caught up in a discourse they do not fully understand but with which they feel strangely comfortable. But even when not understood, such references can be important. As Murray Edelman has observed, politics is a struggle over resources but a struggle over meaning as well.[54]

And these struggles can get complicated. We have seen here that all political crises invite a kind of national self-examination but that these examinations differ depending on the problem at hand. The impeachment proceedings, for example, were a study in political delicacy, with Republicans envisioning a rational electorate that could come to only one conclusion and Democrats warning that same electorate not to make grand decisions for petty reasons. September 11 was another matter entirely. Subsequent to the attacks, the people were again summoned forth but, this time, were asked to marshal their inner resources by reaching out to one another. Eventually, members of Congress moved past the emotional to the practical, reminding the American people that their ultimate strength lay in their pragmatism. When doing all of these things, the nation's leaders used a very old discourse for very new reasons.

Many, of course, find political rhetoric to be banal and insignificant. But our argument here is that its significance lies in its ordinariness, in its sameness. People only use rhetoric, after all, because they have no other choice. If Americans really were good—all the time, to everyone—they would not need to label themselves thusly. If they knew what was ultimately right they could announce those truths once and be done with it. But the American people are both too limited and too diverse to know such things for sure. So they and their leaders make pious declarations, hoping that the sound of their own voices will tell them what to do.

But what happens when a people cannot find a rhetoric that fits? What happens to a country like Afghanistan that knows itself (recently at least) largely by negation? Afghanistan knows it is not Western or Christian or Arab or Russian, and that can be clarifying. But it also knows it is not Pashtun or Uzbek or Tajik alone, and that can be confusing. A nation that cannot find a rhetoric, alas, often cannot find a nation.

We need to know when political language signals what its users have actually experienced and when it reflects their imagined worlds. Both kinds of data are relevant to understanding politics, and both play a role in the practical world as well. Understanding what an electorate actually knows is needed for any sort of rational planning. But knowing what it wants and desires, what frightens and heartens it, is needed for enlightened governance. Great leaders articulate the real and the imagined with equal conviction.

As we have seen here, language deployed during crises can be especially telling. Both the September 11 and impeachment discourses differed from normal electioneering, thereby shedding light on fundamental (if unsettled) aspects of American political experience. And yet the two cases differed from one another as well. That should not be surprising since, on the American plan, collective identity is never whole. In the impeachment case, for example, we found Republicans using a rhetoric that flew in the face of measurable public opinion, and in the aftermath of September 11 we heard the American people praised for being good and generous just hours after nineteen hijackers had declared them neither.

There is much to learn about such matters. How long, for example, can a rhetoric survive when it is undermined by real-world circumstances? Is there an inevitable point of intersection between idealized and actual public opinion, or can both fill the same political space forever? How quickly must a rhetoric of identity adapt to demographic and other changes or to newly formed political coalitions? Do the collective tokens used by ordinary citizens dovetail with those of their leaders, or is there an inevitable disconnect between lay and elite discourse? And we need to ask such questions cross-nationally. Do some nations use collective tokens more self-consciously and uniformly than others? Can such symbols be treated as an unobtrusive measure of a nation's relative political maturity and/or internal harmony? What peculiar blend of ethnic or religious or cultural traditions best predicts how a nation will speak of itself? And are a society's political fractures inevitably found in its public discourse?

This chapter is not the last word on any of these matters, and it is entirely possible that the American case is unique. For many reasons, then, we must develop new and better ways of understanding political language, of learning how a people can reveal all and conceal all simultaneously. Such revelations are inevitably important. Such concealments are inevitably intriguing. We need to understand both.

NOTES

1. B. Anderson, *Imagined Communities* (London: Verso, 1983), 6.

2. For previous studies in this area, see R. P. Hart and S. Jarvis, "We the People: The Contours of Lay Political Discourse," in *The Poll with a Human Face: The National Issues Convention Experiment in Political Communication*, ed. M. McCombs and A. Reynolds (New York: Erlbaum, 1999), 59–84; R. P. Hart and M. Johnson, "Constructing the Electorate During Presidential Campaigns," *Presidential Studies Quarterly*, 29 (1999): 830–49; and R. P. Hart, W. Jennings, and M. Dixson, "Imagining the American People: Strategies for Building Political Community," *Journal of Communication*, 53 (2002): 1–17. Portions of the current chapter derive from R. P. Hart, S. Jarvis, and E. Lim, "The American People in Crisis: A Content Analysis," *Political Psychology*, 23 (2002): 417–37.

3. R. Merelman, *Making Something of Ourselves: On Culture and Politics in the United States* (Berkeley: University of California Press, 1989).

4. R. Scruton, "The First Person Plural," in *Theorizing Nationalism*, ed. R. Beiner (Albany: State University of New York Press, 1999), 290.

5. P. Bourdieu, "Public Opinion Does not Exist," in *Communication and Class Struggle*, ed. A. Mattelart and S. Siegelaub (New York: International General, 1979), 125.

6. M. McGee, "In Search of the People: A Rhetorical Alternative," *Quarterly Journal of Speech*, 61 (1975): 242.

7. G. Baym, "Constructing Moral Authority: *We* in the Discourse of Television News," *Western Journal of Communication*, 64 (2000): 101.

8. See, for example, S. G. Larson, "Public Opinion in Television Election News: Beyond Polls," *Political Communication*, 16 (1999): 133–45; and S. G. Larson, "Who Are 'We'? and What Do 'We' Want? Representations of the Public in Election News," in *We Get What We Vote For—or Do We?: The Impact of Elections on Governing*, ed. P. Scheele (Westport, CT: Praeger, 1999), 68–81.

9. K. Cramer, "Grass-roots Collective Information Processing: Making Sense of Politics Through Group Discussion," paper presented at the annual meeting of the Midwest Political Science Association, Chicago, 1999, 20.

10. C. Miller, "Rhetorical Community: The Cultural Basis of Genre," in *Genre and the New Rhetoric*, ed. A. Freedman and P. Medway (New York: Taylor and Francis, 1994), 67–78. For additional insight on these matters, see V. B. Beasley, "Making Diversity Safe for Democracy: American Pluralism and the Presidential Local Address, 1885–1992," *Quarterly Journal of Speech*, 87 (2001): 25–40.

11. E. T. Lim, "Five Trends in Presidential Rhetoric: An Analysis of Rhetoric from George Washington to Bill Clinton," *Presidential Studies Quarterly*, 32 (2002): 328–66.

12. This is a special concern of Holly Waldren, who, in an imaginative study, analyzed images of the citizenry projected in campaign spots between 1976 and 1996. She found that ordinary citizens were overwhelmingly depicted in the commercials as "recipients" rather than "agents," as political freeriders. A nation that "reinforces the myth of political efficacy while subtly and simultaneously undermining it," says Waldren, threatens that nation's vitality and utility. See H. Waldren, "Representing

the People: An Analysis of Televised Presidential Advertising, 1976–1996," paper presented at the annual meeting of the National Communication Association, New York, 1998, 32.

13. J. Lyon, *Manifestoes: Provocations of the Modern* (Ithaca, NY: Cornell University Press, 1999), 25.

14. C. Willard, *Liberalism and the Problem of Knowledge: A New Rhetoric for Modern Democracy* (Chicago: University of Chicago Press, 1996), 317.

15. For additional insight on this matter see Hart and Jarvis, "We the People."

16. For further details, see ibid.

17. R. Reagan, "Acceptance Speech," Republican National Convention, Detroit, MI, July 17, 1980, *Annenberg/Pew Archive of Presidential Discourse*, CD-ROM (Philadelphia: Annenberg School for Communication, 2000).

18. See M. J. Gerhardt, "The Impeachment and Acquittal of William Jefferson Clinton," in *The Clinton Scandal and the Future of American Government*, ed. M. J. Rozell and C. Wilcox (Washington, DC: Georgetown University Press, 2000), 142–70; M. W. Sonner and C. Wilcox, "Forgiving and Forgetting: Public Support for Bill Clinton During the Lewinsky Scandal," *PS: Political Science and Politics*, 32 (1999): 554–57; and A. J. Miller, "Sex, Politics, and Public Opinion: What Political Scientists Really Learned from the Clinton-Lewinsky Scandal," *PS: Political Science and Politics*, 32 (1999): 721–29.

19. S. Buyer, "Privileges of the House: Impeaching William Jefferson Clinton, President of the United States, for High Crimes and Misdemeanors," 105th Cong., 2d sess., *Congressional Record*, 144 (December 18, 1998): H 11788.

20. J. McGovern, "Privileges of the House: Impeaching William Jefferson Clinton, President of the United States, for High Crimes and Misdemeanors," 105th Cong., 2d sess., *Congressional Record*, 144 (December 18, 1998): H 11820.

21. For further insight into these corpuses, see R. P. Hart, *Campaign Talk: Why Elections Are Good for Us* (Princeton, NJ: Princeton University Press, 2000).

22. These sources included the *New York Times, Newsday, Boston Globe, Boston Herald, Baltimore Sun, Chicago Sun-Times, San Francisco Chronicle, Milwaukee Journal-Sentinel, San Diego Union-Tribune, Houston Chronicle, USA Today, St. Louis Dispatch, Pittsburgh Post-Gazette, Omaha World-Herald, Tampa Tribune, St. Petersburg Times, Hartford Courant, Herald-Sun* (Durham), and *Star-Tribune* (Minneapolis).

23. Several other collective tokens could have been the focus of our scrutiny, but we rejected them for either practical or theoretical reasons. For example, *we/us* was judged too informal, *voters* too restrictive, *citizens* too arcane, *the electorate* too abstract, and *people* too indefinite.

24. We constructed the Scope variable by recording one integer whenever any of the six main variables received a non-zero code, thereby creating a measure of descriptive richness. The resulting metric ranged from a minimum of 1 to a maximum of 6, with a mean of 4.15 and a standard deviation of 1.08.

25. G. W. Bush, "Campaign Speech," Green Bay, WI, September 28, 2000, in *In Their Own Words: Sourcebook 2000*, CD-ROM (Stanford, CA: Political Communication Lab, 2000).

26. Scruton, "The First Person Plural," 290.

27. J. Jackson, Jr., "Airline Baggage Screening." *Congressional Record*, 107th Cong. (October 11, 2001): H 6686.

28. J. Kingston, "America Will Prevail Against This Adversity," 107th Cong., *Congressional Record* (September 11, 2001): H 5502.

29. N. Pelosi, "Authorizing Use of United States Armed Forces Against Those Responsible for Recent Attacks Against the United States," 107th Cong., *Congressional Record* (September 14, 2001): H 5661.

30. T. DeLay, "Civilization Will Defeat Terrorism," 107th Cong., *Congressional Record* (October 5, 2001): H 6417.

31. A. Schiff, "Authorizing Use of United States Armed Forces Against Those Responsible for Recent Attacks Against the United States," 107 Cong., *Congressional Record* (September 14, 2001): H 5646.

32. M. Pence, "America Will Prevail With Strength and Courage," 107th Cong., *Congressional Record* (September 11, 2001): H 5498.

33. See C. C. Arnold, "Reflections on American Public Discourse," *Central States Speech Journal*, 28 (1977): 73–85.

34. For more on these options, see R. Dworkin, *Taking Rights Seriously* (Cambridge, MA: Harvard University Press, 1978); and R. Hofstader, *The American Political Tradition* (New York: Vintage/Random House, 1989).

35. G. Green, "Economic Security and Recovery Act of 2001," 107th Cong., *Congressional Record* (October 24, 2001): H 7277. Extended remarks "Economic Stimulation for Special Interests" (October 24, 2001): H 7221.

36. The specific data are these: The Democrats emphasized the communal (31.2 percent versus 22.5 percent for Republicans) and the intellectual (45.6 percent versus 23.9 percent for Republicans). The Republicans, in contrast, featured the people's axiological qualities (14.1 percent versus 5.4 percent for Democrats) as well as their moral and psychological capacities (76.2 percent versus 54.4 percent for the Democrats).

37. B. Young, "2001 Emergency Supplemental Appropriations Act for Recovery From and Response to Terrorist Attacks on the United States," 107th Cong., *Congressional Record* (September 14, 2001): H 5620.

38. Editorial, "Taking It Slow," *Boston Globe,* September 14, 2001, A22.

39. W. Clinton, "Remarks at the After-School Program Event (Washington, DC, January 26, 1998)," *Washington Post,* sec. A, January 28, 1998.

40. Numerous scholars have documented this trend, but see especially Sonner and Wilcox, "Forgiving and Forgetting."

41. R. Posner, *An Affair of State: The Investigation, Impeachment, and Trial of President Clinton* (Cambridge, MA: Harvard University Press, 1999).

42. The statistical differences are quite pronounced here. The Scope variable ranged from a low of 1 to a maximum of 6. The impeachment remarks averaged 5.31 on Scope, the September 11 speeches 4.63. The campaign comments, in contrast, averaged only 3.69. The relevant chi square for this comparison was robust: F [2,1540] = 370.26, $p < .000$.

43. M. Cook, "Privileges of the House: Impeaching William Jefferson Clinton, President of the United States, for High Crimes and Misdemeanors," 105th Cong., 2d sess., *Congressional Record,* 144 (December 18, 1998): H 11808.

44. R. Kind, "Privileges of the House: Impeaching William Jefferson Clinton, President of the United States, for High Crimes and Misdemeanors," 105th Cong., 2d sess., *Congressional Record,* 144 (December 18, 1998): H 11835.

45. S. Johnson, "Privileges of the House: Impeaching William Jefferson Clinton, President of the United States, for High Crimes and Misdemeanors," 105th Cong., 2d sess., *Congressional Record* (December 18, 1998): H 11784.

46. S. Hoyer, "Privileges of the House: Impeaching William Jefferson Clinton, President of the United States, for High Crimes and Misdemeanors," 105th Cong., 2d sess., *Congressional Record*, 144 (December 18, 1998): H 11789.

47. G. Jacobson, "Impeachment Politics in the 1998 Congressional Elections," *Political Science Quarterly*, 114 (1999): 31–51.

48. For more on the political complexion of Congress at the time, see T. E. Mann and S. Binder, "The 105th: It Could've Been a Contender," *Washington Post*, October 18, 1998, C01.

49. P. Quirk, "Scandal Time: The Clinton Impeachment and the Distraction of American Politics," in *The Clinton Scandal and the Future of American Government*, ed. M. J. Rozell and C. Wilcox (Washington, DC: Georgetown University Press, 2000), 118–41.

50. Rep. Jerrold Nadler, D-New York, December 18, 1998.

51. Rep. Anna Eshoo, D-California, December 18, 1998.

52. T. A. Kazee, "The Congress: The Politics of Impeachment," in *The Clinton Scandal and the Future of American Government*, ed. M. J. Rozell and C. Wilcox, (Washington, DC: Georgetown University Press, 2000), 18–39.

53. Rep. Jim Sensenbrenner, R-Wisconsin, January 14, 1999.

54. M. Edelman, *Constructing the Political Spectacle* (Chicago: University of Chicago Press, 1988).

UNIT 3

THE LANGUAGE OF LEADERSHIP

Unit 2 of this book examined some of the grandest keywords a democracy can conjure up. The words we looked at were small ones—**government,** the **media,** and the **people**—but they described enormously complicated realities. Who, for example, can say they have really met the American people? What simple thing can be said about the federal government in Washington? Given the reach of the communications industries today, does watching FoxNews give one sufficient understanding to comment on the media knowingly? When it comes to entities like these we see the parts but never the wholes. The language of democracy churns constantly because a large and complex nation will not stand still.

In unit 3 we turn away from these amorphous institutions to one embodied in a single individual—the **president.** Any state leader is important, but the American president is unique. With Congress making laws and with the Supreme Court interpreting them, what is left for the president to do? All that remains. Statutorily, the president must be the nation's chief diplomat, manager of an enormous bureaucracy, commander-in-chief of the military, and head appointments officer as well. Culturally, the president must be a father confessor, a role model, and high priest of the nation's rituals. Deprived of a monarchy and with only a few hundred years of national history to depend upon, the American people look to their president for political, financial, and emotional guidance and for safety and protection as well.

Chapter 7 considers how the *president* is used to socialize children. By looking at the way civics textbooks discuss power we can better understand why political indolence is now so attractive for so many. We find the *president* being used to the point of exhaustion in the textbooks, embodying certain models of citizenship and acting as a stand-in for governance itself. That is both good and bad. Tilting their heads toward the presidency can inspire young people, but it can also distance them from the ordinary duties of citizenship. That can be troublesome and it can even be dangerous. We explain why in chapter 7.

Each day, the mass media tell the *president*'s story as well. Chapter 8 looks at fifty years of *Time* magazine coverage and finds it stabilizing the polity. Although some portions of the media may foment cynicism, other portions are oddly establishmentarian. *Time,* and much of the rest of the print press, use presidential history to provide context for current-day events, thereby anchoring its readers politically. Although journalists surely call a spade a spade, they do "system maintenance" work quite often as well. The press focuses mostly on distributive issues—who should get what and how much?—rather than asking deeply axiological questions. Constrained as they are by such habits, the American mass media are hardly insurrectional as a result.

Chapter 9 looks at how incumbent presidents speak of their predecessors. At times we find them doing so in partisan ways but, surprisingly, they also speak of them respectfully, even glowingly, when advancing their various agendas. This explains why the presidency is such a powerful institution: No president starts from scratch. From their first day in office they are surrounded by history. Their daily schedules are dictated by precedent. The people they meet, domestically and internationally, are often prescribed for them. Even the house they live in is encrusted with history. By using the past as they do, presidents reinstitutionalize the office of the presidency, thereby solidifying their own political position and letting the executive branch of government maintain its unique hold over the American people. Keywords are central to all such endeavors.

7

The *President*
Lessons in Political Socialization

In 1831, the American people had an interesting visitor in their midst. Alexis de Tocqueville, a French politician and writer, came to the United States to study its penal system. He completed his mission but did far more as well: He wrote *Democracy in America*, perhaps the finest piece of political sociology every crafted. In it de Tocqueville not only carefully described the new nation but also asked some searching questions:

> How is it that in the United States, where the inhabitants arrived but yesterday in the land they occupy, wither they brought with them neither customs nor memories, where they meet for the first time without knowing each, where, to say it in one word, the instinct of country can hardly exist—how does it come about that each man is as interested in the affairs of his township, of his canton, and of the whole state as he is in his own affairs?[1]

The questions that puzzled de Tocqueville continue to vex anyone familiar with the United States. Yesterday and today, in ways large and small, its people have confronted special challenges in the area of national identity. "Of course I am an American," the patriot declares, but even as he does his interlocutor retorts, "You're certainly not *my kind* of American." American self-knowledge is a powerful and mysterious thing.

Most scholars presume that a nation-state must have, or learn to manufacture, a common identity for its people. Bonds of personal or familial kinship, living together as neighbors in the same geographical region, or joining in community rituals—these and other devices help people learn who they are. For many nations, especially small ones, these processes are natural and inevitable. Other countries struggle mightily with them.[2] The vicissitudes faced by Afghanistan after the U.S.-led removal of the Taliban in 2002 is a case in point. That nation was confronted with insufficient food, medicine, roads, schools, public safety, and economic infrastructure, but these problems paled in comparison to the problem of transforming a largely tribal society into a modern nation with a coherent sense of self.

The American colonists, too, faced challenges, which is why de Tocqueville called them "the most peculiar people in the world."[3] Historian Henry Steele Commager has observed that "in the Old World the nation came before state," while "in America the state came before the nation. In the Old World, nations grew out of well-prepared soil, built upon a foundation of history and traditions; in America the foundations were still to be laid, the seeds still to be planted, the traditions still to be formed."[4] The challenges to the young nation were prodigious: It had no common past or homogenous population or common religious heritage. The extraordinary diversity and size of its land mass presented still other obstacles. For reasons like these, says scholar Daniel Elazar, the United States became a "convenantal arrangement among diverse peoples."[5] In other words, Americans had to rely on the artificialities of rule, law, and contract to regulate themselves and to get a sense of what they might become.[6] As we saw in chapter 6, they had to rely on public discourse to know who they were as well.

The challenges faced in the early republic continue today. In the second half of the twentieth century, the American people tore themselves apart over race relations, the Vietnam war, the emerging women's movement, and the nation's pockets of grinding, unrelenting poverty. Young Americans in particular questioned the authority of governmental institutions. Religious, cultural, and ethnic pots boiled over in the 1960s and 1970s only to be replaced by what many saw as a mindless corporatism in the 1980s. The 1990s brought other challenges as Americans lost confidence in governmental institutions and became disengaged from political activities.

The twenty-first century dawned with the American people again confronting challenges: A Judeo-Christian culture was one thing, but a Judeo-Christian-Muslim culture was quite another.[7] Particularly in the aftermath of the September 11 attacks, the entire concept of what it meant to be an American became problematic. Must one display the American flag on one's front porch or jacket lapel? It is lawful but is it *American* for the government to create strict new regulations regarding search and seizure? Because matters like these have always bedeviled the United States, some method was needed to fashion one people out of many. A nation of tool-makers needed a tool. Public education became that implement.

MAKING AMERICANS

In the United States, citizens are made, not born, and they are made largely through formal education. From the nation's beginnings, public officials saw education as the key to reproducing a citizenry. They were not alone, since many nation-states have relied on schooling to serve governmental interests.[8] But the American case was a special one. As researchers Diane Ravitch and Joseph Viteritti explain, ever since the late nineteenth century Americans "have relied upon government schools as a principle purveyor of deeply cherished democratic values. For many generations of immigrants, the common school was the primary teacher of patriotism and civic values."[9] Things are no different today: The southwestern border of the United States disgorges thousands of potential new Americans each week. Some will stay; some will return; some will be returned. All want to know how to become Americans.[10]

Political socialization involves the "training of individuals for political participation through the inculcation of politically relevant attitudes, values, beliefs, and behaviors."[11] To achieve these ends, early leaders in the United States drafted specific courses on citizenship and required them of all school-children, ensuring that civics and history would become curricular key-stones.[12] From the beginning, the American educational system was designed to create Americans.

National, state, and local governments continue to be concerned about the role played by schools in political socialization.[13] For example, in developing its 1998 civics assessment, the National Assessment Governing Board warned that, once again, the nation was in a "time of heightened public concern about the quality and direction of constitutional government, citizenship, and civic education in America."[14] In the 1990s, two national panels—the National Commission on Civic Renewal and the Council on Civil Society—were established to "study how Americans could revitalize civil society."[15] Also in the 1990s, political scientists called for renewed research on citizenship and youth development,[16] only to be trumped by President George W. Bush himself, who announced a multiyear, $100 million initiative for invigorating citizenship education in the nation's schools.[17]

Despite these efforts, the problem of effectively maintaining civic ties is a vexing one. The 1996 presidential election, for example, produced the lowest voter turnout since 1948.[18] Reflecting on such trends, Jill McMillan and Katy Harriger share a depressing list of problems in the area of political participation:

> Voter studies, public opinion polls, and focus groups tell the same story: American citizens are increasingly likely to believe that political participation makes little difference in their lives, that government is controlled by special interests with money, and that their time and effort are better spent somewhere other than the political arena.[19]

Especially disappointing is the lack of participation by young people. In the 2002 off-year elections, for example, less than a quarter of registered eighteen- to twenty-four-year-olds voted; a great many in that same cohort did not even bother to register at all.[20]

Political attitudes are one thing; political knowledge is another. While scholars often disagree about what sorts of cognitive skills should be expected of informed citizens, most agree that "average Americans' political knowledge is slim and below the standards that should be expected."[21] Researchers are now finding declining levels of political knowledge among young people, less and less interest in public affairs, a disinclination to read newspapers or watch television news, and decreasing party identification.[22] In *Bowling Alone,* Robert Putnam reports that these trends reflect a general disengagement from political, community, and group-based activities in American society.[23]

Political leaders, high school educators, and civic organizations have not stood by idly in the face of such challenges, with the 1980s and 1990s seeing a flurry of activity in this arena. States developed new standards for assessing civic knowledge and attitudes.[24] Civic organizations such as the Close Up Foundation ("the nation's largest nonprofit . . . nonpartisan citizenship education organization") worked "to promote responsible and informed participation in the democratic process through a variety of methods."[25] A massive study of some ninety thousand fourteen-year-olds compared civic knowledge and political attitudes in twenty-four different countries.[26] Students in the United States did well on some items but, overall, their performance was unimpressive.

Why does civic education in the United States produce such unsteady results? One answer might lie in the textbooks used. As the dominant mode of instruction, civics textbooks have been extensively critiqued during the past forty years. When those criticisms reached a peak in the 1960s, textbook publishers responded by creating visually appealing books only to confront charges twenty years later that their publications were vacuous. Other critics have argued that civics textbooks now emphasize pluralism and cultural diversity at the expense of national unity.[27] Political scientists criticize textbooks for offering simplistic views of governmental processes,[28] while others complain that even the best books overlook the controversy and drama of real-world politics.[29] Manufacturing citizens, as it turns out, is no easy matter. Manufacturing good citizens is even harder.

MODELS OF CITIZENSHIP

To get a better understanding of the political socialization process, we did a careful examination of civic textbooks to discover the implicit model of politics fostered therein. In particular, we focused on how the *president* was referred to in the books, in part because so much previous research (tracing back to the classic study of David Easton and Robert Hess in 1962)[30] has found that the chief executive plays an especially powerful role in the psychological world of the American child. Our notion here was that elite portrayals anchor children's perceptions of (1) what is right and wrong about politics, (2) who counts and who is irrelevant, and (3) what political behaviors are worthy of emulation.

Clearly, textbooks provide other information about governance, but it is the president who comes to represent politics as a whole. In addition, the *president* is a linguistic token found in all forms of public discourse (press reports, campaign addresses, popular culture, etc.), thereby becoming a handy tool for comparing texts of varying sorts. Americans may not know very much about the political events of the day, but they almost always have an opinion about the fellow in the Oval Office.

We examined references made to current and past presidents in twenty-seven of the most popular textbooks used in the United States during the last fifty years. Whenever a presidential allusion was found (i.e., a reference to a named chief executive), we identified the specific token used (e.g., Washington, Lincoln) and then gathered relevant contextual information: the unit topic (e.g., basic, legislative, presidency), the political outcome associated with the president (e.g., an articulation of his philosophy, some major policy initiated), the presidential role being performed (e.g., chief of state, head of party), and whether or not a direct quotation was provided.[31]

In some ways our results are not surprising, and in some ways they are extraordinary. Without doubt, for example, the American schoolchild is presented with an elite view of governance in the textbooks, a view that may well distance them from the public sphere since it leaves so little room for the ordinary citizen. Too, the textbooks consistently offered unrealistic portrayals of what a president can accomplish, thereby spawning what general semanticists call IFD Disease—idealization, frustration, demoralization.[32] That is, the books encourage children to tilt their heads upward toward the president (with respect and awe), but later in life they encounter the mean streets of politics. The result: Ideals clash with reality, encouraging the now-matured citizen to quit the political scene. We are promised a rose garden; we get Watergate. Admittedly, there is nothing automatic about all this and some citizens stay buoyant. But given the elite view of politics offered in textbooks, that persistence seems somewhat heroic.

Figure 7.1 illustrates the dramatic use (controlling for number of pages per book) of executive tokens in school textbooks between 1944 and 1999.[33] Some thirty-eight hundred tokens were used, with the high school textbooks of the 1940s and 1950s including comparatively few references to past presidents, focusing instead on the processes of government. Beginning in the 1960s and continuing through the 1990s, however, references to individual presidents increased dramatically, as did the scope of the textbooks themselves. For example, the 1993 version of *West's American Government* used executive tokens in over 26 percent of its pages. But the picture is even starker, since Figure 7.1 does *not* include multiple references to the same president. That is, we did not factor in the "allusive density" of the tokens (to avoid giving undue credit to authors' narrative strategies). So, for example, even though a passage like the following is rife with presidential allusions, we recorded only one token for Ronald Reagan and another for Richard Nixon, and indicated that each had multiple references:

> President Reagan did continue to carry out certain aspects of the new federalism. In 1981, in his first State of the Union Address, President Reagan said that he intended to restore those powers reserved to the states and to the people. His new federalism, similar to Nixon's, was a plan to give the states an increased role in deciding how government revenues should be spent. But Reagan, unlike Nixon, did not want the state and local government to rely as heavily on the federal government's resources. Reagan wanted the state and local governments to spend as much as they raised themselves, but with less federal regulation on how they spent their own revenues. Reagan's attempt to dismantle forty domestic programs at the

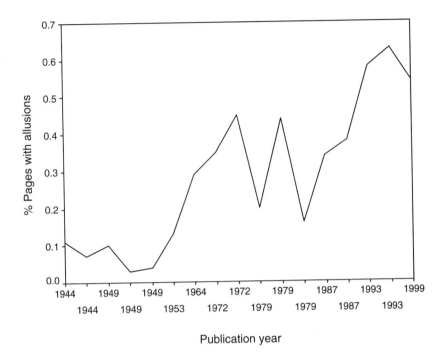

Figure 7.1 Presidential Allusions in Textbooks Across Time.

federal level, including social services, transportation, and community development, was strongly opposed by state governors. They saw Reagan's plan as a ploy to cut federal government expenditures on needed programs.[34]

To understand how presidential tokens can function as a distancing strategy it is useful to acknowledge the essential purpose of civics textbooks. In the preface to the 1999 edition of *Magruder's American Government*, for example, William McClenaghan states that "every edition of this book has had one basic purpose: to describe, analyze, and explain the American system of government."[35] Despite this pledge, the *Magruder* text tells a story of men, not of laws (or legislatures or agencies or parties or caucuses or resolutions or, especially, of principles and values). And that tendency is increasing. The 1949 edition of the *Magruder* text included only seventy-seven presidential tokens, roughly one every ten pages. By 1972, they had quintupled and by 1999 had increased even more. All of this implies that personal rather than formal structures were emphasized, an irony given the structuralism of the 1990s: the emergence of the New Democrats, the changing geopolitics of Eastern Europe (vis-à-vis the United States), the rise of the Gingrich Republicans, a raging Dow Jones average, the third attempted impeachment in a hundred years. There are systemic stories aplenty here, but textbooks know only of presidents.

Textbooks overemphasize not only the influence of the president but also his goodness. For example, in introducing the role of the president, *Magruder's American Government* states, "as President, he is the chief of state, the ceremonial head of the Government of the United States. He is a symbol of the people and of the nation as a whole. He is, in former President Taft's words, 'the personal embodiment and representative of their dignity and majesty.' "[36] Similarly, in the 1993 edition of *West's American Government*, a special feature—"Architect of the American Dream"—introduces the reader to Abraham Lincoln with these words: "The man who preserved the American Union during the Civil War and who proved to the world that democracy could be a lasting form of government was born February 12, 1809, in Hardin, Kentucky, in a one-room, dirt-floor, log cabin."[37] The irony here, of course, is that these antique images were being read by 1990s youngsters with gangsta rap playing in their headphones.

Consistent with these presidential embellishments, the textbooks, regardless of era, described the office of the presidency in olympian terms. While the textbooks of the 1990s sometimes tempered their claims, the power and grandeur of the presidency were nonetheless stressed. For example, *American Civics* announced that the president of the United States is the "busiest man in the world" and then detailed the personal work habits of Truman, Eisenhower, Kennedy, Johnson, and Nixon,[38] ultimately making the chief executive seem a whirling dervish. In doing so, the textbooks reprised the entrepreneurial values lauded in American culture from the time of George Whitfield to that of George Steinbrenner.

In sounding these themes, however, textbooks often become disconnected from popular culture and that is especially problematic when trying to reach young people. The 1988 National Assessment of Educational Progress study found, for example, that almost 30 percent of high school seniors watched television for four or more hours a day and that 72 percent watched for two or more hours each day.[39] Scholars are quick to note that watching that amount of television inevitably directs young people to the contrasts between the world-as-taught and the world-as-witnessed.[40] One author contends, for example, that "those who live on a steady diet of television become trapped. For them, the exceptional becomes the expected and the expected perverse. In such a world, cynicism becomes an intelligent option or, at least, a realistic one."[41]

Textbooks offer a heroic view of governance in which a chief executive's personal qualities overwhelm the institutional challenges he faces. In contrast are the nightly cable talk shows, which lavish detail on politicians' personal foibles. Resolving the disparities between the real and the ideal is not easy for any citizen. But deprived of a sense of historical perspective, it is especially hard for young people. Undaunted by that fact, textbooks continue to trot out what political scientist Thomas Cronin calls a "cult of the presidency," where

> the whole is greater than the sum of its parts. It presents a cumulative presidential image, a legacy of past glories and impressive performances—the exalted dignity of Lincoln, the Wilsonian eloquence, the robust vitality of the Roosevelts, the benign smile and lasting popularity of Eisenhower, the inspirational spirit of Kennedy, the legislative wizardry of Lyndon Johnson, the globe-trotting of the first-term Nixon—which endows the White House with a singular mystique and almost magical qualities. According to this image, the office of the presidency seems to clothe its occupants in strength and dignity, in might and right, and only men of the caliber of Lincoln, of the Roosevelts, or of Wilson can seize the chalice of opportunity, create the vision, and rally the American public around that vision.[42]

Textbooks do not draw upon all presidents equally, as we see in Table 7.1. George Washington, Franklin Roosevelt, Richard Nixon, Thomas Jefferson, and John Kennedy account for over 35 percent of all executive tokens, while presidents like Garfield, Coolidge, McKinley, Harding, Hayes, Polk, and others account for less than 1 percent. Presidents from the twentieth century dominate the textbooks. That makes sense from a journalistic perspective but not from the standpoint of pedagogy. After all, a civics or government course is supposed to awaken youngsters to democracy's enduring features. Still, of the ten most frequently mentioned presidents, seven are from the twentieth century. Only Washington, Jefferson, and Lincoln receive comparable attention. Such presentism makes tactical sense for publishers, but it is the time-transcendent regularities that sustain people's confidence in anything—automobiles, sports teams, computers, governments. Deprived of this sense of continuity, young people are therefore set adrift in a sea of indeterminacies, a condition rife for political cynicism.

But the story becomes even more complicated when we examine the *uses* to which the chief executives are put in the textbooks. Some presidents, like Washington, Adams, Jefferson, and Madison, are used to point up political foundations. That seems logical, as does the fact that references to James Madison account for 60 percent of all tokens deployed in the "basic principles" chapters, thereby securing his standing as the "father of the Constitution." The language used in these fundamentalistic chapters is typically saccharine: "Even though George Washington was born more than two and a half centuries ago, he remains one of the foremost architects of the American dream."[43]

In sharp contrast are the contemporary presidents, who are almost never employed to illustrate basic principles. Instead, they become rooted in the moment. These trends are revealed in Tables 7.2 and 7.3, where we see a clear division between presidents chosen to embody the principles of the nation (its "Chief of State") and those charged with carrying out its business (its "Chief Executive"). So, for example, in 1983 *American Civics* based its comparison of the United States and the USSR on Lincoln's view of the free enter-

TABLE 7.1 Presidential Allusions in Textbooks

Presidential Allusion	Frequency (n = 3807)	Percent Tokens
Washington	331	8.7
F. Roosevelt	324	8.5
Nixon	276	7.2
Jefferson	276	7.2
Kennedy	220	5.8
Johnson	194	5.1
Carter	186	4.9
Wilson	161	4.2
Truman	159	4.2
Lincoln	154	4.0
Eisenhower	147	3.9
Madison	140	3.7
T. Roosevelt	138	3.6
Ford	114	3.0
Jackson	112	2.9
Adams	101	2.6
Reagan	80	2.1
G. H. W. Bush	78	2.0
Taft	54	1.4
Cleveland	49	1.3
A. Johnson	42	1.1
Clinton	42	1.1
Hoover	40	1.0
Monroe	39	1.0
J. Q. Adams	38	1.0
Garfield	30	.08
Coolidge, Tyler, and B. Harrison	29	.08
McKinley	27	.07
Harding	26	.07
Hayes	23	.06
Polk	19	.05
Taylor and W. Harrison	16	.04
Grant and Arthur	14	.04
Buchanan	12	.03
Van Buren	11	.03
Pierce and Fillmore	8	.02

TABLE 7.2 Presidential Roles Emphasized in Textbooks

Chief of State	Chief Executive	Head of Party
Washington	F. Roosevelt	Jackson
Jefferson	Nixon	Cleveland
Wilson	Kennedy	J. Q. Adams
Lincoln	L. Johnson	Clinton
T. Roosevelt	Carter	
Madison	Eisenhower	
Adams	Truman	
Taft	Ford	
Monroe	A. Johnson	
	Hoover	
	Reagan	
	G. H. W. Bush	

TABLE 7.3 Rhetorical Use of *President* Token in Textbooks

Philosophy	Action	Personal
Washington	F. Roosevelt	Eisenhower
Jefferson	Nixon	Hoover
Wilson	Kennedy	Cleveland
Lincoln	L. Johnson	A. Johnson
T. Roosevelt	Carter	J. Q. Adams
Madison	Truman	
	Ford	
	Adams	
	Reagan	
	G. H. W. Bush	
	Clinton	

prise system: "[P]roperty is the fruit of labor; property is desirable; it is a positive good in the world."[44] Ten years later, *West's American Government* used Lincoln to define the essential purpose of government itself:

Governments also provide such services as law enforcement, fire protection, and public health and safety programs. As Abraham Lincoln once said: "The legitimate object of government is to do for a community of people whatever they need to have done but cannot do at all, or cannot so well do for themselves in their separate and individual capacities. But in all that people can individually do for themselves, government ought not to interfere."[45]

In stark contrast are the more recent presidents, who are portrayed as politicians rather than as statesmen, persons who operate in a world of pressing disagreements and immediate consequences. The *principles* upon which they operate—and, indeed, upon which the nation itself operates— are either backgrounded or not mentioned at all. So, for example, we find *Magruder's American Government* using Lyndon Johnson to explain the byways of Washington:

> A President must be willing to bypass the Congress and take the issue to the people. By instinct and experience, I preferred to work from within, knowing that good legislation is the product not of public rhetoric but of private negotiations and compromise. But sometimes, a President has to put Congress' feet to the fire. . . . Sometimes it seemed that the only way to reach the papers and the people was to pick a fight with the Congress, to say mean words and show my temper.[46]

Of the twenty-five presidents accounting for at least 1 percent of the textbook mentions, Theodore Roosevelt and Woodrow Wilson are the only twentieth-century presidents ushered into the ranks of Chief of State; Andrew Johnson is the only non-twentieth-century president framed as a Chief Executive (unhappily, of course). The fact that contemporary presidents are shown floating free of abiding principles is especially important because they also dominate the textbooks' coverage of the executive branch. Of the twenty-five presidents referenced most frequently in the books, eleven are from the twentieth century. Only George Washington received more attention than FDR. In the 1987 textbook *American Government,* for example, a book that contains 254 tokens, Franklin Roosevelt is mentioned twenty-nine times, John F. Kennedy and Lyndon Johnson twenty apiece. The exalted Abraham Lincoln, in contrast, receives far fewer (only nine). On the other side of the coin, one textbook has Jimmy Carter performing herculean duty: showing how public policies are made, demonstrating the relationship between state and local government, and illustrating how public opinion is formed and what impact it has on government.

It is worth stopping for a moment to consider the basic model of citizenship offered in the textbooks. They frame the individual as living in a world (1) dominated by the president, a world in which (2) elites are lavishly praised because they (3) live actively in the present moment while (4) running the national corporation, thereby circumnavigating (5) questions of principle. All of this produces an odd understanding of democracy. It also produces an odd understanding of citizenly duties. Hero-worship, that is, can exalt our vision, but only when we identify with (see ourselves in) the Great Leader. And when governance is restricted to the actions of elites, there is little room for the rest of us. Even worse, there is little for us to do.

The result is a kind of civics education that tempts us with democracy but that keeps us at arms length simultaneously.

MODELS OF GOVERNANCE

Textbooks teach us how to be citizens and they also teach us about governance itself. Generally speaking, the textbooks depict an active, powerful president and a system that works (because of that action, because of that power). *Magruder's American Government* uses the words of that quintessential doer, Theodore Roosevelt, to show how this comes about:

> I declined to adopt the view that what was imperatively necessary for the Nation could not be done by the President unless he could find some specific authorization to do it. My belief was that it was not only [a President's] right but his duty to do anything that the needs of the Nation demanded unless such action was forbidden by the Congress or by the laws. . . . I did not usurp power, but I did greatly broaden the use of executive power. In other words, I acted for the public welfare, I acted for the common well-being of all our people, whenever and in whatever manner was necessary, unless prevented by direct constitutional or legislative prohibition.[47]

Magruder's also contains the familiar photograph of JFK with his back to the camera, head tilted down, to illustrate the centrality of the presidency as well as its burdens. The title accompanying the photo, "Lonely at the Top," adds to its drama.[48] Despite its burdens, however, and despite such problems as war and impeachment, the textbook presidency percolates along in a matter-of-fact, system-works manner.

The textbooks' faith in the system is perhaps most evident in their explanations of controversial events. For example, the Watergate affair, judged by most historians as an egregious use of executive power, is framed in the books as verifying the power of Congress and the steadfastness of the Supreme Court. In the 1979 edition of *American Government: Comparing Political Experiences,* Watergate is used to make a series of mechanistic points about the impeachment process. Similarly, for a chapter on "Congressional Powers" in *American Government: Principles and Practices,* a 1988 textbook, Watergate is used to justify certain powers arrogated to the Senate. In the 1993 version of *West's American Government,* Watergate receives only a single sentence and Richard Nixon's name is nowhere to be found.

We found one detailed discussion of Watergate in our collection of textbooks, one that described the break-in of the Democratic National Committee headquarters, the links between the burglars and the Committee for the Re-Election of the President, and Richard Nixon's efforts to block the actions of Congress and the Courts. The feature concluded with a reassuring prayer: "[T]he challenge to the American Dream is to ensure that the president is never above the law. The American form of democracy is one in which laws rule rather than men and women."[49] In no case, however, did the textbooks speculate about how power is abused in Washington, about the need for oversight of federal agencies, or why Watergate occurred in the first place. In textbook government, institutions always redeem themselves. Our concern, of course, is that such a lesson is likely to be lost on a sixteen-year-old unless that optimistic possibility is considered side-by-side with its darker alternatives.

Only one of the textbooks examined here was published after the impeachment proceedings of Bill Clinton. In 1999's *Magruder's American Government*, Clinton is mentioned on thirty-one pages and accorded seven photographs. The impeachment process is discussed on two pages (illustrating the importance of checks and balances and congressional oversight). The attendant commentary is clear, if antiseptic: "The House approved two articles of impeachment against President Clinton on December 19, 1998. Those charges—of perjury and of obstruction of justice—arose out of the President's 'inappropriate relationship' with former White House intern Monica Lewinsky and his later attempts to cover it up."[50] Impeachment, it would seem, carries little shame. It is a hiccup in the system, a formal, not a moral, breach. The textbooks operate as if the power of governmental actors must be vouchsafed above all else, as if students would run screaming into the night if the *principle of power* were somehow forsaken.

In a similar vein, even though the war in Vietnam tore apart the nation for most of a decade, civics textbooks treat it clinically. In 1972's *Magruder's*, for example, the author stressed the coherence of U.S. policy in Vietnam across the Eisenhower, Kennedy, Johnson, and Nixon administrations, as if the policy's additive aspects compensated for its torments. In 1972, *Magruder's* explained that the purpose of the U.S. mission in Vietnam was to resist aggression, avoid a wider conflict, and bring about a peaceful solution—all under presidential control. By 1999, Vietnam had become an "agonizing and increasingly unpopular war" but the cohesiveness of U.S. foreign policy continued to be stressed, as if the only intolerable mistake were an unplanned mistake.[51] The only chink in *Magruder's* armor was signaled by this: "[T]he war caused many to lose faith in the workings of the American political system."[52] Many indeed.

In short, civics textbooks love power more than anything else. They love the planned use of power most of all. This is not to say the textbooks are witless. But it is to say the *president* hovers so high as to be completely out of sight. It is as if a mortal, vulnerable, president would call undue attention to democracy's problems, as if youth cannot bear the thought of presidents stumbling through life like the rest of us. An even greater fear is that the nation cannot bear the scrutiny of its people. Despite these concerns, the chapter on the presidency in the 1999 *Magruder's* begins with a half-page photograph of Bill Clinton reviewing a British honor guard with the caption, "Symbol of the Nation."[53]

The commitment that civics textbooks have to presidency-centered government often overflows its banks. Whereas discussions of individual presidents make sense in a chapter on the Executive Branch, the *president* does additional work as well. Textbook units focusing on the presidency contain slightly less than 40 percent of all tokens, with the remaining 60 percent exemplifying a wide range of additional topics, especially those related to basic governmental processes. For instance, the 1971 textbook *Civics in Action* contends that:

> Our greatest statesmen have recognized the need for apprentice training in citizenship. Schools are the most important source of such apprenticeship. George Washington urged attention to education. Many of the most famous quotations from Thomas Jefferson dwell upon its importance. James Madison wrote on the same theme: "A popular Government, without popular information, or the means of acquiring it, is but a Prologue to a Farce or a tragedy . . . Knowledge will forever govern ignorance; And a people who mean to be their own Governors must arm themselves with the power which knowledge gives."[54]

Similarly, in the 1964 *Magruder's*, presidential quotations are used to introduce eleven of its forty-three chapters, with presidents setting the scene for discussions of civil rights; suffrage; electioneering; Congress; the departments of State, Agriculture, Commerce and Labor, Health, Education, and Welfare; as well as independent financial agencies and social legislation.

In textbook government, even anti-establishment principles are legitimated by the chief executive. In textbooks adopted throughout the nation after the turbulent protests of the 1960s, for example, Abraham Lincoln was used to illustrate the importance of dissent in American life. In a chapter entitled "Political Alienation and Loyalty," the authors of *American Political Behavior* observed that "Political dissent is a long and honorable American tradition. . . . Throughout our history there have been many great dissenters, including Abraham Lincoln. As a U.S. Congressman he spoke out against American foreign policy during the Mexican War in the belief that President Polk's reasons for fighting the Mexicans were wrong."[55] In life, things happen and presidents act. In textbooks, presidents act and things happen.

It is, of course, important to remember that high school textbooks are written for impressionable young people at a critical juncture in their lives. What great harm is done, some might ask, if the president is overemphasized or if political life appears less chaotic than it really is? Are teachers and textbooks required to tell everything they know about governance at one and the same moment? Is it not prudent, even charitable, to encourage young people to be more idealistic, perhaps even naive, when contemplating the use of power? Shouldn't young people stay young as long as possible?

Our argument is that textbooks go beyond the pale in dramatizing the power of the president and the logic of the political system. Yes, presidents often act bravely and wisely and, yes, democratic systems are probably the supplest of all. Both have stood the nation in good stead for over two hundred years. But it is also true that the models of governance presented in the nation's schoolbooks leave little room for the average person to carry out the duties of citizenship. The portraits painted in the books are rather like those hanging in Vienna's Alte Museum, where one finds paintings from the Middle Ages—pictures of biblical figures, heavenly hosts, ecclesiastical leaders, and emperors great and grand. Across the street lies the Neue Museum, featuring art from the seventeenth century and beyond. There we find still-lifes of bread and cheese, family pets, laborers in their fields, lovers caressing. To cross the street from the Alte to the Neue is to experience the democratization of art. The effect on the visitor is palpable. The images in the Neue draw you in; they seem manageable; they encourage interaction. Civics textbooks should do the same thing.

CONCLUSION

We have focused here on executive tokens, language devices that pass quickly before the eye, presumably without consequence. But keywords have cumulative effects, slowly and insistently telling young people that the public sphere is really a private sphere, that politics is for persons far grander than they. Our argument here is that civics textbooks are not terrible, but they are surely incomplete. Sadly, numerous studies tell us that the political knowledge learned in high school does not survive into adulthood.[56] But as Frances FitzGerald argues, it is not so much the information contained in social studies textbooks that is lacking but the attitudes left behind: "[W]hat sticks to the memory from those textbooks is not any particular series of facts but an atmosphere, an impression, a tone. And this impression may be all the more influential just because one cannot remember the facts and arguments that created it."[57]

Political scientists Matthew Crenson and Benjamin Ginsberg argue that civics education no longer teaches young people "a common set of political ideals and beliefs and to habituate them to the rules of conduct that govern public life in a democracy."[58] Instead, they argue, it creates customers rather than citizens, teaching students a kind of "personal democracy" characterized by volunteerism and service-learning rather than collective, contentious political engagement.[59] It also teaches them a politics of standing-back, of voyeurism. It is no doubt good for young people to respect the *president* and his prerogatives, but when the president takes up all the political oxygen we are endangered.

Citizenship education in the United States is a complicated business. In earlier times a "usable past" based on a storied presidency created a sense of national unity in a country still developing its basic principles and institutions. We need a usable past today as well. But given the vaunted declines in civic participation recently, we need a past that speaks to young people living in a conflict-ridden, overcommunicated society. The *president* is a great and good thing except when he becomes a Sun King. We need more than a

Sun King. We need poll-workers and block-walkers and city council members as well.

We need, that is, a pedestrian politics. We need young people opened up to the messiness and contradictions of democratic life, to its bargains and conflict and compromises, especially its compromises. We need a pedestrian politics that lets students connect the stories they read in textbooks to the lives they live. Textbook authors must learn to break through the clutter vying for students' attention. They need to challenge students, not mollify them, and ensure that their readers do not develop, in Robin Toner's terms, "a happy amnesia about the hardest parts" of their democracy.[60]

Pedestrian politics demands more than stories of presidents. It demands stories of everyday people as well. Textbooks also need a new voice, one that candidly describes the political brambles into which a democracy can fall. We do not need more state and federal standards for testing civic knowledge as much as we need schools to meet the standards of honesty young people demand. Above all, a pedestrian politics cannot be a politics of "looking up." It must be a politics of looking across—at family members and neighbors—and enlisting them in the great experience of democracy. A pedestrian politics is a politics for a busy people. We need a pedagogy for our times.

NOTES

1. A. de Tocqueville, *Democracy in America,* ed. J. P. Mayer, trans. G. Lawrence (New York: Harper Perennial, 1988), 236.

2. For a series of classic treatments of national identity, see H. S. Commager, *The Search for a Usable Past, and Other Essays in Historiography* (New York: Knopf, 1967) and *The American Mind* (New Haven, CT: Yale University Press, 1950); D. Nimmo and J. Combs, *Mediated Political Realities* (New York: Longman, 1983); and E. Shils, *Tradition* (Chicago: University of Chicago Press, 1981).

3. Tocqueville, *Democracy in America,* 201.

4. Commager, *The Search for a Usable Past,* 3.

5. D. Elazar, *The American Mosaic: The Impact of Space, Time, and Culture on American Politics* (Boulder, CO: Westview Press, 1994), 199.

6. For additional discussion of both the need for common bonds and how they were created, see Commager, *The Search for a Usable Past;* R. E. Elazar, *American Political Cultures* (New York: Oxford University Press, 1993); M. Kammer, *People of Paradox: An Inquiry Concerning the Origin of American Civilization* (New York: Oxford University Press, 1972); and R. L. Merritt, *Symbols of American Community, 1773–1775* (New Haven, CT: Yale University Press, 1966).

7. Some of the best reflections on the challenges to American community are contained in E. J. Dionne, *Community Works: The Revival of Civil Society in America* (Washington, DC: The Brookings Institution, 1998); S. Macedo, *Diversity and Distrust: Civic Education in a Multicultural Democracy* (Cambridge, MA: Harvard University Press, 2000); J. S. Nye, P. D. Zeilikow, and D. C. King (eds.), *Why People Don't Trust Government* (Cambridge, MA: Harvard University Press, 1997); and R. D. Putnam,

Bowling Alone: The Collapse and Revival of American Community (New York: Simon and Schuster, 2000).

8. E. H. Wilds and K. V. Lottich, *The Foundation of Modern Education*, 3d ed. (New York: Holt, Rinehart, and Winston, 1964), 261.

9. D. Ravitch and J. P. Viteritti (eds.), *Making Good Citizens: Education and Civil Society* (New Haven, CT: Yale University Press, 2001), 5.

10. Other commentaries on the unique U.S. need to indoctrinate its young are offered by J. I. Goodlan and T. J. McMannon (eds.), *The Public Purpose of Education and Schooling* (San Francisco: Jossey-Bass Publishers, 1997); and S. A. Rippa, *Education in a Free Society: An American History*, 6th ed. (New York: Longman, 1988).

11. T. J. Cook and F. P. Scioli, Jr., "Political Socialization Research in the United States," in *Political Attitudes and Public Opinion*, ed. D. Nimmo and C. M. Borgean (New York: David McKay Company, 1972), 156.

12. Wilds and Lottich, *The Foundation of Modern Education*, 273.

13. For examples of the kinds of civics assessments now being performed, see California Department of Education, "Grade Twelve," in *History-Social Science Content Standards for California Public Schools—Kindergarten Through Grade Twelve*, (Sacramento: California Department of Education, 2000), 54–58; R. G. Niemi and C. Chapman, *The Civic Development of 9th- Through 12th-Grade Students in the United States: 1996* (Washington, DC: U.S. Department of Education, Office of Educational Research and Improvement, November 1998); Council of Chief State School officers, *Civics Framework for the 1998 National Assessment of Educational Progress: The NAEP 1998 Civics Report Card for the Nation* (Washington, DC: U.S. Department of Education, Office of Educational Research and Improvement, National Center for Educational Statistics, 1999).

14. Council of Chief State School Officers, *Civics Framework*, ix.

15. Ravitch and Viteritti, *Making Good Citizens*, 4.

16. J. Torney-Purta, "Comparative Perspectives on Political Socialization and Civic Education," *Comparative Education Review*, 44 (2000): 89.

17. Story accessed on the website of the National Endowment of the Humanities, http://www.neh.fed.us/news/archive/20030501.html (June 3, 2003).

18. M. M. Conway, *Political Participation in the United States*, 3d ed. (Washington, DC: CQ Press, 2000).

19. J. McMillan and K. J. Harriger, "College Students and Deliberation," *Communication Education*, 51 (2002): 237.

20. M. B. Marklein, "Students Electing to Participate," *USA Today*, November 5, 2002, D1.

21. D. A. Graber, *Processing Politics: Learning from Television in the Internet Age* (Chicago: University of Chicago Press, 2001), 43. Graber is summarizing the position of other social scientists when arguing that the average citizen is "moderately well-informed" (45). Scholars supporting the position of the ill-informed citizen are M. Delli Carpini and S. Keeter, *What Americans Know About Politics and Why It Matters* (New Haven, CT: Yale University Press, 1996).

22. Putnam, *Bowling Alone*.

23. Ibid.

24. See Niemi and Chapman, *Civic Development; Civics Framework for the 1998 National Assessment of Educational Progress; History-Social Science Content Standards for California Public Schools*.

25. See http://www.closeup.org/aboutcuf.htm (June 5, 2003).

26. J. Torney-Purta, J. Schwille, and J. Amadeo, *Civic Education Across Countries: Twenty-four National Case Studies from the IEA Civic Education Project* (Amsterdam, The Netherlands: International Association for the Evaluation of Educational Achievement, 1999).

27. J. J. Patrick, *ERIC Digest: High School Government Textbooks* (Bloomington, IN: ERIC Clearinghouse for Social Studies/Social Science Education, 1988); C. Harrington, "Textbooks and Political Socialization," *Teaching Political Science*, 7 (1988): 481–500, M. Janowitz, *The Reconstruction of Patriotism: Education for Civic Consciousness* (Chicago: University of Chicago Press, 1983).

28. H. B. Barger, "Suspending Disbelief: The President in Pre-College Textbooks," *Presidential Studies Quarterly*, 20 (1990): 55–70, and "Demythologizing the Textbook President: Teaching About the President After Watergate," *Theory and Research in Social Education*, 4 (1976): 51–66; T. E. Cronin, *The State of the Presidency*, 2d ed. (Boston: Little Brown and Company, 1980).

29. Patrick, *ERIC Digest*, 2.

30. D. Easton and R. Hess, "The Child's Political World," *Midwest Journal of Political Science*, 6 (1962): 229–46.

31. Some of the methods used and data reported here were originally presented in D. Smith-Howell, "Using the Past in the Present: The Rhetorical Construction of the American Presidency," unpublished Ph.D. dissertation, University of Texas at Austin, 1993.

32. See W. Johnson, *People in Quandaries: The Semantics of Personal Adjustment* (New York: Harper, 1946).

33. The use of executive tokens is not so dramatic in eighth-grade textbooks. The eighth-grade textbooks examined do not include books adopted for use after 1993.

34. *West's American Government* (St. Paul: West Publishing Co., 1993), 96.

35. W. A. McClenaghan, *Magruder's American Government* (Needham, MA: Prentice-Hall, 1999), vi.

36. W. A. McClenaghan, *Magruder's American Government* (Boston: Allyn and Bacon, Inc., 1972), 282.

37. *West's American Government* (1993), 360.

38. W. H. Hartley and W. S. Vincent, *American Civics*, 4th ed. (New York: Harcourt Brace Javanovic Publishers, 1983), 85.

39. R. G. Niemi and J. Junn, *Civic Education: What Makes Students Learn* (New Haven, CT: Yale University Press, 1998), 92.

40. Ibid., 95–96.

41. R. P. Hart, *Seducing America: How Television Charms the Modern Voter*, rev. ed. (Thousand Oaks, CA: Sage Publications, 1999), 82.

42. Cronin, *The State of the Presidency*, 84.

43. *West's American Government* (1993), 42.

44. Harley and Vincent, *American Civics*, 24.

45. *West's American Government* (1993), 6.

46. McClenaghan, *Magruder's American Government* (1999), 358.

47. Ibid., 355. Bracket and second ellipsis in original.

48. Ibid., 360.

49. *West's American Government* (1993), 397.

50. *Magruder's American Government* (1999), i.

51. *Magruder's American Government* (1972), 344.

52. *Magruder's American Government* (1999), 445.

53. Ibid., p. 315.

54. R. E. Gross and V. Devereauz, *Civics in Action* (Palo Alto, CA: Field Educational Publishing, Inc., 1971), 23.

55. H. D. Mehlingher and P. J. John, *American Political Behavior* (Lexington, MA: Ginn and Company, 1972), 154.

56. Graber *Processing Politics*, 46–47.

57. F. FitzGerald, *America Revised: History Schoolbooks in the Twentieth Century* (New York: Vintage Books, 1980), 18.

58. M. A. Crenson and B. Ginsberg, *Downsizing Democracy: How America Sidelined Its Citizens and Privatized Its Public* (Baltimore: Johns Hopkins University Press, 2002), 6.

59. Ibid.

60. R. Toner, "Ugly Echoes: A Sanitized Past Comes Back to Haunt Trent Lott," *New York Times*, December 15, 2002, Section 4, 1.

8

The *President*
How Institutions Preserve
Themselves

S eymour Martin Lipset, the only person to have served as president of both the American Sociological Association and the American Political Science Association, is an especially keen observer of political life. In his sociological classic, *Political Man*, Lipset examines the conditions needed for democracy to flourish, ultimately arguing that the system's legitimacy is its key factor. Says Lipset:

> Legitimacy involves the capacity of the system to engender and maintain the belief that the existing political institutions are the most appropriate ones for the society. The extent to which contemporary democratic political systems are legitimate depends in large measure upon the ways in which the key issues which have historically divided society have been resolved.[1]

But what are these "key issues"? What does it take for a government to last? Why do some countries have six different leaders in five years? For Lipset, all states are inherently fragile, constantly being challenged by those inside and outside, by factors both technological and social. Political scientist Jonathan Lemco adds to these observations, noting that "twenty-seven of the forty-four federations formed in the past two hundred or so years across the globe have failed either by breaking apart or by becoming fully centralized unitary states."[2] In recent years, the world has witnessed chaos in countries where governmental structures failed to function or functioned counterproductively—Kosovo, Albania, Chechnya, Northern Ireland, the Palestinian Authority. Despite its several challenges, however, the United States has been a model of political stability. Why?

In the past fifty years, the United States has faced numerous challenges. The disputed presidential election of 2000, the impeachment of Bill Clinton, the terrorist attacks of September 11, the Watergate affair and subsequent resignation of President Richard Nixon, the Vietnam War and its attendant domestic disturbances, the civil rights movement of the 1950s and 1960s, and the assassinations of John F. Kennedy, Martin Luther King, Jr., and Robert Kennedy (and the near-assassinations of Gerald Ford and Ronald Reagan) were all enormously consequential events, any one of which could have compromised the political system. Reading any newspaper during the past fifty years would reveal still other tensions—between Republicans and Democrats; between state and local government; among advocates for women's, labor, and gun rights organizations. Miraculously, the United States managed to fight world wars and deal with constant domestic turmoil without splitting apart. This is a historical curiosity, but it is more than that— it is a fact that allows 285 million Americans to go about their daily lives with hope in their hearts.

This chapter looks at one, humble adjunct to the creation of political legitimacy. It begins by assuming that no single factor—a strong economy, plenty of available land, or technological know-how—is alone capable of sustaining a nation. It assumes, instead, that stability requires many things, some of which are found within the nation's citizens and institutions. It assumes, further, that quite subtle forces—how people talk to one another, for example— can slowly build the understandings needed to keep political bonds intact. And it assumes, finally, that the nation's mass media are implicated in this process, that they can promote societal values even when critiquing them or when dispassionately analyzing political institutions and actors. We can observe all of this when the media discuss the nation's *president.*

THE AMERICAN CASE

Nothing about the United States is simple. While there is general acknowledgment that the nation has been remarkably stable despite its continual stresses and strains, scholars are not sure why this is so. Political scientist Courtney Brown, for example, notes that the United States has managed to achieve "regime stability" even when beset by political change. He observes that "the American electorate often experiences electoral changes that would be considered unstable or volatile in other national settings. The strength of the democratic institutions and the failure of the American government to collapse are facts that should not cloud one's ability to recognize and to characterize the scope and magnitude of the mass electoral changes that do occur."[3] If we take Brown at his word, it appears that (1) the United States is constantly changing but that (2) those changes are masked by certain systemic regularities. The United States is, in that sense, oxymoronic, a nation that prides itself on inventing new things—new computers, new movies, new epicurean delights—even as it repeats old patterns. How can all this be true?

Political institutions help: a Constitution, a functioning legislature, well-established political parties, careful regulation of money and banking, a stable currency, predictable cycles of leadership, the peaceful exchange of governing authority.[4] As we saw in chapter 7, having citizens undergo similar cultural indoctrinations also helps build a sense of identity. Collective identity is important because people seem instinctually threatened by the odd and the foreign—at least at first. They also fear precipitousness. While Central American, Eastern European, and African nations alike have been brought to their knees by sudden, violent changes in leadership, Americans somehow adjusted when a Southern populist succeeded an East Coast brahmin on one awful morning in November 1963 (LBJ and JFK), when a genial centrist succeeded a controversial internationalist in 1974 (Ford and Nixon), or when the loser of the popular vote moved into the Oval Office at the turn of the century (G. W. Bush). Making these transitions successfully, says one scholar, is "an unambiguous indicator of high political legitimacy" for a nation.[5]

The United States has also managed to ward off the religious turmoil that has savaged so many other countries. It has done so by effecting a kind of truce between Church and State, giving the former honorific duties and the latter temporal control. As one author notes, a "rhetoric of civic piety" has evolved in the United States to enforce this contract, thereby giving both Church and State the freedom (and dignity) needed to maintain cordial relations.[6] The power of that contract—and the stability it purchases—is remarkable given the myriad of issues it superintends—abortion, most notably, but also Christian–Muslim tensions, the taxation of Church property, public aid to private schools, support of Israel, and so forth.

Historically, America's civic associations (the VFW, the PTA, the League of Women Voters, Junior Achievement) have also helped maintain political traditions and given people needed points of contact. Equally important are the nation's mass media, although they play a more ambiguous role. Early in the twentieth century, for example, John Dewey and Walter Lippman famously debated the press's potential for keeping people informed (Dewey was more optimistic than Lippman). Since that time, the politics of the mass media has been analyzed by hundreds of scholars, one of whom is Patrick O'Neil. He argues:

> There is a common assumption that a strong connection exists between mass communication and democracy. Simply put, the assumption is that for democracies to function, civil society requires access to information as a means to make informed political choices. Similarly, politicians require the media as a way in which they can take stock of the public mood, present their views, and interact with society. The media are thus viewed as a vital conduit of relations between state and society.[7]

While the mass media have always flourished best in democratic societies, their relations with a democratic State are never unproblematic, as we saw in chapter 5. For some, the mass media are a truly malevolent force.[8]

Other observers judge them less harshly but see them as destabilizing. As James Fallows contends in *Breaking the News*, media antipathies toward the political process often seem responsible for Americans' frustrations with politics.[9] Because readers emulate writers, these critics contend, political cynicism is compounded. When that happens, the media are charged with undermining the tenets of both democracy and journalism.[10] The very titles of recent books point up these tendencies: *Democracy Without Citizens, Peep Show, The Governing Crisis,* and *Spiral of Cynicism.*[11]

One of the most vigorous contemporary discussions focuses on the media's alleged "liberal bias."[12] Pundits such as Ann Coulter have drawn a crowd with *Slander: Liberal Lies About the American Right,* as has Bernard Goldberg with his bestseller *Bias: A CBS Insider Exposes How the Media Distort the News.*[13] In addition, political activist Brent Bozell and researcher Robert Lichter have opened up the Media Research Center in Washington, DC, an operation that patiently tracks the media's daily outpourings in an (inevitably successful) attempt to find a liberal slant to the news. As a result, the Lefty Journalist and Maligned Rightist have become protagonists in a continuing American morality play, which, as we saw in chapter 5, is one of the media's best stories about itself.

More dispassionate research has failed to find clear indications of bias,[14] although some scholars (e.g., Kuypers' *Press Bias and Politics*) have argued that the mainstream press can be almost anti-democratic.[15] More often, though, scholars agree that the media have a "narrative bias." requiring reporters to give storylike qualities to the often uninterpretable facts of everyday life. As a result, characters like Conflict, Grandeur, Chance, Surprise, and Destiny trod the stage, with the day's events fitted into a preestablished script. All this makes the news constantly interesting, fueled by a "melodramatic imperative" toward politics.[16]

Other scholars tell a far different story about the press, arguing that the news is fundamentally conservative because its personnel are socialized by corporations which are themselves disciplined by market forces.[17] Scholar/activists like Noam Chomsky in *Manufacturing Consent* and *Media Control: The Spectacular Achievements of Propaganda* make the case acidly, contending that oligarchical forces impinge on the newsgathering business, often without the reporter knowing it.[18] As a result, giant corporations are let off the hook for their misdeeds, and business leaders (e.g., Ted Turner, Jack Welch, Bill Gates, etc.) are turned into role models, if not demigods. Marxists like Stuart Hall push the matter further, arguing that late capitalism has turned reporters into cheerleaders, making them incapable of discovering the news that really needs reporting.[19]

We focus on less lofty matters here, although we want to shed some light on this liberal/conservative debate. To get a better understanding of the stabilizing role played by the mass media, we examine how they treat one of the most powerful keywords of all, the *president.* Admittedly, by focusing on the most exalted character in the American pantheon, we could be charged with stacking the deck in favor of the Chomsky/Hall side of the argument. But our purposes are more descriptive than polemical: We want to see if the mass media are part of the nation's governing apparatus and, if so, how they perform those duties.

Our answer is that the media both stabilize and legitimate the polity. These are separate functions. Saddam Hussein, for example, ran a highly stable government that was seen as illegitimate by most (non-Baathist) Iraqis.

In contrast, a government can be comparatively unstable (for example, Italy's at almost any point in the latter half of the twentieth century) without losing fundamental legitimacy. The long-term importance of legitimacy over stability cannot be gainsaid. It is not surprising, for example, that the mass media have flourished (often in eye-popping ways) in modern Italy even as they were brutally suppressed in Saddam's Iraq.

And what of the American case? To answer that question, we tracked the *president* token (i.e., all named persons who held the office prior to the current chief executive) in the pages of *Time* magazine from January 1945 through December 2000. *Time* was chosen because it is an undeniably popular newsmagazine, because it has been published continuously (in roughly the same format) for over eighty years, because it reaches a national audience, and because it has been the focus of considerable prior research.[20] *Time*'s reporters also write in an accessible style, making idiomatic contact with the American people on a weekly basis. As a result, *Time*—the coffee-table magazine—has an unusual ability to affect what ordinary Americans think about their political system.

To make our investigation manageable, we analyzed one article per month for each of the fifty-six years studied, resulting in a cache of 672 news stories. Each presidential token in the articles was examined in ways similar to those described in chapter 7, including the type of article in which the token appeared (e.g., column, cover story, or general report), the political associations ascribed to the chief executive (i.e., personal, philosophical, or policy-based resemblance to a predecessor), the topic of the article (e.g., domestic, international, or mixed), the political role focused upon (e.g., chief of State, chief executive, or head of party), and the token's judicial function (i.e., endorsement, criticism, illustration, or neutral).

ACHIEVING LEGITIMACY

Of the 672 articles studied here, 275 (40.9 percent) contained allusions to past presidents. In other words, two out of every five *Time* articles preserve a "tissue of historicity" by constantly contrasting the sitting chief executive to those who served in the position earlier. This emphasis on the past is a curious fact for a *news* magazine. It must also be unsettling for the sitting president, who is measured each day by his predecessors' yardstick. It made comparatively little difference whether the story was a general report, a cover story, a political commentary, or a personality profile. *Time* forces the chief executive to keep his peers close to his chest.

Over the time period studied, personality profiles were dominant (34.1 percent), but in the last twelve years (the Bush and Clinton presidencies), general reports and cover stories containing historical allusions increased, perhaps reflecting a stylistic change for *Time*. Regardless of the format, however, the past abides in the present, a sharp contrast to the presentism found in the school textbooks analyzed earlier.

Occasionally, the presidential allusions become almost comically thick. For example, in an otherwise pedestrian article analyzing the federal budget in light of the 2000 presidential campaign, *Time* set out on an invigorating historical journey:

> Ever since Adams and Jefferson, there has been a tradition of father-son rivalry in the White House. Eisenhower helpfully told reporters he couldn't think of a single idea Nixon contributed during their eight-year tenure together. Hubert Humphrey died politically in Lyndon Johnson's war. When George Bush promised a "kinder, gentler nation" in 1988, he meant kinder and gentler than Ronald Reagan's.[21]

What is one to take away from this excursion? The story is nominally about potential tensions between a lame-duck president (Bill Clinton) and a vice president (Al Gore) trying to make his way on the campaign trail. But *Time* tells a story that places current White House tensions in a grander perspective, thereby telling an institutional as well as a personal tale.

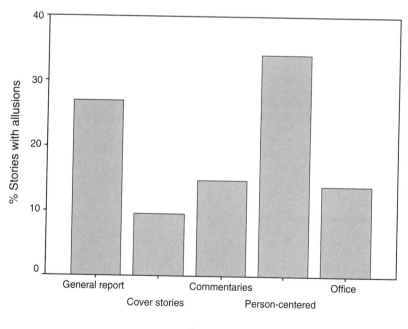

Figure 8.1 Presidential Allusions in *Time* Magazine by Story Type.

The range of presidential tokens used by *Time* is also considerable, with thirty-six of the past forty presidents mentioned at least once in the 275 articles. Naturally, founders like Washington, Adams, and Jefferson were mentioned frequently, but *Time* also emphasized contemporary icons like John F. Kennedy (17.2 percent of all tokens) and Franklin D. Roosevelt (11.3 percent). Ronald Reagan has also moved into those ranks in recent years. With only twelve years of articles (1988–2000) and two successors (G. H. W. Bush and Clinton) in his wake, Reagan nevertheless managed to account for 8.5 percent of all presidential allusions in our database.

Any good reporter, of course, understands that current events must be put "in perspective" for the reader. Toggling back and forth between the past and the present performs that function, but it does two other things as well: (1) It creates a certain seamlessness for the polity, and (2) it discovers an underlying rationality to all events, even unexpected ones. Even better, it makes unexpected events seem expected, thereby giving the reader a sense that all is well with the world. The result is a constant foreshadowing, an approach that lets the reporter philosophize a bit even when issuing a rather ordinary report about the 1992 primary campaign:

> The New Hampshire results suggested an emerging seriousness and impatience in American voters, a sense that they are groping into difficult political and moral territory, often well in advance of both the politicians and media. The usual American political apparatus seemed to be malfunctioning, defective—incapable of bringing along plausible leaders, Presidents, as it once did. The party of Franklin Roosevelt, Harry Truman, and John Kennedy was fielding another B-team. So it seemed to many voters, who also thought that the Republicans had a President—and Vice-President— of unusual weightlessness.[22]

Using the past in these ways casts an institutional patina over *Time*'s coverage, and that sometimes plays to the advantage of a new president. From inauguration day forward, the chief executive becomes ensconced in the lives of his predecessors—for good and ill. Because he is being judged by their standard, that can seem a diminution. At the same time, however, being judged by a *presidential* standard gives the new chief executive a weightiness the ordinary politician does not have. We see such elevation-by-assessment in *Time*'s treatment of George H. W. Bush's inaugural address:

> If George Bush signaled anything by proclaiming a "new breeze" it was a new altruism, a move away from the Reagan era's tacit approval of selfishness, an end to the glorification of greed. . . . John Kennedy's "ask not" formulation was better put, and Eisenhower's too: "A people that values its privileges above its principles soon loses both." But Bush's simplicity was profound, and more in keeping with his underlying message.[23]

By describing the presidency in "collectivist" terms like these, *Time* emphasizes the transience of the officeholder even as it highlights the office's indomitability, thereby performing an almost anthropological function. As we observed in chapter 4, rituals spring up to cope with liminal moments—moments of transition, marginal moments. A presidential inaugural is one such moment, a time when the past—the known—becomes oddly juxtaposed to the unknown—the future. Baptisms, bar mitzvahs, weddings, retirement dinners, and funerals all share these qualities of liminality. They tempt us with growth even while making us stare into the abyss. Such moments require a grand rhetoric. Hugh Sidey of *Time* magazine obliges:

> We are in America so young in years; yet we suddenly seem old from responsibility. Just 20 years ago, poet Robert Frost came to town to recite at John Kennedy's Inauguration: "Such as we were we gave ourselves outright/ . . . To the land vaguely realizing westward,/But still unstoried, artless, unenhanced." Kennedy answered: "The torch has been passed to a new generation of Americans." Ike huddled in his coat, white scarf up around his neck on that day. When the Inaugural was over, the defeated Richard Nixon slipped down the Senate steps of the Capitol front and disappeared into the dark back seat of a limousine, little realizing that he would return in eight years as President. And as Reagan prepared for his Inaugural, Nixon watched from New York, still a power in American Government, his presence felt through people and policies that took root in his time in the White House. The past holds us.[24]

A rhetoric this rich performs an incorporating function, but it also creates great expectations for the new president. As a result, allusions to past presidents are found more frequently in the early days of a presidency rather than later on. For example, almost 40 percent of *Time*'s tokens during the George H. W. Bush presidency occurred in a single year—1989. Similarly, 41 percent of the tokens found during the Clinton presidency appeared in 1993. This sort of "frontloading" has always been true of *Time*'s coverage, but it has become more dramatic in recent years, perhaps suggesting an increasing political (or social or psychological) anxiety on the part of the American people. Is the world moving too fast for us? Has the postmodern condition finally settled in?

There is a simpler explanation—American politics has become more contentious in recent years, and that makes voters nervous, especially during presidential transitions. In addition, as we will see in chapter 10, voters' partisan identities have become unstable, with third-party candidacies growing apace and with the number of political Independents now rivaling those of Democrats and Republicans. It would be foolish to conclude from these facts that the American mass media—patriots that they are—deploy an institutionalizing rhetoric to paper over the nation's political cracks. Nevertheless, there is little doubt that *Time* works hard to provide historical context for unexpected or problematic events, as we saw during the Clinton transition:

> As bad as the current climate is between the White House and the military, Clinton's problems are not unique. "Almost every President has had trouble with the military and the Chiefs," says presidential historian Michael

Beschloss. John Kennedy's war-hero status could not protect him from criticism when he refused to provide air cover for the Bay of Pigs landing. Lyndon Johnson's Joint Chiefs threatened a mass resignation over his policy of graduated escalation in Vietnam. And Dwight Eisenhower's five stars provided no cover when he tried to cut the Air Force budget.[25]

Here is a curious feature of *Time*'s news stories: Even when addressing the chief executive's *personal* qualities, the magazine treats them institutionally. Allusions to past presidents occur more often in *Time*'s personal profiles than in its cover stories, news commentaries, or general reporting. Surely that is strange. It makes sense to compare presidents' ideas about international relations or to contrast how one chief executive deals with the labor unions versus another. Far odder is to compare their personality quirks, but that is exactly what happens 43.5 percent of the time (as we see in Figure 8.2), a number that dwarfs tokens focusing on political philosophy (30.8 percent) or executive actions (15 percent).

Is *Time* trying to turn political science into political psychology? Rhetorically, at least, such an approach makes narrative sense. Narratives, after all,

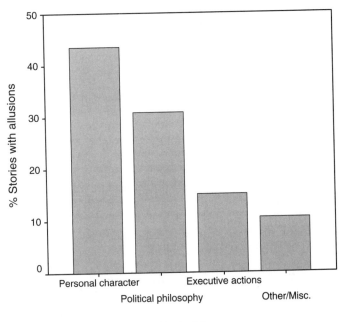

Figure 8.2 Focus of Presidential Stories in *Time* Magazine.

move best when describing an individual's personal foibles or their inner longings. Goaded by scholars such as James David Barber (author of *The Presidential Character*),[26] the media may have come to believe that an ideal personality exists and that it best predicts success in the Oval Office. This is a reasonable, although untested (probably untestable), assumption. Tested or not, *Time* focused on the "inner president" in March 1965:

> Addressing himself thus, Johnson was never more powerful. Other Presidents have lamented the plight of the Negro but have skirted the hard words necessary to describe the depth of the Negro's deprivation. But Johnson believes with Teddy Roosevelt that the Presidency is a "bully pulpit," and with Truman, who once said, "It is only the President who is responsible to all the people." And so, on the night before and straight up to the time he arrived at the Capitol, he dwelt deeply on his subject, philosophizing, penciling, revising, emphasizing. Now he was ready.[27]

The fact that the preceding scene focuses on one of the most fundamental legislative initiatives of the nation's history seems less important to *Time* than did LBJ's emotional readiness for the challenge. The fact that *Time* had no real data about such matters seems a mere quibble in the presence of such moving cadences.

Strengths are one thing, weaknesses another, but weaknesses are also part of *Time*'s institutional story. In July 1978, for example, the magazine tied Jimmy Carter's leadership problems to a variety of personal flaws inevitably magnified by life in the White House. Said *Time:*

> It is not unusual for a President to falter as he approaches mid-term, and this has to be especially true in an era of unprecedented media exposure. The once fresh face and crisp new manner have become familiar as the local grocer's. What may have been entertaining idiosyncrasies, like Truman's salty language, Eisenhower's chronic golfing and Carter's reflexive grin, can become slightly irritating. No longer larger than life, as on the triumphant eve of Inauguration, the mid-term President starts looking all too vulnerably human.[28]

At the hands of *Time*, then, the president is constantly tied to the past. This is not to say that *Time*'s readers awake each morning to yet another Groundhog Day, but it is to say that each day eerily resembles the one that preceded it. In the pages of *Time*, presidents come and presidents go but, even as they go, they return—this time to help interpret the actions of their successors. This gives *Time*'s coverage a rather ghostly quality. But theirs is a comforting wraith, one that uses the *president* to keep things in place, to give the office perpetual legitimacy. *Time* leads no revolutions and, in that sense, it continues in the tradition of its founder—Henry R. Luce. But this is not *Time*'s story alone. The American mass media respect institutions because they themselves are a Fourth Estate. This results in legitimacy for everyone.

ACHIEVING EFFECTIVENESS

According to Seymour Lipset, it takes more than legitimacy to render a polity stable. It also takes effectiveness. The trains must run on time, the armies must fight well, the politicians must balance the budget (eventually). Societies that are "high on the scales of legitimacy and effectiveness," says Lipset, maintain their political traditions as well as their principles of governance.[29]

The mass media can help adjudicate this question of effectiveness. By constantly setting expectations for the chief executive, expectations based on the actions of his predecessors, *Time* and the other news organs hold the president's feet to the fire. Sometimes these disciplinary practices are subtle. For example, *Time* often sets the stage for an upcoming event by reminding readers what occurred under similar circumstances in times past, thereby ensuring that the current chief executive does not overstep his bounds. We see all of this when *Time* reported on John Kennedy's forthcoming meeting with Nikita Khrushchev in May 1961:

> In the past, U.S. Presidents, ranging from Franklin Roosevelt through Harry Truman to Dwight Eisenhower, have never fared too well in face-to-face meetings with Soviet dictators—even when the U.S. was dealing from strength. There was no doubt that Jack Kennedy, his New Frontier foreign policies currently in a state of some disarray, was taking a chance.[30]

Time's implicit warning here is that Kennedy is in some danger of overplaying his hand since he does not have the negotiating power held by previous presidents. *Time* therefore uses reactionary criteria to judge a potentially radical moment, an approach that encourages President Kennedy to trim his sails.

This sort of forecasting gives *Time*'s coverage an almost oracular quality. In addition, it helps establish policy boundaries by "herding" the chief executive constantly, keeping him from veering too far right or too far left. For example, in one article *Time* lionized the centrist instincts of George H. W. Bush by reminding readers of the less palatable (if more visionary) alternatives to his approach:

> Yet this was no nuclear abolitionist, no Jimmy Carter daring to dream about the "elimination of all nuclear weapons from this earth." Nor was it Ronald Reagan, putting his faith in a pure defense that would render nuclear weapons "impotent and obsolete." Instead, it was classic George Bush, a traditionalist and pragmatist, striving for boldness without undermining a quality he values even more: prudence.[31]

On other occasions, *Time* uses a sharper dialectic to establish acceptable boundaries. This is a classic journalistic move in which "both sides" are given an equal opportunity to speak, after which some midpoint is endorsed. The trick, of course, is to judiciously select those representing the different sides of the argument. That lets the journalist, not the disputants, dictate the terms of the discussion. We see all this in operation when Bill Clinton gave his maiden speech to the U.S. Congress in 1993. "If a presence haunted the halls of Congress last Wednesday night," *Time*'s coverage began, "it was not Kennedy or Roosevelt or any of the other 20th century Democrats who beckoned the citizenry to sacrifice. It was Ronald Reagan." *Time* then drove its point home: "'Government is not the solution to our problems,' Reagan said in 1981. 'Government is the problem.' 'I believe government must do more,' the young apostate [Clinton] declared 12 years later."[32]

The rhetoric of reporting is interesting. In this case, for example, *Time* locates Clinton on the political map by using his predecessors—not some fringe group, not some erstwhile activist—to determine his position. In doing so, *Time* curtails the president's potential range of motion. It is little wonder, then, that American politics is so often an incrementalist politics.

As we see in Figure 8.3, *Time*'s judgments are fairly well balanced between endorsement (35.4 percent) and criticism (28.7 percent) and that, too, is part of the journalistic art. As Daniel Hallin argues, two-sidedness is a kind of sidedness, of course, an approach that keeps radical options at bay.[33] That approach also sets the *criteria* by which political effectiveness can be judged.

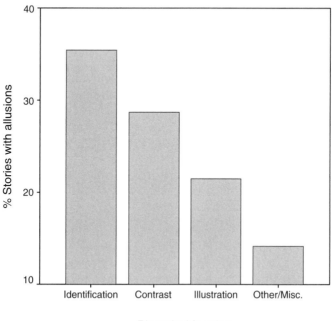

Figure 8.3 Function of Presidential Allusions in *Time* Magazine.

Sometimes, the judgments are harsh. When *Time* took the early measure of the Nixon administration, for example, it encouraged several former presidents to haunt the new office-holder:

> In a hundred days, Franklin Roosevelt led a foundering society back to self-confidence and no President since 1933 has been allowed to forget it. John Kennedy complained shortly before assuming power: "I'm sick of hearing about a hundred days, I'm not Roosevelt, and these aren't the '30s." But the legend persisted. Lyndon Johnson, in fact, encouraged comparisons, and with pockets stuffed full of legislative box scores he could show by certain singular mathematics a better record than that of his old mentor, F.D.R.[34]

Time drives the dagger in further: "Richard Nixon has been positively silent; there are no legislative compilations in his coat pocket; he does not even have a slogan for his administration; he has brought no peace, slowed no inflation, cleansed no air and water, uplifted no ghettos."[35] One hundred days. So little done. What must Nixon be thinking?

Occasionally, *Time* is fickle, attesting to another of the attractions of buying ink by the barrel. Six weeks after having lauded the young presidency of Bill Clinton, for example, the magazine urged him to get a move on, observing that one hundred days—one hundred days—had already passed and that Clinton had only arrogance to his credit. "All presidents are arrogant of course," *Time* opined, "the problem is undisciplined arrogance." With Clinton having "threatened to withhold patronage from Democratic defectors and to campaign against Republican opponents," he resembled his role model, Franklin Roosevelt. So far, so good. Then *Time* delivered the coup de grâce: "But F.D.R. wooed the G.O.P. assiduously."[36]

In pursuing the course it does, *Time* largely resembles its counterparts in the journalism business. Being a weekly rather than a daily news organ, however, *Time* can draw a somewhat bigger picture. That makes it an unusually good vehicle for seeing how the presidency maintains itself. *Time*'s strategies—of helping set the president's agenda, of suggesting what is possible and impossible, of deciding how the chief executive should be evaluated, of praising the president when he is good and scolding him when he is bad—are all executed within an institutional frame, and that frame is, itself, an argument. It is an argument for looking back before going forward, of balancing east with west, of finding a center that holds. For both good and ill this produces an American kind of politics.

CONCLUSION

In this chapter, we have found that the news is old. It is old even when it is new. The *president* is never allowed to shake his predecessors, being constantly tethered to the nation's past. How curious for a nation that prides itself on its inventiveness, that tires so quickly of hula hoops and cell phones.

The news coverage examined here is stolid, anchoring the nation's present in its past, its future in its past as well. There is a timidity to all of this, an unwillingness to move forward too precipitously. This timidity would surprise a marketing professional; it would not surprise a structuralist.

The data reported here suggest that the Marxist critics are partly right and partly wrong when it comes to popular journalism. *Time* is not a toady when it comes to presidential politics, but it is not terribly brave either. It tends the nation's institutions, never really challenging the existing order in fundamental ways. It calls a spade a spade but never really demands a new deck of cards. It certainly never cashes in its chips.

The nation's press is more good than bad. It scrutinizes governmental actions carefully and, if governments fall because of that scrutiny, that is as it should be.[37] The nation's press has a storied history in this regard, and muckraking is part of the national pulse. Throughout its history the press has reported change, turbulence, and conflict and somehow the nation has survived. It has also allowed existing social and economic structures to stay dominant but, contrary to the Marxist critics, that does not necessarily mean it has lulled "the population into a mindless acceptance of the status quo."[38] The American press constantly wrangles with government. It celebrates Roy Peter Clark's dictum: "Without journalism, democratic life dies from lack of oxygen. Without democracy, journalism loses its heartbeat."[39]

This chapter has told a tale of stability. *Time* assimilates the new chief executive into the institution of the presidency and reminds him of its traditions constantly. It is, in that sense, the nation's civics teacher. That is exactly how Henry R. Luce wanted it. In the prospectus he developed to inaugurate Time, Inc., Luce declared that keeping people informed "is the only axe this magazine has to grind. The magazine is one of news, not argument, and verges on the controversial only where it is necessary to point out what the news means."[40] What Luce did not say, but what we have observed here, is that his magazine would also become a vehicle for maintaining the nation's prerogatives. The result is the nation described by Seymour Martin Lipset: "The United States has developed a homogenous culture in the veneration accorded the Founding Fathers, Abraham Lincoln, Theodore Roosevelt, and their principles."[41] *Time* magazine is part of that homogeneity, part of that veneration. It keeps the waters calm.

NOTES

1. S. M. Lipset, *Political Man: The Social Basis of Politics,* exp. ed. (Baltimore: Johns Hopkins University Press, [1960] 1981), 64.

2. J. Lemco, *Political Stability in Federal Governments* (New York: Praeger, 1991), 1.

3. C. Brown, *Ballots of Tumult: A Portrait of Volatility in American Voting* (Ann Arbor: The University of Michigan Press, 1991), 3.

4. See E. Lehman, *The Viable Polity* (Philadelphia: Temple University Press, 1992).

5. Ibid., 153.

6. R. P. Hart, *The Political Pulpit* (Lafayette, IN: Purdue University Press, 1977). For an update on such matters, see the twenty-five-year retrospective on this book presented in the *Journal of Communication and Religion*, 25 (2002): 1–148.

7. P. H. O'Neil, "Democratization and Mass Communication: What Is the Link?" in *Communicating Democracy: The Media & Political Transitions*, ed. Patrick H. O' Neil (Boulder, CO: Lynne Rienner Publishers, 1998), 1.

8. Lehman, *The Viable Polity*, 110–11.

9. J. Fallows, *Breaking the News: How the Media Undermine American Democracy* (New York: Pantheon Books, 1996).

10. J. L. Downie and Robert G. Kaiser, *The News About the News: American Journalism in Peril* (New York: Alfred A. Knopf, 2002), 9. See also R. A. Pride, "Media Critics and Newsgroup-Embedded Newspapers: Making Attentive Citizens Attentive," in *The Public Voice in a Democracy at Risk*, ed. Michael Salvador and Patricia M. Sias (Westport, CT: Praeger, 1998), 127–48.

11. R. M. Entman, *Democracy Without Citizens: Media and the Decay of American Politics* (New York: Oxford University Press, 1989); L. Sabato, M. Stencel, and S. R. Lichter, *Peep Show: Media and Politics in an Age of Scandal* (Lanham, MD: Rowman & Littlefield, 2000); W. L. Bennett, *The Governing Crisis: Media, Money, and Marketing in American Elections* (New York: St. Martins, 1992); and J. N. Cappella and K. H. Jamieson, *Spiral of Cynicism: The Press and the Public Good* (New York: Oxford University Press, 1997).

12. It is important also to recognize that numerous authors doubt the notion of the liberal bias in the news. See, for instance, D. Niven, *Tilt? The Search for Media Bias* (Westport, CT: Praeger, 2002); and E. Alterman, *What Liberal Media? The Truth About Bias and the News* (New York: Basic Books, 2003).

13. A. H. Coulter, *Slander: Liberal Lies About the American Right* (New York: Crown, 2002); and B. Goldberg, *Bias: A CBS Insider Exposes How the Media Distort the News* (Washington, DC: Regnery Publishers, 2002).

14. See, for example, the research reported in R. P. Hart, *Campaign Talk: Why Elections Are Good for Us* (Princeton, NJ: Princeton University Press, 2000), 169–98.

15. J. A. Kuypers, *Press Bias and Politics: How the Media Frame Controversial Issues* (New York: Praeger, 2002).

16. M. B. Hovind, "The Melodramatic Imperative: Television's Model for Presidential Election Coverage," in *The Electronic Election: Perspectives on the 1996 Campaign Communication*, ed. L. L. Kaid and D. G. Bystrom (Mahwah, NJ: Erlbaum, 1999), 15–27.

17. The best commentary of this sort is the pioneering work of Gaye Tuchman. See her *Making News: A Study in the Construction of Reality* (New York: Free Press, 1978).

18. E. S. Herman and N. Chomsky, *Manufacturing Consent: The Political Economy of the Mass Media* (New York: Pantheon, 1988); and N. Chomsky, *Media Control: The Spectacular Achievements of Propaganda* (New York: Seven Stories Press, 2002).

19. Hall's critiques of news production are spread throughout his writing, but a pungent version appears in *The Hard Road to Renewal: Thatcherism and the Crisis of the Left* (London: Verso, 1988).

20. See, for example, M. Grossman and M. J. Kumar, *Portraying the President: The White House and the News Media* (Baltimore: Johns Hopkins University Press, 1981); T. E. Patterson, *Out of Order* (New York: Vintage Books, 1994); and R. P. Hart, D. Smith-Howell, and J. Llewellyn, "News, Psychology, and Presidential Politics," in

The Psychology of Political Communication, ed. A. Crigler (Ann Arbor: University of Michigan Press, 1996), 37–64.

21. "Can This Marriage Be Saved?" *Time*, July 12, 1999, 26.

22. "Voters Are Mad as Hell," *Time*, March 2, 1992, 18.

23. "A New Breeze Is Blowing," *Time*, January 30, 1989, 17–18. Communication scholar Robert Denton observes that this rhetoric of transformation is often more important for the electorate than for the new president: "Americans want and need to believe that the common man they elevated to the Presidency is a 'Lincolnesque' bearer of infinite wisdom and benevolence. The perceived qualities are confirmed as soon as the candidate takes the oath of office." See R. E. Denton, "On 'Becoming' President of the United States: The Implications of the Office with the Officeholder," *Presidential Studies Quarterly*, 13 (1983): 373.

24. "A Moment of Special Glory," *Time*, January 26, 1981, 26.

25. "Semper, Phooey," *Time*, April 12, 1993, 34.

26. J. D. Barber, *The Presidential Character: Predicting Performance in the White House*, 2d ed. (Englewood Cliffs, NJ: Prentice-Hall, 1977).

27. "A Meeting of History & Fate," *Time*, March 26, 1965, 20.

28. "A Problem of How to Lead," *Time*, July 1978, 10.

29. Lipset, *Political Man*, 69.

30. "Toward Vienna," *Time*, May 26, 1961, 14.

31. "Toward a Safer World," *Time*, October 7, 1991, 18–19.

32. N. Gibbs, "Working the Crowd," *Time*, March 1, 1993, 19.

33. D. Hallin, *The "Uncensored War": The Media and Vietnam* (New York: Oxford University Press, 1986).

34. "Nixon's First Quarter," *Time*, April 25, 1969, 19.

35. Ibid.

36. "The First 100 Days," *Time*, May 3, 1993, 47.

37. For more on this line of thought, see D. Graber, *Mass Media and American Politics*, 5th ed. (Washington, DC: CQ Press, 2000), 21.

38. L. Bogart, *Commercial Culture* (New York: Oxford University Press, 1995), 60.

39. R. P. Clark, "Introduction," in *The Values and Craft of American Journalism: Essays from the Poynter Institute*, ed. R. P. Clark and C. C. Campbell (Gainsville: University Press of Florida, 2002), 1.

40. R. T. Elson, *Time, Inc.: The Intimate History of a Publishing Enterprise, 1923–1941* (New York: Atheneum, 1986), 8–9.

41. Lipset, *Political Man*, 68.

The *President*
Managing Democratic Tensions

In the trying times of the early 1940s, with a world war raging in Europe and just ten months before the United States itself would be attacked at Pearl Harbor, Franklin Delano Roosevelt declared that "democracy is not dying." A curious statement, but one befitting a time when the entire concept of a people living freely was being challenged by a gaggle of totalitarians. "We know it," continued Roosevelt, "because democracy alone, of all forms of government, enlists the full force of men's enlightened will. We know it because democracy alone has constructed an unlimited civilization capable of infinite progress in the improvement of human life."[1]

Almost fifty years later, also during a presidential inauguration, George Herbert Walker Bush reflected on the "stunning fact" that the nation had endured for two hundred years after its violent, revolutionary beginning.[2] Eight years later, Bill Clinton pledged to keep "democracy forever young, . . . flexible enough to face our common challenges."[3] At around that same time, *Magruder's American Government* reminded high school students that "democracy is not inevitable. It does not exist in the United States simply because Americans regard it as the best of all possible political systems. Nor will it continue to exist for that reason. It will continue to exist only for as long as we, the people, continue to subscribe to—and practice—those concepts."[4]

Why is the rhetoric of democracy so filled with doom and gloom? Why is its ephemeral nature continually stressed? How can a modern people, a people fascinated by controlled, technological efficiency, celebrate something so precarious? On Flag Day, Memorial Day, the Fourth of July, Labor Day, Veterans Day, Thanksgiving, and Presidents' Day Americans are told that they are a lucky, not an entitled, people. How can they find comfort in that?

The question becomes richer: Why do the American people continue to debate the very fundaments of their culture? Why do some burn the American flag to prove they have the freedom to do so? What sort of a patriotic act is it to lie down in front of an Army tank? to burn one's draft card? to march in protest when one's fellow citizens are in harm's way in some distant clime? If democracy has the capacity to "advance our common dreams,"[5] why are its tenets a constant source of friction, even combat, among its adherents? With Americans having learned about the glories of their political system since grade school, why are they, as grownups, continually nagged about their civic duties? Is democracy not strong enough to stand on its own, powerful and silent?

Apparently not. Democracy needs chatter. A democracy is too preposterous a notion to be erected and then forgotten. Like all political systems, democracy requires a rhetoric, but it has special needs as well. It needs an adaptable rhetoric to let it cope with a large and contentious society. This chapter tells the story of that rhetoric and how its primary icon, *the American president*, meets the emotional needs of its people and gives them a sense of direction. This rhetoric is trotted out in Washington each day to make democracy seem less preposterous.

THE FRAGILE DEMOCRACY

As Courtney Brown has observed, the United States has enjoyed "regime stability" in the midst of constant "electoral volatility" during its short history.[6] Political elections remind us of that fact. Normally, both the winner and the loser celebrate the end of a campaign by singing the praises of democracy. The conclusion of a campaign is, as discussed in chapter 8, a liminal moment, a time of transition. People feel fragile during such moments: Will the transition be an orderly one? Will the new president upset the stock market? Will my taxes go up? All elections prompt these uncertainties, but the presidential election of 2000 was a special case. If ever a string of epithets could have been expected from the candidates it was at the end of that campaign, a campaign in which the winner was the loser and the loser the winner. But that formulation of the 2000 election is itself controversial, which is why the outcome of the campaign was determined by the Supreme Court of the United States.

No epithets, no obscenities, were heard on December 12, 2000, the day the campaign was decided. All that was heard was the siren song of democracy. The winner-turned-loser, Al Gore, sang its notes when declaring the election had been decided "through the honored institutions of our democracy."[7] The Electoral College victor, George W. Bush, reminded the nation of the also-contested election of 1800, which marked "the first transfer of power from one party to another in our new democracy."[8] It is easy to dismiss these sentiments as mere words, disingenuous attempts to hide the candidates' true feelings at what must have been an awful time for them. Skeptical though they were when listening, however, most Americans demanded nothing less from the candidates. Gloating by Bush and sour grapes from Gore were clearly unacceptable. Democracy needed a duet.

Three years later—predictably—the music became more discordant, as nine Democratic contenders began thumping lecterns throughout the country to negate the injustice done their party in the previous campaign. But presidential elections are only one sign of electoral volatility. In the past twenty years, citizen referendums have become a regular feature of state and local governments. These petitions have changed how some states raise revenue, how long an elected figure may serve in office, and even whom can get married.

Another source of volatility is that between state and federal government. In the spring of 2003, for example, George W. Bush campaigned for a federal tax cut at a time when most state legislatures needed tax increases to make their budgets balance. Attesting to the madness that is sometimes politics, Nebraska's Democratic senator supported the president's tax proposal while its Republican governor rejected the idea of infusing federal tax dollars into the state budget. Ultimately, the U.S. Senate approved the proposed tax cut by a 51–49 vote, with the vice president casting the deciding vote and with only two Democrats supporting it and three Republicans voting against their party leaders.[9] The *New York Times* celebrated this auspicious moment scathingly: "[T]wo misguided, poorly timed tax bills from the House and the Senate . . . will not provide the short-term stimulus the country needs but will almost surely cause economic problems for the future."[10] No doubt the president sighed.

At around that same time, fifty-one Democratic legislators left the state capital in Austin for a sojourn in Ardmore, Oklahoma, thereby denying the Republican-led House the head-count it needed to secure a quorum sufficient for passing a bill that would have redistricted Democrats into oblivion. The Democratic representatives returned only after the date for approving new legislation had passed.[11] All of these events occurred in the spring of 2003 even as federal investigators probed such corporate titans as Enron, WorldCom, and Martha Stewart and as Congress passed—and the courts denied—new regulations over campaign financing. Democracy, it seems, is never quiet.

As we saw in chapter 4, lay distrust of politics also complicates governance. In *A Necessary Evil: A History of American Distrust of Government*, Garry Wills contends that government is only grudgingly accepted in the United States because anything beyond a necessary minimum "instantly cancels one or another liberty."[12] Public opinion polls show that Americans venerate the American system of government but decry the politicians in their midst.[13] But even as they decry the politicians in their midst, they return incumbents to Congress about 90 percent of the time. Clearly, the concept of democracy appeals to most Americans and its practices disturb them. The U.S. political system gets its energy from this tension between expectation and reality.

In this chapter, we illustrate how presidential discourse responds to the strains of republican life by examining a large number of speeches from 1945 through 2000, focusing particularly on *president* tokens (i.e., named occupants of the Oval Office). We found over eleven thousand tokens in the more than forty-two hundred speeches we examined, roughly 2.7 tokens per speech.

We coded each speech for token frequency, political associations (i.e., personal, philosophical, or policy-based resemblance to the speaker), the token's judgmental function (endorsement, criticism, illustration, or neutral), and the use of direct quotations. In addition, situational data were gathered, including genre (ceremony, briefing, political rally, press conference), audience (national, local, press, special interest), and location (Washington, DC; U.S. regions; or international).[14] By mapping these allusions, we hoped to discover one of the nation's main strategies for managing its tensions.

USING THE PAST

Before discussing these strategies, however, we might reflect on why a president would refer to his predecessors at all. Chapters 7 and 8 hint at potential answers: doing so makes a new president feel part of the institution and gives the people a sense of continuity, thereby making them institution-regarding. That is, even though the president is arguably the most powerful leader in the world, his authority is temporary and limited by law and circumstance. Domestically, for example, members of the opposing party, fractious reporters, and a temperamental public constantly bedevil him. Becoming the national historian gives him an edge. As communication scholar Bruce Gronbeck argues, the past is "an ally of legitimation processes, a vehicle for sanctifying institutional authority, authorizing acts of power, and articulating codes of collective and individual conduct."[15]

All this seems reasonable enough, but its effects are sometimes odd. For example, near the end of his first inaugural address, Ronald Reagan—who came to Washington to disassemble as much of the federal government as possible—wrapped himself in its mantle instead:

> At the end of this open mall are those shrines to the giants on whose shoulders we stand. Directly in front of me, the monument to a monumental man, George Washington, father of our country. A man of humility who came to greatness reluctantly. He led America out of revolutionary victory into infant nationhood. Off to one side, the stately memorial to Thomas Jefferson. The Declaration of Independence flames with his eloquence. And then, beyond the reflecting pool, the dignified columns of the Lincoln memorial. Whoever would understand in his heart the meaning of America will find it in the life of Abraham Lincoln.[16]

Twelve years later, another partisan came to town, this time promoting an activist federal government. Unlike Reagan, Bill Clinton found change, not continuity, in the nation's history:

> Americans have ever been a restless, questing, hopeful people. And we must bring to our task today the vision and will of those who came before us. From our Revolution to the Civil War, to the Great Depression, to the civil rights movement, our people have always mustered the determina-

tion to construct from these crisis the pillars of our history. Thomas Jefferson believes that to preserve the very foundations of our Nation, we would need dramatic change from time to time. Well, my fellow Americans, this is our time. Let us embrace it.[17]

In these ways, presidents make an ally of history because they have comparatively little else to sustain them. Presidents make no laws, after all, and, technically speaking, they do not even make wars. Congress does those things and more. The Supreme Court interprets the laws Congress makes, and even the president's cabinet officers must be approved by the Senate. The president gets to appoint the heads of government agencies and, in a nation of some three million federal workers, that is not an insignificant source of influence.[18] But mostly presidents persuade. They jealously guard that power, refusing to squander it on doomed social policies or ill-conceived alliances. They align themselves with White House traditions constantly, often reinterpreting those traditions when so doing. As Richard Neustadt said of Harry Truman, he "saw the office as a living chain of presidents . . . each a trustee for those following after."[19] That strategy has intimidating possibilities.

We found that all presidents invoked the past regularly (see Figure 9.1). Dwight Eisenhower was the more sparing in this regard (roughly one-sixth of his speeches contained presidential allusions), while Lyndon Johnson used them most often (almost 40 percent of his speeches contained such tokens). Regardless of ideology (John Kennedy used presidential allusions as often as Ronald Reagan) or personal style (Harry Truman and George H. W. Bush behaved similarly), the presidents regularly dipped into the past. They did so infrequently during press conferences but quite often during ceremonies, rallies, and briefings. Although they spoke on the campaign trail of "bringing a new voice to Washington," they all became disciplined by the past once they arrived. Their reasons for doing so varied, and that is the story of this chapter.

THE THERAPEUTIC PAST

From their earliest days on the planet, people have gathered on ceremonial occasions to share communal truths. Sometimes these gatherings matched the phases of the moon, sometimes the crop cycles or the seasons. People have painted their bodies during rituals, sung melodies near a flickering campfire, danced until the sun came up. Ceremonies often match the phases of human life—birth, adolescence, marriage, death. The language of rituals is also interesting. Sometimes only the elders spoke, sometimes only the men. In the most traditional societies, ceremonial roles were highly prescribed, no variations permitted. As Maurice Bloch has said, in such societies "the orator's words are almost entirely not his own, in the sense that he sees them as handed down from the ancestors. He will have learned all the

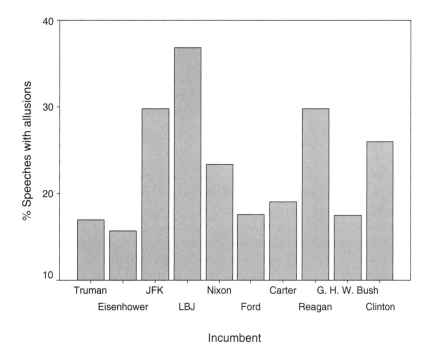

Figure 9.1 Allusions to Predecessors by Individual Presidents.

proverbs, stories and speech forms and his main aim is to repeat them as closely as possible."[20]

But the most important thing about rituals is that they are a public way of doing group emotion. Rituals do therapeutic work, purging people's fears and anxieties and replacing them with hope and anticipation. For these reasons, politicians like rituals. They like them because the rules guiding them are known and because emotional work is more enjoyable than ideological work. People inevitably feel better after a ceremony. Politicians like that feature too.

Presidents of the United States superintend the nation's most important rituals. As one researcher reports, over 40 percent of a chief executive's speechmaking is now done in ritualistic settings, and that proportion has increased steadily during the last fifty years.[21] With presidents having to cope each day with what Spiro Agnew called the "nattering nabobs of negativism" in Washington, DC, rituals can soothe a president's soul. When conducting such rituals, presidents often embrace their predecessors. Abraham Lincoln, Thomas Jefferson, and George Washington—that eternal trio—account for 50 percent of all tokens used by recent presidents in public ceremonies. They constitute the nation's "foundation myth," its bedrock under-standings.[22]

Rituals are never innocent, however. For example, Bill Clinton once deliv-ered a speech at the Jefferson Memorial on the 250th anniversary of Thomas Jefferson's birth. He did so early in his administration (in April 1993), but he had already hit several bumps in the road by then, having had to withdraw the name of Zoë Baird, and later Kimba Wood, to be attorney general; hav-ing blundered into an untimely discussion of gays in the military; and already seeing problems to come over his wife's complex program for national health care. Three months in office and the storm clouds were already brewing. So Clinton asked Thomas Jefferson to help him explain why change was needed in Washington:

> We are the inheritors of Jefferson's rich legacy. On this the 200th anniver-sary of his birth, we can honor him best by remembering our own role in governing ourselves and our Nation: to speak, to move, to change, for it is only in change that we preserve the timeless values for which Thomas Jef-ferson gave his life, over two centuries ago.[23]

Clinton's behavior was not unique. The "presidential past" constantly beckons and, when it does not, the current chief executive asks it to beckon:

- *Bill Clinton:* "Remarks at the Dedication of the Harry S. Truman Build-ing," September 22, 2000.
- *George H. W. Bush:* "Remarks at the Luncheon Commemorating the Dwight D. Eisenhower Centennial," March 27, 1990.
- *Ronald Reagan:* "Remarks at the FDR Library 50th Anniversary Lun-cheon," January 8, 1989.
- *Gerald Ford:* "Remarks at the Lincoln Birthday Celebration," February 12, 1975.
- *Richard Nixon:* "Dedication of Woodrow Wilson International Center for Scholars," February 18, 1971.
- *Lyndon Johnson:* "Remarks on the 175th Anniversary of George Wash-ington's Inaugural," April 30, 1964.
- *Dwight Eisenhower:* "Remarks at the Dedication of Theodore Roosevelt Home," June 14, 1953.
- *Harry Truman:* "Independence Day Address at Home of Thomas Jeffer-son," July 4, 1947.

Rituals are concocted situations. We concoct them to take our minds off our worries, and we do so arbitrarily. July 3 or July 5 would have been per-fectly acceptable days upon which to celebrate the nation's heritage, but *July 4* sounds better—for reasons no historian can fully document. But approxi-mations are good enough when it comes to ritual, although the emotional register must be on key. In ritualistic settings, all the women are strong, all the men good-looking, and all the children above average.

Ceremonies focus on values, not policies. In the spring of 1998, for example, just after Bill Clinton was accused of having an affair with a young intern, he spoke about the importance of public service, using, ironically enough, John Kennedy's legacy to support his arguments. In doing so, Clinton tapped into a battle metaphor that reflected his own sense of siege at the time:

> John Kennedy made us believe that in public service you could fight for the things that ought to be fought for; you could fight against the things that ought to be fought against; and that the sole purpose of power, fleeting though it is, was to be applied to the best of your God-given ability to those worthy goals.

The conclusion to Clinton's remarks was even more telling, especially in light of his then-tarnished image:

> I hope that the children of this age will find a way to believe in America the way President Kennedy helped me to believe in America and to believe that the political process leaves the ultimate power in the people and gives its elected Representatives a precious chance just to bring out the good and stand against the bad. It is the eternal human obligation. He made it seem like fun and noble and good. The least we can do is to keep the torch burning.[24]

Lyndon Johnson provides another example of rhetorical therapy. During a speech at the Lincoln Memorial during a round of intense protests about Vietnam and civil rights, Johnson patiently explained the nature of Lincoln's character:

> The true quality of Lincoln emerges, I think, from the fact that for four long brutal years he never permitted his anguish and doubt to deter him from acting. He recognized that the evidence he had to go on was very incomplete. Yet he made a total commitment to action. And this commitment, while always total, was never fanatical. Lincoln's mind was always open. He was always searching for a new light. He was looking for a better policy. His intelligence never rested. The consequence was that, as he forced himself to confront changing reality he never ceased to grow.[25]

Who is Johnson talking about here? himself or Abraham Lincoln? His remarks reflect a kind of emotional triangulation, with Lincoln standing in for Johnson and also for us. The result is a pleasing package that may not be all that inaccurate, if we are to believe historian Richard Current: "Lincoln had all the doubt and determination of Lyndon B. Johnson."[26]

There is no more dramatic example of history's therapeutic possibilities than that provided by Richard Nixon on his last day in office. The newly disgraced Nixon quoted Theodore Roosevelt's remarks on the death of his wife and then continued in this way: "That was T. R. in his twenties. He thought the light had gone from his life forever—but he went on. And he not only became President but, as an ex-President, he served his country, always in the arena, tempestuous, strong, sometimes wrong, sometimes right, but he was a man."[27] The political psychologists could have a field day with Nixon's remarks, containing as they do images of youth, manhood, battle, service, and indomitability. His remarks are also dualistic in the extreme: light versus dark, male versus female, error versus rectitude, today versus tomorrow. These forty-nine words condense the enigma that was Richard Nixon.

We do not pay our presidents to work out their emotional needs in public, but they do so anyway, turning their predecessors into doppelgangers, shadowy figures who walk before them and pave the way. A doppelganger is a "double-walker" who casts no reflection but who ministers to its counterpart nonetheless. In the preceding examples, it is hard to know who is figure and who is ground—the sitting president or his predecessor. If that leads to confusion, it is a confusion chief executives find useful.

THE EVOLVING PAST

Presidential tokens do psychological work, but they also serve practical functions, one of which is so obvious that it seems unremarkable: Presidents frame themselves as inheritors of an incomplete tradition. For this stratagem to work, the president must channel his forebears into the present. This makes the president something of an empty vessel. It also makes him conservative, clinging to the past to generate the authority needed to move forward. Most remarkably, it invents "coattails" for the president to grasp. In the world of presidential rhetoric, nothing is ever new.

Bill Clinton, one of the youngest presidents to sit in the Oval Office, was never new. When it came to healthcare, he was as old as Richard Nixon: "Under this health care security plan, every employer and every individual will be asked to contribute something to health care. This concept was first conveyed to the Congress about 20 years ago by President Nixon."[28] Six months later, Clinton aged again: "Many of you in this audience remember when Franklin Roosevelt led the struggle to create Social Security. You were there when John Kennedy and Lyndon Johnson fought to create Medicare, a solemn pact with our senior citizens." He then became ancient: "Many of you also remember, I hope, that Franklin Roosevelt and Harry Truman . . . all tried and failed in the face of special interest opposition to guarantee health security for all Americans. But we can do it this year, and we must."[29]

Given the disaster that was the Clinton healthcare system, we will never know its true progenitor—the think tanks in Washington or the mind of FDR. But rhetoric has its own logic, its own science and history as well. Rhetoric asks us to overlook the niggling details so that some sort of agreement can be reached. In his well-known address of November 3, 1969, for example, Richard Nixon used a tissue of history to rally the nation in support of the Vietnam War: "Three American presidents [Kennedy, Eisenhower, and Johnson] have recognized the great stakes involved in Vietnam and understood what had to be done." He concluded thusly: "Fifty years ago, in this room and at this very desk, President Woodrow Wilson spoke words which caught the imagination of a war-weary world."[30]

This sort of bridge-building often transcends party lines. So, for example, when Ronald Reagan invoked the sainted John Kennedy in behalf of his 1981 tax cut, he blazed a path he would travel for another eight years.[31] During his time in office, Reagan delivered 379 speeches containing presidential allusions, a total surpassed (proportionally) only by Lyndon Johnson. This is a curious duo—the disestablishmentarian Reagan and the institutionalist Johnson. What the latter attempted to build in five years, the former tried to undo in eight. But both wanted to be seen as mere cogs in the presidential machinery, dutifully following their predecessors.

Why did Ronald Reagan, a person who wanted to radically alter the role of the federal government, need institutional history to make his case? The apparent answer: Campaigning is one thing; governing is quite another. During his presidency, Reagan used Franklin Roosevelt to defend his Strategic Defense Initiative,[32] Harry Truman to justify his Central American policy,[33] John Kennedy to warrant increased support for the Pentagon,[34] Lyndon Johnson to advance his program for reduced federal spending,[35] and Richard Nixon to improve Sino-American relationships.[36] Perhaps because he ran for office as an outsider, perhaps because he was a centrist disguised as a conservative, or perhaps because he saw utility in a Trojan Horse strategy, Reagan had an unusual fondness for the past.

It is easy to underestimate strategies like Reagan's. Surely few listeners would notice, never mind be affected, by such appeals. We disagree. We see such devices as powerful precisely because they seem insignificant, because they pass through the mind so quickly. A president who does history's bidding is, in a sense, not an individual at all. He is the past made present, an incarnation of all that is good now returned. Content analysis calls our attention to these patterns and asks us to take their additive effects seriously. Using these devices, a genial man like Ronald Reagan seems even more genial, a catholic politician, not a partisan. Reagan spoke for all presidents and they for him.

THE TACTICAL PAST

Despite what the laudatory inscriptions say on the monuments, presidents are partisan creatures. They run for office to change things, and, once elected, they do all in their power to trump their opponents. This is hardball politics, and it is a game Americans love to play. Campaigns, naturally, bring such partisanship to the surface. Between 1945 and the present three incumbent presidents have lost their reelection efforts and three incumbent vice presidents have failed to move up to the Oval Office. At the same time, however, *presidential* campaigning is complicated because, when running for reelection, a president must preside over the nation and bash his opponents simultaneously. Ronald Reagan did so amiably: "Well, to all of you who knew the party of FDR and Harry Truman and JFK and that tradition, let us say to you—and I do know how you feel, because I was there myself once—walk with us down the new path of opportunity, and we'll save this country in a bipartisan way."[37]

The first president Bush was no Ronald Reagan, but he too poached in Democratic territory. When traveling through Wisconsin in the fall of 1992, for example, Bush was reminded that "forty-four years ago next month, another incumbent President came through Waukesha."[38] Bush admitted that he differed a bit from Harry Truman (and that he voted against him in 1948), but declared them kinfolk nonetheless. Their records of military service were comparable, said Bush, they both ran for reelection as underdogs, they confronted hostile Congresses, and they—the Missouri pol and the Yale preppie—had a similar fondness for plain speech. Bush then transported himself into the soul of Harry Truman and exorcised Bill Clinton in the process:

- Harry Truman said, "The buck stops here." On issue after issue, Governor Clinton says, "First, let's blame George Bush," and then, "I'll get back to you later with an answer.". . . .

- Harry Truman was a man of decisiveness not equivocation. He'd find little in common with Governor Clinton. . . .

- You know, many people thought Harry Truman would lose in 1948. But he said what was on his mind. He didn't worry about the press. And he never lost faith in the United States of America. . . .

- And like Harry Truman, I believe a new age of America beckons and that we can reap the benefits. With your help come November we will match our global victory with economic security here at home.[39]

Presidents used tokens less often during elections than ceremonies, but they still used them prodigiously.[40] They sometimes used several at the same time, although some did so more than others (Harry Truman lectured an entire nation about presidential history during his whistlestop tour of 1948, for example, while Richard Nixon avoided that approach). Most candidates were neither shy nor discriminating when doing so. In 1980, for example, Jimmy Carter jealously guarded his party's turf:

We'll win because we are a party of a great President who knew how to get re-elected—Franklin Delano Roosevelt. And we are a party of a courageous fighter who knew how to give 'em hell—Harry Truman. And as Truman said, he just told the truth and they thought it was hell. And we're the party of a gallant man of spirit—John Fitzgerald Kennedy. And we're the party of a great leader of compassion—Lyndon Baines Johnson, and . . . [41]

Later in that same speech, Carter jealously guarded the Republicans' turf as well: "Where is the conscience of Lincoln in the party of Lincoln? What's become of their traditional Republican commitment to fiscal responsibility?"[42]

Sometimes this business of presidential allusions can be complicated, as, for example, when it moves to the meta-discursive level. For example, Jimmy Carter once tried to make a campaign issue out of Ronald Reagan's lack of rhetorical propriety:

> My Republican opponent quite often quotes the eloquent words of Franklin D. Roosevelt. On occasion he quotes Harry Truman. On occasion he quotes John Fitzgerald Kennedy. But then a couple of months ago in an interview with *Time* magazine, he said, and I quote him: "If you look back, you find that those great social reforms didn't work." And he continues to say that the compassionate programs of the New Deal were actually based on fascism. Franklin D. Roosevelt wouldn't approve of a candidate who said that quoting his own words.[43]

Carter shows here that the past is not static—it is constantly being negotiated. Professional historians know that to be true, of course, but politicians have discovered the principle as well.

Campaign rhetoric is not always honorific. Each party has its skeletons, and a favorite campaign tactic is to open the other fellow's closet door. George H. W. Bush was not above that tactic, once bypassing his immediate opponent in 1992 to take a shot at the sainted carpenter from Plains: "Go back to Jimmy Carter. Interest rates were 21 percent. Inflation was 15 percent. The 'misery index,' unemployment, inflation added together, it was invented by the Democrats, went right through the roof."[44] Perhaps Mr. Bush was exacting revenge here for Harry Truman's autopsy of the Hoover administration some years earlier: "We remember Mr. Hoover himself was a great efficiency expert. We remember how he selected one of the richest men in American to be his Secretary of the Treasury. But efficiency wasn't enough 20 years ago, and efficiency isn't enough today."[45]

Allusions like these are a kind of definition-by-negation, a way of backing into a position or of not taking a position but appearing to have done so. Presidential allusions are quick, efficient signals that have little semiotic value (they are bereft of specific content) but still give audiences the sense that something important is happening. These allusions fly by quickly during a campaign, sometimes nettling an opponent and clouding the issues as well. Nobody did that better than Ronald Reagan, a man who governed like a Republican but who spoke like a Democrat: "To all those Democrats who were loyal to the party of F.D.R., Harry Truman, and J.F.K, but who see that its current leaders have changed it . . . we say to them: Our arms are open. Join us."[46]

CONCLUSION

Politics is never easy. This chapter has isolated three of its challenges: (1) Guiding a nation composed of free-thinking people puts constant pressure on that nation's leader; (2) cyclical changes in leadership make it hard for a single, coherent view of the world to develop; (3) partisan skirmishes can force a president to choose between governing and competing. These tensions can be sharp ones, but the president is not without his allies. Rhetoric is one such ally. It offers therapeutic help to cope with the rigors of governance, intellectual help to make the world seem cohesive, strategic help to make partisanship an advantage. For most presidents, these moves become second nature.

As one scholar notes, "Rhetoric gives us something to think about as well as something not to think about."[47] Presidential allusions are a simple, powerful way of distracting the American people. They can be powerful since, as Charles Elder and Roger Cobb observe, people instinctively respond to symbols having high affect and valence but underdeveloped meanings.[48] In other words, the very *saying* of Franklin Roosevelt's name unleashes associations in some Americans that bypass their brains on the way to their hearts. The *Roosevelt* keyword turns public memory into a political tool.

There is danger in that. A distracted people has no focus, overvalues the insignificant, and does not know where to turn. When the past is perverted—to soothe a president's soul or to cloud the issues of the day—the electorate suffers, the least discriminating among it the most. But the past can also be a bounty. As Henry Steele Commager declares, finding a "usable past" is crucial to nation-building,[49] and, as John Bodnar notes, the past performs best when helping a polity deal with current issues insightfully.[50]

Barry Schwartz, in *George Washington: The Making of an American Symbol*, eloquently describes the power of the past for the present:

> The Washington image, along with the ideals associated with it, has maintained its hold on American society for more than two hundred years. It has been evoked and reinforced by periodic commentaries in schools and the mass media, and by the material sign of the Washington cult—its icons, shrines, place names, and observances. By their common exposure to these media, millions of people are drawn into a moral communion, and through this relationship the continuity of their political tradition is reinforced. The commemoration of Washington thus provides a continuous American interpretation of American life.[51]

According to Schwartz, this is collective memory at its best, anchoring a society and giving it vision. But as scholar Barbie Zelizer warns, how we remember a thing and what we do with those memories is ultimately most important.[52] Splendid though he was, George Washington cannot help us formulate policies about cloning, abortion, space exploration, the Middle East, urban gentrification, terrorism, the V-chip, or even capital punishment. We, Washington's descendents, must work out those problems for ourselves. Empirically, the past is past; phenomenologically, it is a contrivance. Especially in the presence of our most talented politicians, we dare not forget that distinction.

We are all creatures of the past as we have come to know it. We need to know it better. Democracies can be undone by a misremembered past, an overly pontifical past, an exploited past. We need to maintain our historical attachments but only to those portions of the past that still offer guidance. Although short, the history of the United States has much to teach—the courage of the Puritans but also their ethnocentrism; the imagination of the robber barons but also their thievery. "History," declared Ronald Reagan, "is not only made by people; it is people. And so history is, . . . as heroic as you want it to be, as heroic as you are."[53] Perhaps. But history can also be banal and sectarian and rapacious and indolent. We need a history that teaches us better than that.

NOTES

1. F. D. Roosevelt, "Third Inaugural Address," in *American Freedom Library: Today's Issues, Traditional Values Electronic Library*, ed. (Orem, UT: Western Standard Publishing Company, 1998).

2. G. H. W. Bush, "Inaugural Address," January 20, 1989, Washington, DC, in *Public Papers of the President: 1989* (Washington, DC: U.S. Government Printing Office, 1989), 1.

3. W. J. Clinton, "Inaugural Address," January 20, 1997, Washington, DC, in *Public Papers of the President: 1997* (Washington, DC: U.S. Government Printing Office, 1997), 43–44.

4. W. A. McClenaghan, *Magruder's American Government* (Needham, MA: Prentice Hall, 1999), 15.

5. W. J. Clinton, "Inaugural Address," in *Public Papers: 1997*.

6. C. Brown, *Ballots of Tumult: A Portrait of Volatility in American Voting* (Ann Arbor: University of Michigan Press, 1991), 2–4.

7. As quoted in K. Ritter and B. Howell, "Ending the 2000 Presidential Election," *American Behavioral Scientist*, 44 (August 2001): 2316.

8. Quoted in ibid., 2324.

9. "Midlanders Key to Tax Cut Package," *Omaha World-Herald*, May 16, 2003, www.omaha.com (June 19, 2003).

10. Editorial, "Sleight of Hand on Capitol Hill," *New York Times*, May 18, 2003, WK12.

11. For more on this story, see the *Omaha World-Herald*, May 16, 2003, www.omaha.com (June 16, 2003).

12. G. Wills, *A Necessary Evil: A History of American Distrust of Government* (New York: Simon & Schuster, 2002), 15.

13. See, for example, V. Braitwaite and M. Levi (eds.), *Trust and Governance* (New York: Russell Sage, 1998).

14. The speeches examined were from the *Public Papers of the Presidents* beginning in 1945 with Harry Truman. The content of the *Public Papers* has varied over the years, with additional details (such as brief remarks to the press) being constantly added. A significant problem with this collection is its inconsistency in indexing through the years. For many years, the indices seem complete, but those from 1969 to 1977 and from 1989 to 2000 were either incomplete or references to former presidents were omitted. Despite these deficiencies, every effort was made to tally all presidential allusions in all speeches. As more presidential documents become digitized, the hand-coding procedures used here will no longer be necessary.

15. B. Gronbeck, "Ronald Reagan's Enactment," in *Form, Genre, and the Study of Political Discourse,* ed. H. W. Simons and A. A. Aghazarian (Columbia: University of South Carolina Press, 1986), 226.

16. R. Reagan, "Inaugural Address," January 20, 1981, Washington, DC, in *Public Papers of the President: 1981* (Washington, DC: U.S. Government Printing Office, 1981), 3.

17. W. Clinton, "Inaugural Address," January 20, 1993, Washington, DC, in *Public Papers of the President: 1993* (Washington, DC: U.S. Government Printing Office, 1993), 1.

18. For additional information about the federal payroll, see the U.S. Department of Labor's Bureau of Labor Statistics, http://www.bls.gov/home.htm (June 17, 2003).

19. R. E. Neustadt, "Truman in Action: A Retrospect," in *Modern Presidents and the Presidency,* ed. M. Landy (Lexington, MA: Lexington Books, 1985), 6.

20. M. Bloch (ed.), "Introduction," in *Political Language and Oratory in Traditional Society* (London: Academic Press, 1975), 8.

21. R. P. Hart, *The Sound of Leadership: Presidential Communication in the Modern Age* (Chicago: University of Chicago Press, 1987).

22. D. Nimmo and J. Combs, *Subliminal Politics: Myths and Mythmakers in America* (Englewood Cliffs, NJ: Prentice-Hall, 1980), 33.

23. W. Clinton, "Remarks on the Observance of the 250th Anniversary of the Birth of Thomas Jefferson," April 13, 1993, Washington, DC, in *Public Papers: 1993,* 424. While the *Public Papers* have Clinton saying "200th anniversary," the title of the speech is "Remarks on the Observance of the 250th Anniversary of the Birth of Thomas Jefferson."

24. W. Clinton, "Remarks at the John F. Kennedy Presidential Library Foundation Dinner," March 2, 1998, Washington, DC, in *Public Papers of the President: 1998* (Washington, DC: U.S. Government Printing Office, 1998), 315–16.

25. Lyndon B. Johnson, "Remarks at a Ceremony at the Lincoln Memorial," February 12, 1967, Washington, DC, in *Public Papers of the President: 1967* (Washington, DC: U.S. Government Printing Office, 1967), 177.

26. R. Current, "The Lincoln Presidents," *Presidential Studies Quarterly,* 9 (1979): 31.

27. R. Nixon, "Remarks on the Departure from the White House," August 9, 1974, Washington, DC, in *Public Papers of the President: 1974* (Washington, DC: U.S. Government Printing Office, 1974), 632.

28. W. Clinton, "Address to a Joint Session of the Congress on Health Care Reform," September 22, 1993, Washington, DC, in *Public Papers: 1993,* 1562–63.

29. W. Clinton, "Remarks at a Health Care Forum," March 21, 1994, Deerfield Beach, FL, in *Public Papers of the President: 1994* (Washington, DC: U.S. Government Printing Office, 1994), 507.

30. R. Nixon, "Address to the Nation on the War in Vietnam," November 3, 1969, Washington, DC, in *Public Papers of the President: 1969* (Washington, DC: U.S. Government Printing Office, 1969), 902, 909.

31. R. Reagan, "Remarks and Question and Answer Session with State and Local Officials During a White House Briefing on the Economic Recovery," May 28, 1981, Washington, DC, in *Public Papers of the President: 1981* (Washington, DC: U.S. Government Printing Office, 1981), 468.

32. R. Reagan, "Toasts of the President and Prime Minister Margaret Thatcher of the United Kingdom at a Dinner at the British Embassy," February 20, 1985, http://www.reagan.utexas.edu/resource/speeches/1985/22085f.htm (June 18, 2003).

33. R. Reagan, "Address to a Joint Session on Congress on the State of the Union," January 27, 1987, Washington, DC, in *Public Papers of the President: 1987* (Washington, DC: U.S. Government Printing Office, 1987), 57.

34. R. Reagan, "Radio Address to the Nation on Armed Forces Day and Defense Spending," May 18, 1985, http://www.reagan.utexas.edu/resource/speeches/1985/51885a.htm (June 18, 2003).

35. R. Reagan, "Remarks at a Fundraising Luncheon in Billings, Montana, for United States Senate Candidate Larry Williams," August 11, 1982, http://www.reagan.utexas.edu/resource/speeches/1982/81182b.htm (June 18, 2003).

36. R. Reagan, "Remarks to Chinese Community Leaders in Beijing, China," April 27, 1984, http://www.reagan.utexas.edu/resource/speeches/1984/42784a.htm (June 18, 2003).

37. R. Reagan, "Remarks at a Reagan-Bush Rally," Louisville, KY, October 7, 1984, in *Public Papers of the President: 1984* (Washington, DC: U.S. Government Printing Office, 1984), 1464.

38. G. H. W. Bush, "Remarks at the Republican Party Labor Day Picnic," September 7, 1992, Waukesha, WI, in *Public Papers of the President: 1992* (Washington, DC: U.S. Government Printing Office, 1992), 1485.

39. G. H. W. Bush, "Address at the Republican Party Labor Day Picnic in Waukesha, Wisconsin," September 7, 1992, http://bushlibrary.tamu.edu/papers/1992/92090701.html (June 19, 2003).

40. Situational use of presidential allusions was apportioned as follows: ceremonies (37 percent); political rallies (22.3 percent); briefings (20.6 percent); press conferences (10 percent); organizational meetings (8 percent); miscellaneous (2 percent).

41. J. Carter, "Remarks Accepting the Democratic Nomination at the Democratic National Convention," August 14, 1980, New York, in *Public Papers of the President: 1980* (Washington, DC: U.S. Government Printing Office, 1980), 1532.

42. Ibid., p. 1538.

43. J. Carter, "Remarks to Senior Citizens," October 15, 1980, Boston, in ibid., 2245.

44. G. H. W. Bush, "Presidential Debate," October 19, 1992, East Lansing, MI, in *Public Papers: 1992*, 1857.

45. H. Truman, "Address in St. Paul at the Municipal Auditorium," October 13, 1948, St. Paul, MN, in *Public Papers of the President: 1948* (Washington, DC: U.S. Government Printing Office, 1948), 772–73.

46. R. Reagan, "Remarks at a Reagan-Bush Rally," September 3, 1984, Cupertino, CA, in *Public Papers: 1984*, 1226.

47. Hart, *The Sound of Leadership*, 69.

48. C. Elder and R. Cobb, *Political Uses of Symbols* (New York: Longman, 1983), 58.

49. H. S. Commager, *The Search for a Usable Past, and Other Essays in Historiography* (New York: Knopf, 1967).

50. J. E. Bodnar, *Remaking America: Public Memory, Commemoration, and Patriotism in the Twentieth Century* (Princeton, NJ: Princeton University Press, 1992).

51. B. Schwartz, *George Washington: The Making of an American Symbol* (New York: Free Press, 1987), 205. For other work along these same lines, see T. Brown, *JFK: History of an Image* (Bloomington: Indiana University Press, 1988); and M. D. Peterson, *Lincoln in American Memory* (New York: Oxford University Press, 1994).

52. B. Zelizer, "Reading the Past Against the Grain: The Shape of Memory Studies," *Critical Studies in Mass Communication*, 12 (1995): 217–18.

53. R. Reagan, "Remarks at a Fundraising Reception for the John F. Kennedy Library Foundation," June 24, 1985, Washington, DC, in *Public Papers of the President: 1985* (Washington, DC: U.S. Government Printing Office, 1985), 815–16.

UNIT 4

THE LANGUAGE OF CAMPAIGNING

Unit 3 examined the fundamental tensions of a democratic system. We asked how children learn the principles of governance, whether the media are a helpmate or a hindrance to democracy, and how the chief executive copes with political conflict when advancing his programs. In each case, we found keywords (in this case, allusions to former **presidents**) playing important but overlooked roles. The past, we found, is not one thing but many things. Events and persons from yesteryear are constantly being reborn and then sent out to do more work. Death has dominion over many things, but not rhetoric. Because of keywords, the past becomes only another kind of present in political affairs.

In unit 4 we move from institutional maintenance to the turbulence of political campaigns. Campaigns have always been noisy affairs, but they have never lasted as long, cost as much, or been as electronic as they are today. Modern campaigns bustle with an entirely new set of activities: National candidates charter jets to fly from place to place; the press trails along in its own aircraft; fund-raising is done during black-tie soirees and in the poultry yards of Iowa; and websites are used to build up a candidate, to tear down an opponent and, again, to raise money. Strategy questions, not policy questions, have become the journalist's stock-in-trade, and televised advertising has become an art form. If Candidate A makes a gaffe at ten o'clock in the morning, Candidate B will have an uplinked response ready by noon. Even when the campaign is over it is not really over since, as Sidney Blumenthal states, presidents are now in permanent campaign mode. The good news in winning an election is that one has received a new job. The bad news is that campaigning for reelection begins next week.

We discuss the language of campaigns in unit 4. Chapter 10 examines the **party,** that left-for-dead institution that is both accepted and reviled in the United States. Scholars have studied parties from every conceivable angle—their history, their organization, their financing, their convenings—but few have looked at what is said about them. We do that here, finding that journalists and politicians speak of parties differently and that those differences became more pronounced after 1980. In addition, the rise of the Independent changes what everyone thinks of parties, and that adds a new complexity to political calculations in the United States. Ultimately, politicians and their parties are joined at the hip, and that is a curse and a blessing for both.

Chapter 11 focuses on political ***promises,*** those much-maligned statements that publicly commit an elected official to taking action or, at least, that appear to do so. While scholars have often investigated whether or not campaign promises have been fulfilled (they have, for the most part), few have looked at what promises sound like. We do so here, finding that promises are rather careful, rather positive, rather self-risking, and often rather bold as well. Promises have dropped off in recent years, and that, we argue, may cost the political process some of the hope and imagination it needs.

Chapter 12 focuses on the ***consultant,*** the newest keyword in American politics and one of the most evocative. We describe the growing dominance of consultants in campaigns and inquire into how that affects what the average voter thinks about politics. Consultants add an element of mastery to campaign coverage, with the press fascinated by consultants who pull the rabbit out of the hat time and time again. In many ways, what people think about consultants dovetails with what they think about politics generally, and that, we argue, could become a worrisome thing indeed.

10

The *Party*
An Irrepressible Institution

Thomas Jefferson was a legacy waiting to happen. President John F. Kennedy once sang his praises in a room filled with Nobel prize laureates: "I think this is the most extraordinary collection of talent, of human knowledge, that has ever been gathered together at the White House, with the possible exception of when Thomas Jefferson dined alone." Thomas Jefferson, author of the Declaration of Independence, founder of the Library of Congress, father of one of the country's most prestigious public universities, and crafter of the Louisiana Purchase, is cherished to this day by both Republicans and Democrats. But Jefferson did not return the compliment. He once said that a political party is "the last degradation of a free and moral agent." "If I could not go to heaven but with a party," Jefferson vowed, "I would not go there at all."[1] Thirty-five years later, Jefferson changed his tune when observing that "Men by their constitutions are naturally divided into two parties: (1) Those who fear and distrust the people and wish to draw all powers from them into the hands of higher classes. (2) Those who identify themselves with the people, have confidence in them. . . . In every country, these two parties exist."[2]

Why did Jefferson come down firmly on both sides of the issue? Political scholar Gary Orren notes that a great many of Jefferson's fellow Founders were opposed to parties but eventually embraced them for one simple reason: They proved indispensable. Orren says that parties are needed in the United States for two reasons:

First, America retains an archaic, eighteenth century form of government in which power is fragmented within and among many institutions which share authority. The vast number of veto points in this system makes action difficult and inaction easy. Parties serve as a method for aggregating popular choices, tying these conflicts over courses of action to a broader program, and thus making compromise rather than veto the general form of resolution. Second, the demand for widespread popular participation emerged earlier and has proceeded further in the United States than elsewhere. The American public has achieved a greater voice in political affairs through the steady extension of the franchise, increases in the number of public officials subject to popular approval at the polls, and the involvement of citizens in the selection of party nominees. Political parties are needed to harness the participation of a powerful citizenry and fashion a coherent message out of the din of voices.[3]

Even though parties serve these important functions, Orren reminds us that "in no other democracy does the anti-organizational spirit run deeper."[4] Because parties challenge the individualistic and populist spirit of American culture, they are both accepted and reviled.

Other scholars have noticed this unique American attitude toward parties, but none has asked the kinds of questions guiding this chapter: How are parties talked about in the United States, and what does such talk do for us? During a political campaign, that is, some of our loudest voices—those of political candidates and the mass media—talk about parties constantly. What are they saying, and why are they saying it? Have they, like Jefferson, said different things at different times? If so, what motivated these changes? expediency? morality? philosophy? culture? And when parties are discussed, how is that talk received by voters? The term *party* is not a large word, but it does considerable work. We examine that work here.

UNDERSTANDING PARTIES

Political scientist Stephen Frantzich has said that studying political parties "is like trying to herd snakes. Everything is slippery—from the definitions to the measurements of existence and strength."[5] Not surprisingly, given the complex feelings Americans have about parties, they have been studied from a thousand vantage points: as protectors of the political system,[6] as historical benchmarks,[7] as cross-cultural phenomena,[8] as an emotional lever during political campaigns,[9] as a source of cognitive cues for would-be voters,[10] as a method for disciplining elected officials,[11] as a means of achieving social reform,[12] as a way of protecting ordinary people from economic elites,[13] and as a sign of modernity itself.[14]

Scholars have also examined historical trends in this area, prompting Cornelius Cotter to suggest that a "deathwatch" over parties has been conducted since the 1960s. Indeed, the "decline of parties thesis" has prompted some strong statements. Researcher Jack Dennis, for example, once announced the imminent "demise of a once prominent institution of American government and politics,"[15] but John Bibby responded with this: "[T]wo-party politics is highly compatible with American society, culture, and governmental structures."[16] Larry Bartels was even bolder: "[T]his conventional wisdom regarding the 'decline of parties' is both exaggerated and outdated."[17]

All of this commentary about the relative health of parties overlooks a more basic question: Why talk about them at all? If parties have died, why not give them a decent burial and forget them? If they are flourishing, why not respond with trumpets? Clearly, observers have enjoyed driving stakes into the hearts of the parties only to see them stagger back once again, the zombies of modern politics. Parties bother people, and they bother them greatly. Why?

To answer that question it is useful to examine what has been said about parties. The morning newspaper is a good place to start since, as Kevin Phillips argues, the "party candidate" has been largely replaced by the "media candidate."[18] The media make the news, and the news gives the candidates visibility. The media sell advertising, and advertising makes the candidates formidable. The media commission polls, and the polls become an alternate political reality. In such a game, the parties are clearly on the sidelines. Whereas it took Stephen Douglas fifty-nine ballots to be nominated for president by the Democrats when they convened in 1860, a century-and-a-half later John Kerry considered dipping into his wife's fortune to finance the political spots he would need to win the Iowa and New Hampshire primaries.

Not surprisingly, then, the parties are jealous of the media. They have reason to feel that way since, as Michael Robinson has found, coverage of the parties is overwhelmingly negative.[19] Thomas Patterson reports similar findings, contending that when media institutions organize campaigns they leave little room for parties (as witnessed, for example, by declining network coverage of party conventions).[20] In trying to understand why Bill Clinton (in 1993) and Newt Gingrich (in 1995) were not rewarded for their policy successes by the mass media, Patterson writes that "ingrained cynicism rather than knee-jerk liberalism is the media's real bias. Reporters have a decidedly low opinion of politics and politicians, and it slants their coverage of Republicans and Democrats alike."[21]

Martin Wattenberg raises a different point. In his content analysis of campaign newspaper coverage from 1952 to 1980, Wattenberg found that journalists are more likely to focus on individual candidates than on party structures and preferences. In interpreting his findings, Wattneberg writes that "although the total number of campaign-related stories declined in this period, the actual number of mentions of presidential candidates stayed relatively stable. In contrast, the number of instances in which parties were mentioned by name fell precipitously." But Wattenberg's story goes even deeper: "More theoretically important than the raw count of mentions, however, is the ratio between coverage of candidates versus that of parties." While the raw number of candidate mentions outnumbered party mentions during this thirty-year period, "the ratio increased from about two to one in the 1950s to roughly five to one by 1980."[22] For Wattenberg, then, the issue is not just one of media tone but also one of party eclipse, which raises the most unsettling question of all for the parties: Is disrespectful coverage better than no coverage at all?

Some observers respond in the affirmative. Journalist Joann Byrd believes, for example, that coverage equals power and that journalists' failure to cover the parties (especially minor parties) violates their duty to defend free speech and independent thinking.[23] Adding data to that claim, Diane Francis reports that after a powerful television station stopped granting media coverage to the Quality Party of Canada, it dropped from 6 percent to 1 percent in the polls.[24] Ian Ward found that to be true in Australia as well.[25]

And what of the United States? Again according to Wattenberg, there has been movement away from party-brokered electioneering to a media-inspired focus on candidate personalities.[26] The result, says Wattenberg, is that "the parties are losing their association with the candidates and the issues," thereby making it "increasingly difficult for Americans to see the relevance of political parties."[27] The media's heavy focus on candidates—their viewpoints, their families, their eccentricities—turns them into voters' intimate companions. In such an arrangement, who needs parties?

We must also ask what it means for American politics when the candidates, not the parties, occupy center stage during campaigns. Researchers are just beginning to unpack that question. Some are speculating that it could eliminate long-standing party allegiances by voters,[28] thereby leading to financial difficulties for the parties (and hence their ability to "grow" future candidates at the grassroots level)[29] as well as to decreased party influence in the policy-making process (who needs parties, after all, when one has C-SPAN?).[30] In addition, it opens up the entire question of whether hammering out a party platform is worth the strife (since candidates often depart from it during the heat of a campaign).[31] When candidates begin to worry about "building coalitions" rather than "rallying the party," says Mathew McCubbins, campaigns will become less predictable because coalitions can shift so rapidly in a just-in-time society.[32]

All these matters are of great importance, but we ask humbler questions here. If politicians no longer need political parties, do they mention them at all? When they do discuss them, what do they say? If the mass media are now running our campaigns, does that mean they can ignore party activities entirely? Or does the press treat the parties dismissively, calling into question their relevance in an age of declining group memberships and civil associations? There is also the positive scenario. Perhaps the "decline of the parties" thesis is overstated. Perhaps candidates sing the parties' praises. Perhaps discussing party activity still provides a convenient shorthand for the mass media, a way of clarifying electoral options for voters and, hence, a way of stabilizing the political cosmos. There is also the question of how rhetoric relates to reality. Parties could be dying in the United States but still have rhetorical power. Or, conceivably, they might not be mentioned as often as they once were but still wield great influence in the candidate-vetting process. Ultimately, our central question is this: Is *party* still a keyword in American politics. We shall argue here that it is.

As in other chapters, our approach will be content analytic and we will focus particularly on presidential campaign speeches and newspaper articles generated during the last fourteen presidential elections. As in other chapters, we drew these materials from the archives of the Campaign Mapping Project (see chapter 1). In this particular case, the keyword-in-context program located 1,346 instances of *party* (and its two main cognates, *parties* and *partisan*) in the campaign speeches and 11,669 more such tokens in the news coverage. To reduce this count to a manageable size, we drew a stratified sample of terms, randomly selecting twenty-five tokens per year per genre, ultimately producing a sample of 692 statements that were then coded by a team of trained researchers.[33]

The analytical scheme used in this chapter is inspired by theoretical work in the area of political parties. For example, to get rhetorical data about the party decline thesis, we examined the *role* ascribed to the parties (i.e., whether they were said to be part of the problem or part of the solution); *potency* (whether they were taking charge or being acted upon);[34] and *position* (whether they were elite organizations, part of government, or a mass phenomenon).[35] To assess the political environment ascribed to parties, the variables *time* (present, past, future);[36] *valence* (positive, negative, balanced); and *associations* (those interacting with the parties—party officials,[37] candidates,[38] interest groups,[39] and voters[40]) were assessed. Finally, to drill a bit deeper into the texts themselves, the variables *behavior* (the parties' actions, whether intellectual, psychological, or sociological in nature) and *qualities* (adjectives characterizing the party—e.g., clear, unified, placid, etc.) were added. This complex of categories gave us a rich understanding of how parties are discussed in public today.

THE RESILIENT PARTY

Martin Wattenberg's *The Decline of American Political Parties* has been a key source for understanding the nature of partisanship in the latter twentieth century, and for good reason: He was the first scholar to track how parties have been treated in media coverage and to compare the resulting patterns to public opinion data. Using a different (and more diverse) cache of news coverage, we found that Wattenberg was largely correct when reporting that *party* references declined steadily between 1952 and 1980. But what about the last twenty years? As Figure 10.1 shows, things have changed. Parties are on something of an upswing in news coverage. Moreover, as Figure 10.2 reports, the ratio between candidate mentions and party mentions (one of Wattenberg's key concerns) has also leveled off, tempering the conclusion that candidate-centered campaigns have driven parties into the dust. As Figure 10.1 reports, it is *the candidates* who have been making the parties seem obsolete.

What can we learn from these data? For print news, at least, *party* references increased in the late 1970s, a time that Bartels calls "the nadir of party identification in the American public."[41] Why the resurgence? There are several possibilities. The decline of Jimmy Carter's presidency and the rise of Reagan Republicanism—a rise accompanied by the newly coined Reagan (blue-collar) Democrats—perhaps convinced the press that a new chapter was being written in U.S. politics. That story continued when power shifted in the Senate (in 1986) to the Democrats and then again in 1992 when they took control of the White House. The new face of partisanship morphed once

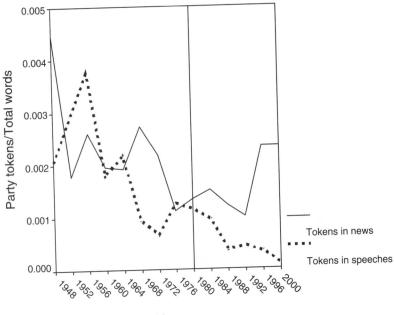

Figure 10.1 *Party* References Across Time. (Vertical axis at 1980 marks the endpoint of Wattenberg's [1996] content analyses of media coverage.)

again in 1994 when Newt Gingrich and colleagues rolled into the House of Representatives. All of these stories were partisan stories, and all were conflictual as well. The press may sometimes get bored with party labels, but they always love a good fight.

The story of 1980–2000 was an economic story as well, with financing campaigns becoming more and more expensive, thereby making the parties quite literal brokers. The story also has a series of subplots: the decline of the Old Democrats (Jimmy Carter versus the House Democrats) and the rise of divided government (Ronald Reagan and Tip O'Neill), followed by the era of the New Democrats. One could tell the history of American politics at the end of the twentieth century without discussing parties, but that would be an inadequate history indeed.

So what can one say about Wattenberg's notion of party decline? From the standpoint of news coverage, that thesis will have to be put on hold until the politics of the New Millennium becomes clearer. Surprisingly, though, the Wattenberg thesis holds quite well for political candidates. They have never been more beholden to the parties for fund-raising than they are at

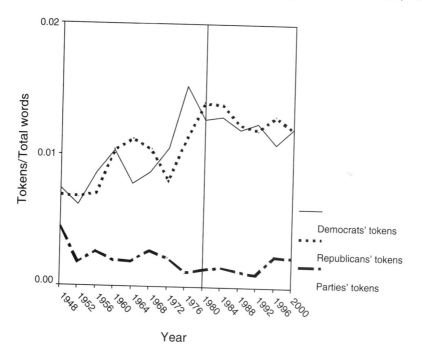

Figure 10.2 *Party* and Candidate References in News Reports. (Vertical axis at 1980 marks the endpoint of Wattenberg's [1996] content analyses of media coverage.)

present, but they have also never been less inclined to tip their hats in their direction. Research shows that candidates have even eschewed partisan language during convention acceptances, a daunting sort of ingratitude indeed![42]

The difference between the press and the candidates may simply be one of role: The tale of the 1980s and 1990s was one of changing party dynamics, and the press dutifully told that tale. Presidential candidates, in contrast, do not tell stories; they make them. They have also been laboring under a major constraint—voters' growing restiveness about the very concept of partisanship. John Anderson was part of that story in 1980, as was Ross Perot in 1992 and Ralph Nader in 2000. Their candidacies and the growing disinclination of voters to identify themselves as Democrats or Republicans may have caused the candidates to trim their sails. During this same time, the parties themselves were changing. They no longer gave out jobs for votes, as did the Democrats in Chicago's heyday, and the corporations no longer jumped when the Republican party told them to jump, in part because of a complex labor pattern in a world of multinationals, in part because so many corporate CEOs had been raised in the rambunctious 1960s, and in part because the high-tech sector had a new corporate sociology that was socially progressive and fiscally conservative. All of these forces, alone and collectively, have made candidates loath to discuss partisan issues. The press and the politicians—same world, different jobs.

THE EMPOWERED PARTY

When political professionals look at parties they ask these types of questions: Can the Republicans pass the budget they want? Is candidate Watson attractive enough to get statewide Democratic support? Will the president's party on Capitol Hill support his agenda? These are questions about power. When it comes to politics, the only things seemingly worth discussing in the newsroom—or in the cloakroom—are who can twist an arm and who cannot, who is in the arena and who is on the sidelines? Whenever parties are discussed, the question of power commands.

As Table 10.1 illustrates, parties are more likely to be treated as actors than as recipients of action (46.4 percent in speeches, 47.1 percent in news—see Potency variable), and that is especially true when politicians do the talking. Parties are also more likely to be constructed as elite entities than as instruments of the people (86.2 percent in speeches, 65.0 percent in news—see Position variable). And when parties are discussed, the past and the future inevitably give way to the present (speeches = 78.3 percent, news = 96.4 percent—see Time variable). Contrary to popular opinion, parties are treated as forces to be reckoned with, at least rhetorically. The death knell for parties may have been sounded too soon.

Admittedly, we are operating at the microtextual level here, paying attention to words immediately adjacent to *party* tokens. From a rhetorical viewpoint, these stylistic clusters are only part of the story. Ideas, arguments, evidence, and themes also affect how a message is interpreted. But sometimes these particularities can be important, especially when they cascade over an audience time and time again: "the two major parties," "a great political party," "it's never easy to throw a party out of the White House," "strong leadership of both parties," and "leaders of our party in Congress."

Celebrity, it has been said, substitutes for royalty in the United States, monarchialism being singularly inappropriate in a shirtsleeved democracy. In politics, that instinct results in a constant emphasis on party leadership. Said John Kennedy: "I think what counts are the men that the political parties put up, and I think party labels mean a good deal."[43] Twenty-four years later, Ronald Reagan tweaked his opponents in a similarly hierarchical way: "[W]hat has happened to the party of Harry Truman and Scoop Jackson? I was once a member of that party, and for a great part of my life, myself."[44] The modern reincarnation of Ronald Reagan—George W. Bush—liked this strategy so much he retrofitted it for the 2000 campaign: "Al Gore leads the

TABLE **10.1** Rhetorical Features of *Party* Tokens (in Percentages)

Variable	Usage	News Coverage	Candidate Speeches
Role	Part of the solution	26.4	39.1
	Part of the problem	22.9	20.3
	As conflicted	0.7	0.7
	Uncertain	50.0	39.9
Potency	Unclear	9.3	34.8
	As actor	47.1	46.4
	As recipient	43.6	18.8
Time	In present	96.4	78.3
	In past	3.6	19.6
	As potential	0	2.2
Valence	Identity	39.3	18.8
	Positive	16.4	31.9
	Negative	27.1	21.7
	Balanced	14.3	12.3
	Unclear	2.9	15.2
Associations	Same party	10.7	13.8
	Different party	10.0	28.3
	Politician of same party	32.9	15.2
	Politician of different party	1.4	4.3
	Voters/citizens	21.4	22.5
	Political interest group	0.7	0.7
	Other	18.5	8.6
	No other entity mentioned	4.3	6.5
Position	Elite	65.0	86.2
	Mass	17.1	2.9
	Global	17.9	10.9
Task	Mobilization	16.4	11.6
	Campaign	69.3	52.2
	Governing	7.1	22.5
	Mixed	7.2	13.7
Behavior	Intellectual body	12.9	12.3
	Acting body	33.6	16.7
	Feeling body	8.6	8.7
	Unclear	45.0	62.3
Qualities	Action	0.7	0.7
	Emotion	22.9	11.6
	Unity	32.9	21.7
	Ideology	1.4	3.6
	None	42.1	62.3

party of Franklin Delano Roosevelt—but the only thing he has to offer is fear itself."[45]

Experts have long debated whether the essence of a political party can be found in its connections to governmental operations, in its unique organizational dynamics, in its grassroots membership patterns, or in the men and women who lead them.[46] Our data clearly support the emphasis on leadership. In news coverage, parties are four times more likely to be depicted as elite operations than mass operations. This tendency is even stronger among the candidates, who refer to elites thirty times more often than the laity. Sometimes the rhetoric sounds triumphalist, but more often it is distinguished by its absence of lay markers. This is an odd finding, especially when one considers how frequently the heads of U.S. Steel or General Motors sing the praises of the American worker. There are no assembly lines in the Democratic party, however.

There are a few exceptions to these patterns. One occasionally finds reference to "party worker enthusiasm" or "the party faithful." But both reporters and politicians are members of the Beltway Club, so they tend to talk in the same clubby way. Richard Nixon was a card-carrying member of that club, and he was also diffident in the extreme. So when he referenced the hoi polloi it was a noteworthy moment:

- We ask you to work and vote for us, remembering you're working and voting not just for a man, not just for a party, but for what is best for America.[47]

- Go out and not just vote, but work as you never have before, remembering that you're working not just for a man, not just for a party, but that you're working for America and for the cause of peace and freedom for all mankind.[48]

- Carry it for the Senate, carry it for the governorship, carry it for the Congress, remembering that you're working not just for a party, but for what is best for America and all the world.[49]

- Missouri is always a close state, and it's going to take a lot of work to win it, but it can be won if you work not just for our party, and not just for a man.[50]

Richard Nixon the populist? Bill Clinton was a far more natural populist, but even he talked about parties in elite ways. On election eve in 1996, outside the Merrimack Restaurant in Manchester, New Hampshire, surrounded by the hundreds of loyalists who dogged his every step in the campaign, even in this most proletarian of settings, Clinton had only stars in his eyes:

I was so happy and proud when I stood here on this stage this morning and I listened to [congressional candidates] Arnie and Joe and Dick and [Governor] Jeanne Shaheen talk about what they wanted to do and why they were running and what they represented. And I heard, I guess it was Joe who said [Senator] Warren Rudman said that the Democrats had become the moderate party. I think the Democrats have become the modern party as well, the party of the future. America has always needed at times of great changes in how we work and live and relate to each other and the rest of the world a modern moderate party, a common sense but vital, vigorous centrist party moving this country forward. That's what you see on this stage [this morning].[51]

Glorious speaker though he was, there is a danger in Clinton's remarks. Imagine how different the speech would have sounded if he had profiled some of the campaign workers in the crowd, a few of the thousand young faces who had duplicated flyers for him or brought coffee to him or written op-eds for him or driven him from Dover to Durham to Danbury. From the party's perspective, Clinton's is a rhetoric of proclamation, not a rhetoric of recruitment. Such a rhetoric can be energetic (Clinton's was surely that), and it can make potential followers see themselves in partisan terms (as Bartels and Wattenberg might suggest).[52] But an elite rhetoric can also be distancing, and that can hurt a party. Sensing that, the Republicans used a grassroots approach during the 2002 midterm elections, a comparatively new plan for them. If that strategy works, both parties may begin to shift the power trajectories noted here.

THE NONPARTISAN PARTY

As mentioned earlier, one of the major challenges political parties face in the United States at the turn of the century is the challenge of recruitment, a problem exacerbated by the image of parties as rigidly ideological, goose-stepping to a march now out of date. Young people, especially, are turned off by groups unwilling to respond to new realities or to experiment with fresh ways of solving problems. The parties must answer such charges. A key-word now rising in popularity, *the Independent,* offers to save young voters from political orthodoxy. But here is an ironic fact: Our data do *not* show that the press and the political establishment emphasize partisanship. The parties have their problems, but, rhetorically at least, they are not problems of their own making.

As revealed in Table 10.1, neither the intellectual (12.3 percent for candidates, 12.9 percent for news—see Behavior variable) nor ideological (3.6 percent for candidates, 1.4 percent for news—see Qualities variable) aspects of the parties are emphasized. Parties are also more likely to be depicted as part of the solution (39.1 percent for candidates, 26.4 percent for news—see Role variable) than as part of the problem (20.3 percent for candidates, 22.9 percent for the news). In addition, they are placed in negative Contexts far less often by the press (only 27.1 percent) than one might have expected in the "only good news is bad news" era. The candidates also stress the positive more than the negative (31.9 percent versus 21.7 percent—see Valence variable). Naturally, these are only linguistic data. The parties do other things to get themselves in trouble—raising obscene amounts of money and picking sorry candidates, for example. But our findings show that their speech is less doctrinaire than one might have suspected.

We want to be careful to stress here that the "anti-partisan" tone appears *when parties themselves are the object of attention.* Without question, the mass media like a good brawl, but they tend to emphasize interpersonal rather than systemic conflict. For example, the following story appeared in the *Los Angeles Times* in 1948 and featured then-Governor Earl Warren (the future Supreme Court Justice). To modern ears, Governor Warren's remarks will seem unusually generous, even antique. After all, Warren ran for governor on both the Democratic and Republican ballots in California, so one could assume he would pull his punches. Although Warren's case may not be typical, we found no real changes in partisanship over time. Said the *Los Angeles Times*:

> Warren touched upon the growth of political parties in this country as vehicles of expression for the people. People from all walks of life can be found in both major parties, he said. "In both parties there are those who would say that all good flows from their own party and all political evil from the other," Warren continued. "But the vast majority of Americans know that this is not true. They know that good Americans are to be found in both parties. They realize there are progressives and conservatives in the ranks of both. No party has a patent on progress, a copyright on governmental principles or a proprietary interest in the advances made. . . . I believe that our best chance of preserving responsible government under the two party system depends upon how wholesome our campaign can be, how free they are from the prejudice of party, class or race, and upon the extent to which we can unify rather than divide our people."[53]

Warren is both thoughtful and balanced here. Because he is dealing with genuinely fundamental issues, there is a courtliness to his remarks and a system affirmation as well. Things are different when the press focuses on *individuals.* Unlike the Warren quotation, the following passages will be depressingly familiar to modern readers, containing as they do all of the partisan-sniping exempted from the *party*-centered news just discussed:

- *1984:* "House Speaker Thomas P. (Tip) O'Neill Jr. (D-Mass.) this week criticized Reagan for visiting campuses across the country and spreading a gospel of selfishness."[54]
- *1988:* Several Democrats charged that Vice President Bush, the Republican Presidential nominee who in President Reagan's first term was head of a drug task force aimed at blocking drug smuggling at the borders, failed in his role.[55]
- *1992:* Defense Secretary Dick Cheney, once a fiercely partisan GOP congressman, now turns political questions away with a wry smile.[56]
- *1996:* "The United States has a negative net worth," Perot said. "The blame must be shared by Democrats and Republicans alike."[57]

- *2000:* This week, the Republicans were trumpeting the governor's new slogan, "Real plans for real people," and the Democrats were replying with the taunt, "George Bush's real plans hurt real people."[58]

By transferring ideology to political actors, the news insulates the party system itself. Naturally, such personalizing strategies can cause voters to reject the candidates as well as the parties they represent. But as media scholars contend, personalization often exempts larger social structures from coming under attack. That can be both good and bad.[59] By locating ideology in actors—who can be voted out of office—rather than within the party system, the media may contribute to what Denis McQuail calls their most powerful effect: protection of the status quo.[60]

If the press is system preservative, political candidates are even more so. We found they tended not to make an issue of party affiliation. That is an irony since so many of our data derived from hotly contested elections. But campaigns present a dilemma to candidates: Stress your opponent's group connections to mobilize your own partisans but, in so doing, depict yourself as narrow-minded to those you hope will cross over. Stressing partisanship can also make a candidate seem desperate, which may be why research shows that the more optimistic candidate usually wins the race in the United States.[61] And so new mantras have developed in American politics, ones that voters may not fully believe but which they like hearing nonetheless: "Cross party lines," "this party will not create divisions," "put aside partisan feelings," and "put progress ahead of partisanship."

For James Madison, faction was the greatest danger to the young American polity, and his fear is still the nation's fear. It was not Lyndon Johnson's greatest fear (he reserved that for being bored) but it was high on his list. As a result, he parsed his words with supreme care:

> President Hoover was a Republican. I am a Democrat. But his hopes for America and my hopes for America, his hopes for humanity and my hopes for humanity are not partisan. . . . Now, in this campaign, you will have a decision to make. Two weeks from yesterday you will go and select your leaders for this country and the leaders for the free world for the next 4 years. You have two issues that stand out: Shall we continue the foreign policy of bipartisanship, where Senator Arthur Vandenberg, a Republican, worked with President Truman, a Democrat, to stop the Communists in Greece and Turkey? Shall we follow the bipartisan policy of President Dwight D. Eisenhower, who worked with Lyndon Johnson, a Democratic leader of the Senate, in the crisis in the Strait of Formosa, when our country was united and we put our country ahead of our party? Shall we follow the policies of Senator Dirksen and Senator Hickenlooper, who worked with John Fitzgerald Kennedy in the Cuban missile crisis and in the test ban treaty? Or shall we go off on another adventure to fly to evils that we know not of on a very dangerous course?[62]

There are, to be sure, many examples in our dataset of candidates blasting their opponent's party. Too, because we focused on general elections rather than primaries, we may have been spared the rankest instances of partisan-ship. But our data were fairly consistent across time, and that suggests that presidential politics is more generous than many would have guessed. The American people have never loved parties, in part because they are cabalis-tic and in part because they are run by elites. But the two-party system is also a prized American icon. That may explain why candidates and the press have treated it so carefully. The fact that campaign rhetoric more often attacks individual candidates than party structures may be too fine a dis-tinction for some observers, given how ugly American politics can become. We feel, however, it is a distinction of some importance, both politically and culturally.

THE ENDURING PARTY

As numerous observers tell us, the news requires drama. According to Lance Bennett, they generate such qualities in three ways: by personalizing things (i.e., giving preference to individual actors rather than ideas or social sys-tems); by violating expectations (e.g., featuring unlikely occurrences); and by making things seem fragmented (when, for example, they lift actors out of context and put them in unstable situations).[63] This makes the news inter-esting but, for Bennett, it also trivializes politics and robs it of its institutional character. It also makes voters think less critically about their political options.

Using Bennett's criteria, parties may not seem very useful to the news since they feature groups rather than individuals,[64] stability rather than change,[65] cooperation instead of competition,[66] and loyalty versus insurrec-tion.[67] How boring. But consider what an establishmentarian force (like a party) looks like when bumping up against something brash and dynamic (like a political candidate). It looks like the-man-against-the-machine, a clas-sic tale (one thinks of Willy Loman) that works well in the theater as well as in the newspapers. It also works well for dramatizing parties. In the 1960s that story focused on party apparatus: Could it adapt to new political reali-ties? Later, the story reversed itself: Could the candidate woo a changing constituency? In both cases the party's durability was emphasized. That durability becomes a foil for the forces of change in the news narrative.

The classic example occurred in 1968 when the Democratic party was going through extraordinary upheaval, as a ragtag collection of activists threatened the party's grey beards and when a charismatic malcontent, Sen-ator Eugene McCarthy, played the party spoiler. The story of the 1968 cam-paign was a story of institutional solidarity in the face of massive social change. Poor Hubert Humphrey was caught in the middle. The difficulty of Humphrey's situation can be seen in the following news excerpt, a story that appeared on October 28, just eight days before the fall election:

Sen. Eugene J. McCarthy (D) of Minnesota was quoted in a Washington dispatch to the *London Times* as saying he will announce his support for Vice President Hubert H. Humphrey in California next Wednesday.

Louis Heren, Washington correspondent of the *Times,* reported: "Late, but certainly better late than never, the Democratic Party will go to the polls on Nov. 5 more or less united." Mr. Heren said he learned of Senator McCarthy's decision to back Mr. Humphrey for president from the Senator himself on the night of Oct. 24. He said Senator McCarthy "remains unenthusiastic about the Vice President's candidacy but has finally decided that he cannot avoid making a choice." In an introduction to Mr. Heren's story, the *Times* said:

Together with President Johnson's decision to exert his influence with the conservative wing by campaigning on Mr. Humphrey's behalf, this suggests that much of the Democratic Party is at last rallying behind its candidate. The McCarthy decision is expected to narrow, if not close, the gap between Mr. Humphrey and Mr. Richard Nixon, the Republican candidate," the *Times* said.[68]

The scene shifted in the 1970s. Democratic constituencies continued to morph, and the Republicans were challenged internally as well. If the question in 1968 was whether the candidate could stomach the party, the story in 1976 was just the opposite:

The latest survey indicated that both Carter and Ford were having problems holding on to the support of their own parties. Carter's support among Democrats has declined 11% in the last month. Ford has slipped 8% among Republicans. Meanwhile, the number of undecided Democrats has nearly doubled, to 17% from 9%. The number of undecided Republicans also has risen, but less dramatically, to 12% from 10%. In a normal election, voters become increasingly committed to a candidate as balloting nears.[69]

The pot continued to boil. By 1992 both the Republicans and the Democrats had changed considerably. The Democrats had gotten more ethnic and more feminine, the Republicans richer and more religious. Both parties confronted internal strife and, as before, the candidates had to dance nimbly— they were good loyalists but they were not marionettes. The *New York Times* even had to mix metaphors to capture Bill Clinton's approach: "Clinton Pursues Party Sweep Without Whispering a Hint." The news text explained Clinton's dilemma:

Something is conspicuously missing from Bill Clinton's speeches in these concluding weeks of the 1996 campaign. As much as he wants his party to recapture control of the Senate and House of Representatives on Nov. 5, he is careful to avoid explicitly partisan appeals. "Voters are suspicious of partisanship," a Presidential aide said. "So he is not going to go out there and ask them to give him a Democratic Congress so he can push through a Democratic program. You can't throw it in people's faces that way, at least in his view, or you'll remind a lot of them that they'd rather not see a concentration of power in one party's hands. The degree to which we succeed in this is the degree to which we don't push the issue too hard."[70]

Clinton's situation shows that parties are still a problem. They are stolid. That is their glory and that is their curse. It is also their news peg. The mass media keep telling that story, a story of individual candidates facing a structuralist dilemma: Become part of the organization but do not become absorbed by it. That dilemma provides efficient plot lines for the media even while placing tremendous pressure on candidates and parties alike.

Parties are politics writ small. They have the characteristics of all groupings—internal squabbling, leadership challenges, a search for focus. That makes them attractive to the press. A party is something you can get your hands around. But party news is too often shallow and, as we have seen here, too often personalistic. One would hope for more. Parties have been, after all, central to democratic life. They have been useful in organizing elections and providing deliberative space for committed partisans. To reduce them to their corporate and strategic dynamics is to diminish what they are and what they might become. Having said that, a careful study of the news text shows that the two-party system abides. Its endurance gives American politics a needed sense of continuity and voters at least two points of political orientation. Parties are imperfect and the news is imperfect, but together they tell a useful story.

CONCLUSION

This chapter confirms some expectations about party dynamics in the United States and it challenges others. The term *party* is not discussed as often as it once was, but it is still treated with deference—by candidates as well as the media. Our data show a consistently empowered entity, one that endures. At the same time, many have stripped parties of their ideological natures, and that has turned them into mere organizations. That approach has two effects: (1) It lets candidates reach beyond party boundaries to attract Independents and nonaligned voters (thereby creating the Age of the Republicrat), and (2) it lets the press turn a political story into a social story, thereby increasing its dramatistic reach.

Historically, party labels have proved useful as "cognitive shortcuts" for voters and they have helped journalists organize the political world. Anything that is two-dimensional, after all, is useful to the news text: The American League needs the National League as Israel needs Palestine and as Hertz needs Avis. Binaries are a stock source of conflict, and they help simplify things. As we have seen here, however, the party dialectic has shifted from one of identity (Can the party find a candidate?) to one of division (Can the candidate accept the party?). Today, parties are the constant and candidates are the variable.

There has been a resurgence of the party story since 1980. This may be because of simple political determinacies since the parties have been challenged by internal divisions in recent years. There are other forces at work as well: The money being raised for candidates is party money and even the much-heralded political action committees are, in essence, party satellite operations. The parties have also been a good source of plot lines because of concerns about the rising Independent. For all of these reasons, party news is good news for the press.

The situation is somewhat different for candidates, who increasingly run away from party labels. They have always done so in the general election, but even primaries have become problematic. In the summer of 2003, for example, Howard Dean traveled about the United States accompanied by eight other Democratic candidates for president. But Dean was the only one who called people back to the "real" Democratic party. His colleagues stressed issues, not identity, an approach that was in keeping with the political orthodoxy of the last twenty-five years.

Will parties survive? Some doubt they will. Americans, after all, are no longer a nation of joiners or, at least, they no longer join the kinds of organizations their parents and grandparents once joined. They are, instead, information addicts. They live in an age when all that is known to humankind can be had with a Google search. Do such people need guidance from political parties? Is not a party label a sign that one cannot think for onself? Not surprisingly, political professionals scoff at these questions, noting that "power collects" in the United States and it has always collected. There *will* be groups, they *will* be organized, and they *will* have power. Parties will persist, the professionals argue, because politics persists.

Our data show that the death of the parties has been prematurely announced. Parties are less a symbolic resource for candidates than they once were, but they are still treated gingerly, and gingerliness is a sign of respect. The parties are more useful to the media, for both intellectual and rhetorical reasons, and that bodes well for their continued visibility. In both quantitative and qualitative ways, then, we find there is still life in the *party*.

NOTES

1. T. Jefferson, "Letter to Francis Hopkinson, March 13, 1789," in *The Writings of Thomas Jefferson*, vol. 7, ed. Andrew A. Lipscomb and Albert Ellery Bergh (Washington, DC: Issued under the auspices of the Thomas Jefferson memorial association, 1903–04), 300.

2. T. Jefferson, "Letter to Henry Lee, August 10, 1824," in *The Writings of Thomas Jefferson*, vol. 16, ed. Andrew A. Lipscomb and Albert Ellery Bergh (Washington, DC: Issued under the auspices of the Thomas Jefferson memorial association, 1903–04), 73.

3. G. R. Orren, "The Changing Styles of American Party Politics," in *The Future of American Political Parties: The Challenge of Governance*, ed. J. L. Fleishman (Englewood Cliffs, NJ: Prentice Hall, 1982), 4–5.

4. Ibid, 5.

5. S. Frantzich, *Political Parties in the Technological Age* (New York: Longman, 1989), 8.

6. J. Aldrich, *Why Parties? The Origin and Transformation of Party Politics in America* (Chicago: University of Chicago Press, 1995); and E. E. Schattschneider, *Party Government* (New York: Holt, Rinehart and Winston, 1942), 1.

7. R. Hofstadter, *The Idea of a Party System: The Rise of Legitimate Opposition in the United States, 1780–1840* (Berkeley: University of California Press, 1972).

8. K. Janda, *Political Parties: A Cross-National Survey* (New York: The Free Press, 1980).

9. See Schattschneider, *Party Government*; A. Downs, *An Economic Theory of Democracy* (New York: Harper, 1957); J. A. Schlesinger, "The New American Political Party," *American Political Science Review,* 79 (1985): 1152; F. Sorauf and P. A. Beck, *Party Politics in America,* 6th ed. (Glenview, IL: Scott, Foresman and Company, 1988).

10. A. Campbell, P. E. Converse, W. E. Miller, and D. E. Stokes, *The American Voter* (New York: Wiley, 1960), 120; S. Popkin, *The Reasoning Voter* (Chicago: University of Chicago Press, 1991), 14.

11. D. W. Brady, *Critical Elections and Congressional Policy Making* (Stanford, CA: Stanford University Press, 1988); G. M. Pomper, *Passions and Interests: Political Party Concepts of American Democracy* (Lawrence: University of Kansas Press, 1992).

12. N. Polsby, *Consequences of Party Reform* (Oxford: Oxford University Press, 1983); S. L. Maisel (ed.), *The Parties Respond: Changes in the American Parties and Campaigns,* 3d ed. (Boulder, CO: Westview Press, 1998).

13. W. D. Burnham, "The Changing Shape of the American Political Universe," *The American Political Science Review,* 59 (1965): 27.

14. J. Linz and A. Stepan, *Problems of Democratic Transition and Consolidation* (Baltimore: Johns Hopkins University Press, 1996); P. Schmitter and T. Karl, "What Democracy Is . . . and Is Not," in *The Global Resurgency of Democracy,* 2d ed., ed. L. Diamond and M. Plattner (Baltimore: Johns Hopkins University Press, 1996), 49–62.

15. J. Dennis, "Trends in Public Support for the American Party System," *British Journal of Political Science,* 5 (1975): 230.

16. J. F. Bibby, "In Defense of the Two-Party System," in *Multiparty Politics in America,* ed. P. S. Herrnson and J. C. Green (Lanham, MD: Rowman & Littlefield, 1997), 73–74.

17. L. Bartels, "Partisanship and Voting Behavior, 1952–1996," *American Journal of Political Science,* 44 (2000): 35, 44.

18. K. Phillips, *Mediacracy: American Parties and Politics in the Communications Age* (Garden City, NY: Doubleday, 1975).

19. M. Robinson and M. Sheehan, *Over the Wire and on TV: CBS and UPI in Campaign '80* (New York: Russell Sage Foundation, 1983).

20. T. E. Patterson, *Out of Order* (New York: Vintage Books, Random House, 1984), 227.

21. T. E. Patterson, "Bad News, Period," *PS: Political Science and Politics,* 29 (1996): 17.

22. M. Wattenberg, *The Decline of American Political Parties, 1952–1996* (Cambridge: Harvard University Press, 1998), 93. Specifically, Wattenberg asks: "[A]re political parties in fact now receiving less coverage in election reporting, compared to candidates, than in the past?" (92). He tests this hypothesis "on a limited basis" by examining the content of election coverage between 1952 and 1980 in two major metropolitan newspapers (*Chicago Tribune* and *Washington Post*) and three national weekly magazines (*Newsweek, Time,* and *U.S. News and World Report*). His research team examined articles between September and October for each of these years; their charge was to "count the number of times political parties were mentioned by name

in the stories and headlines compared to presidential candidates. In addition, on a more subjective level, coders were instructed to look for and count the number of substantive linkages between parties and candidates in the content of the stories" (92). They found that "the number of instances in which parties were mentioned by name in the stories fell precipitously" (93) and the ratio of candidate mentions to party mentions "increased from about two to one in the 1950s to roughly five to one by 1980" (93).

23. J. Byrd, "Giving People What They Deserve: Why Cover Minor Political Parties?" *Media Studies Journal,* 12 (1998): 26.

24. D. Francis, "Muzzling the Minority Voice in Quebec," *Macleans,* 109 (1996): 13.

25. I. Ward, "'Media Intrusion' and the Changing Nature of the Established Parties in Australia and Canada," *Canadian Journal of Political Science,* 26 (1993): 478.

26. M. Wattenberg, *The Rise of Candidate-Centered Politics: Presidential Elections of the 1980s* (Cambridge: Harvard University Press, 1991).

27. Ibid., x, 89.

28. R. B. Rapoport, "Partisanship Change in a Candidate-Centered Era," *Journal of Politics,* 59 (1997): 185.

29. G. S. Pastor, W. J. Stone, and R. B. Rapoport, "Candidate-Centered Sources of Party Change: The Case of Pat Robertson," *Journal of Politics* 61 (1999): 423.

30. K. D. Patterson, A. A. Bice, and E. Pipkin, "Political Parties, Candidates, and Presidential Campaigns: 1952–1996," *Presidential Studies Quarterly,* 29 (1999): 26.

31. L. S. Maisel, "The Platform Writing Process: Candidate-Centered Platforms in 1992," *Political Science Quarterly,* 108 (1992): 671.

32. M. McCubbins, "Party Decline and Presidential Campaigns in the Television Age," in *Under the Watchful Eye: Managing Presidential Campaigns in the Television Era,* ed. M. McCubbins (Washington, DC: Congressional Quarterly, 1992), 30.

33. Specifically, to draw this sample, we did the following: First, we stratified on speaker to accommodate a mixture of statements by Democratic and Republican nominees (although, because there were only 17 instances of *party* in the 1988 campaign, our sample for speeches is 342). Second, we further stratified on newspaper type to ensure a mixture of news outlets in the press coverage data. Some of the methods used and data reported in this chapter were originally presented in S. Jarvis, "The Talk of the Party: Partisanship in American Political Discourse, 1948–1996," unpublished Ph.D. dissertation, University of Texas at Austin, 2000.

34. D. Broder, *The Party's Over* (New York: Harper and Row, 1972); Schlesinger, "The New American Political Party," 1152.

35. G. M. Pomper, "The Alleged Decline of American Parties," in *Politicians and Party Politics,* ed. J. Geer (Baltimore: John Hopkins Press, 1998), 14–39; V. O. Key, Jr., *Politics, Parties and Pressure Groups* (New York: Crowell, 1946).

36. W. D. Burnham, *Critical Elections and the Mainsprings of American Politics* (New York: Norton, 1970); W. N. Chambers and W. D. Burnham, *The American Party Systems: Stages of Political Development* (New York: Oxford University Press, 1975), v.

37. Key, *Politics.*

38. Wattenberg, *Decline.*

39. Key, *Politics.*

40. M. Ostrogorski, *Democracy and the Organization of Political Parties,* ed. S. M. Lipset (New York: Doubleday Anchor, 1902/1964).

41. L. Bartels, "Partisanship and Voting Behavior, 1952–1996," *American Journal of Political Science,* 44 (2000): 36.

42. Wattenberg, *Decline,* 221, 222.

43. J. Kennedy, "Campaign Speech," Indianapolis, IN, October 4, 1960, *Annenberg/Pew Archive of Presidential Discourse,* CD-ROM (Philadelphia: Annenberg School for Communication, 2000).

44. R. Reagan, "Campaign Speech to Congregation of Temple Hillel," Valley Stream, NY, October 26, 1984, *Annenberg/Pew Archive of Presidential Discourse,* CD-ROM (Philadelphia: Annenberg School for Communication, 2000).

45. G. W. Bush, "Campaign Speech to Rising Generation Visioneering Incorporated," MI, October 19, 2000, in *In Their Own Words: Sourcebook 2000,* CD-ROM (Stanford, CA: Political Communication Lab, 2000).

46. For a discussion of where party might reside, see V. O. Key, Jr., *Politics, Parties and Pressure Groups* (New York: Crowell, 1946); F. Sorauf and P. A. Beck, *Party Politics in America,* 6th ed. (Glenview, IL: Scott, Foresman and Company, 1988); G. M. Pomper, *Passions and Interests: Political Party Concepts of American Democracy* (Lawrence: University of Kansas Press, 1992).

47. R. Nixon, "General Speeches, Speech 5," Vancouver, WA, September 13, 1960, *Annenberg/Pew Archive of Presidential Discourse,* CD-ROM (Philadelphia: Annenberg School for Communication, 2000).

48. R. Nixon, "General Speeches," Long Island, NY, September 28, 1960, *Annenberg/Pew Archive of Presidential Discourse,* CD-ROM (Philadelphia: Annenberg School for Communication, 2000).

49. R. Nixon, "General Speeches," Charleston, WV, September 27, 1960, *Annenberg/Pew Archive of Presidential Discourse,* CD-ROM (Philadelphia: Annenberg School for Communication, 2000).

50. R. Nixon, "General Speeches," Springfield, MO, September 21, 1960, *Annenberg/Pew Archive of Presidential Discourse,* CD-ROM (Philadelphia: Annenberg School for Communication, 2000).

51. W. J. Clinton, "Campaign Speech Outside the Merrimack Restaurant," Manchester, NH, November 4, 1996, *Annenberg/Pew Archive of Presidential Discourse,* CD-ROM (Philadelphia: Annenberg School for Communication, 2000).

52. See Bartels, "Partisanship," 44; Wattenberg, *Decline,* 4.

53. "Warren Calls for Unity in Major Utah Address," *Los Angeles Times,* September 17, 1948, A1.

54. "Conservatism on Upswing Among College Students," *Christian Science Monitor,* November 1, 1984, A1.

55. "Democrats Criticize Bush's Role as the House Takes Up Drug Bill," *New York Times,* September 8, 1988, A25.

56. "Back at the White House, Most Eyes Are on Arkansas," *Los Angeles Times,* September 5, 1992, A1.

57. "Debate 'Confused,' Perot Says," *Washington Post,* October 7, 1996, A6.

58. "With Its Independent Streak, Wisconsin Remains a Tossup," *New York Times,* September 22, 2000, A19.

59. S. Hall, *The Hard Road to Renewal: Thatcherism and the Crisis of the Left* (London: Verso, 1988).

60. D. McQuail, *McQuail's Mass Communication Theory,* 4th ed. (London: Sage Publications, 2000).

61. R. P. Hart, *Campaign Talk: Why Elections Are Good for Us* (Princeton, NJ: Princeton University Press, 2000).

62. L. B. Johnson, "Campaign Speech," Belleville, IL, October 21, 1964, *Annenberg/Pew Archive of Presidential Discourse,* CD-ROM (Philadelphia: Annenberg School for Communication, 2000).

63. W. L. Bennett, *News: The Politics of Illusion*, 2d ed. (New York: Longman, 1988).

64. Schlesinger, "The New American Political Party," 1153.

65. Downs, *Economic Theory of Democracy*, 25.

66. J. Schumpeter, *Capitalism, Socialism and Democracy* (New York: Harper and Row, 1942), 283.

67. Chambers and Burnham, *The American Party Systems*, 5.

68. "McCarthy Quoted as Set to Support Humphrey," AP-UPI wire story, October 28, 1968.

69. "Poll Finds Growing Voter Confusion," *Los Angeles Times*, October 18, 1976, A1.

70. "Clinton Pursues Party Sweep Without Whispering a Hint," *New York Times*, October 23, 1996, A1.

11

The *Promise*
Imagining the Future Together

With Felicity McKevitt

W hen running for president in 1988, George Herbert Walker Bush had one of the spiffiest résumés of any candidate in the twentieth century. Born the son of a U.S. senator, Bush was a student leader at the prestigious Phillips Academy in Andover, Massachusetts; one of the youngest pilots in the Navy during World War II; and recognized for bravery after being shot down by Japanese aircraft. After the war, Bush was inducted into Phi Beta Kappa at Yale University, held several appointed posts (ambassador to the United Nations, chairman of the Republican National Committee, chief of the U.S. Liaison Office in the People's Republic of China, and director of the Central Intelligence Agency), and was twice elected vice president under Ronald Reagan. Impressive as his qualifications were, they were not the talk of the 1988 presidential campaign. That distinction went to a single line from his speech at the Republican National Convention when he told the American people this: "Read my lips: No new taxes."[1]

When delivering his speech, Bush was behind in the polls and needed a post-convention bounce. He got one. His carefully crafted phrase became the most versatile locution of the campaign: Bush repeated it constantly on the stump, as did his opponent (derisively, to be sure); print and broadcast journalists also used it as a news peg for their economic coverage during the campaign. The phrase had legs even after the election. It was resuscitated by the press in 1990 when then-President Bush signed legislation increasing taxes by $164 billion over five years, and it also became a mantra for the Democratic party during the 1992, 1996, and 2000 campaigns.

What made this phrase so memorable? Why did it have so many different uses? Why did it become a sorry signpost along an otherwise distinguished career path? The answer: Bush made a promise, and people remember such things. The late New York City mayor Fiorello LaGuardia recognized that when musing that "the first task of a statesman is to disappoint supporters and break campaign promises." A half-century later, voters still believe LaGuardia—that candidates will say or do anything to get elected. That belief, coupled with an avalanche of attack ads, strategy-centered campaign coverage, government scandals, and talk-show rantings, have made the American people distrustful of public officials.

It is commonly thought that politicians make promises all the time. But is that true? Others assume that after Bush's mistake, no other candidate would follow in his footsteps. Is that true? Still others say that those who distrust promises and those who appreciate them cannot possibly be the same people. Is that true? Here, we examine over fifty years of campaign rhetoric (1948–2000) to see what promises sound like. Keying on the linguistic token *promise* and its variations, we look at the obvious and nonobvious ways in which politicians have made commitments to the electorate. Our approach is necessarily blunt and cannot possibly capture all the ways candidates make commitments. (It is noteworthy, for example, that our technique would not have caught the infamous "read my lips" statement since it did not include the *promise* token). Still, we found 619 promises in the 550 speeches we inspected, a bit more than one promise per outing.

Promises have not disappeared over the years and so we must ask why. Are promises an addiction worse than cocaine, a substance without which politicians cannot soar to the heights? Or are promises instigated by the press, with their demands for a new scoop each day? Do voters themselves require some Grand New Vision every four years that will make their lives tolerable? Perhaps American culture is to blame. The old Puritan vision of the United States as a "shining city on a hill" seems to have set Americans on that course, so perhaps their history is their future. It is worth remembering, for example, that that old Puritan vision was one of Ronald Reagan's favorites, an image he used to support his economic, domestic, international, and even environmental agendas.[2] And so we ask: If nobody likes promises, why do politicians keep making them?

UNDERSTANDING PROMISES

Campaign promises are part of the electoral landscape. They pop up with the regularity of bluebonnets in the Texas hill country. Promises are offered in the meetings of neighborhood associations and in congressional races alike, sometimes memorably but often in supremely mundane ways. As common as promises are, we know comparatively little about them. A handful of scholars has studied them, and this is one of their more surprising findings: Presidents usually work to fulfill their promises. Gerald Pomper's analysis of party platforms shows that to be true for most chief executives.[3] When such promises were not fulfilled, says Pomper, it was because of clashes with Congress, conflicts with higher-priority items, or changes on the domestic or international scene.

Using a variety of research techniques, other scholars have followed Pomper's lead. Michael Krukones studied the in-office behavior of eleven presidents, Jeff Fishel examined chief executives in the 1960s through 1980s, and Carolyn Shaw did an in-depth study of Bill Clinton's 1992 campaign promises.[4] All found the same thing: Politicians generally try to keep their promises. Peter Kinberg reports that that was especially true of pledges based on party platforms.[5] Still other scholars found that politicians avoided making promises when trouble loomed on the horizon. That is, when tempted to make promises that would be difficult to fulfill (e.g., universal health care after the 1992 Clinton debacle), candidates backed off.[6] Political promises may not be the indiscriminate things some think them to be.

How do the media treat politicians' promises? They often distort them. In one study focusing on tax issues, for instance, it was found that journalists ignored promissory details in a mad rush to report that a specific promise had been made.[7] A similar conclusion was advanced by Kathleen Hall Jamieson and her colleagues.[8] They found that journalists habitually separated politicians' claims from the evidence supporting them, making citizens think that empty promises had been made when, in fact, they had been backed up rather well. Such techniques, the researchers report, lead to an underinformed public.

In another study, Thomas Patterson concluded that "the press makes [fatuous promises] appear to be the norm."[9] Even though most campaign pledges are fairly sincere, he notes, the press frames them as strategic tools needed to win an election rather than as policy tools to guide the nation. Broken promises, or compromises between the president and Congress, received far more attention than earnest attempts to fulfill campaign pledges, Patterson reports. Such news coverage typically implies that personal factors (e.g., a politician's motives) overrode their institutional obligations. The story of the untrustworthy politician, says Patterson, is simpler and more appealing than one of Constitutional checks and balances.

While helpful, these studies do not tell us what promises sound like. It is the sound of promises, we argue, that embodies their strengths and weaknesses. To get a better understanding of them we ask a series of basic questions: (1) When are the American people most likely to hear campaign promises? (2) What sorts of candidates—challengers or incumbents, Democrats or Republicans, winners or losers—are most likely to make them? (3) What makes a promise sound like a promise rather than, say, like a declaration or a prediction? (4) How reasonable are the promises politicians make?

In answering these questions, we rely on what has come to be known as speech act theory. A speech act is the basic unit of language containing meaning. A sentence is often thought to be the elementary speech act, but it can also be embodied in a word or phrase as long as it follows the rules for accomplishing the implied action. So, for example, "I do" typically gets one married, but responding to the preacher's question with "It's O.K. with me" would be sufficient *if it met society's requirement for the act of marrying.* Speech act theory focuses not so much on what is said but on what is done when something is said. It has been used to examine the implicit bargains made in marital and family settings, the ways immigrants learn to fit in to a new culture, how children discover what it means to sound "grown up," the strategies for making a story sound real rather than fictional, and how people become assimilated into business routines.[10]

We are interested in such performative actions here. As J. L. Austin wrote, "When I say 'I promise,' a new plunge is taken: I have not merely announced my intention, but, by using this formula (performing ritual), I have bound myself to others and staked my reputation in a new way."[11] For Austin, when a political candidate says, "I pledge to cut your taxes," the candidate is doing as well as saying. Voters usually understand both sets of messages because they have learned their culture's performative rules for promises. In contrast, a candidate who claims that taxes have gotten too high is merely "observing" or "surmising." For complex reasons, we view such speech acts as less consequential than the act of "promising."

John Searle has identified several ways in which promising is more than vocalizing. He states that when speakers make promises, they imply that (1) they intend to accomplish some future action, (2) they assume they have the hearer's approbation to do so, (3) they would not do so in the normal course of events, (4) they will make every effort to follow through on their promises, and (5) they recognize that the hearer holds them responsible.[12] Because of the promises contained within promises, Searle says, they have practical, moral, and political dimensions and therefore catch our attention.

Guided by these assumptions, we set out to analyze the political promises made during the last fourteen presidential elections. All speeches in the Campaign Mapping Project's textbase were searched for promissory tokens, resulting in 619 snippets for analysis.[13] Given our concern for speech act theory, we concentrated on promissory tokens that assumed actional ("I promise") versus nominal ("these promises") status in the sentence. Such tokens were identified by a keyword-in-context program that isolated the twenty words preceding and following the target phrase, thereby letting us capture the sense in which a word was being used.

In terms of basic information, we noted the speaker's party (Democrat, Republican), his incumbent status (challenger, current office-holder), and the outcome of the race (winner, loser). To get a better sense of how the tokens functioned, we examined the promise's locus (self- or other-centered), its tone (positive or negative), and its emphasis (i.e., was it a values-based promise or a policy promise?). We also catalogued the promise's complexity (how much background knowledge did it require of a hearer?) by noting whether it was framed in personal, collective, castigatory, or substantial ways.[14] Finally, we took note of the promise's attainability, the extent to which it fell within the duties of the office of the president.[15] Our findings ran the gamut from the expected to the surprising, but we came away from our study with a healthy respect for political promises.

PROMISSORY PATTERNS

Even though it is common to disparage campaign promises, Table 11.1 reports that they are, in fact, rather modest in nature. They were a bit more positive than negative, more self-promoting than other-disparaging, and

Table 11.1 Rhetorical Features of Campaign Promises (in Percentages)

		Total (n = 619)	Democrats (n = 175)	Republicans (n = 444)	Challengers (n = 442)	Incumbents (n = 117)	Winners (n = 293)	Losers (n = 326)
Locus	Own	56.4	56.0	56.5	55.4	58.8	58.7	54.3
	Others'	43.6	44.0	43.5	44.6	41.2	41.3	45.7
Tone	Positive	51.1	50.8	51.1	50.9	51.4	54.9	47.5
	Negative	48.9	49.1	48.9	49.1	48.6	45.1	52.5
Complexity	Insubstantial	52.3	45.7	55.0	52.5	52.0	54.6	51.2
	Substantial	47.7	54.3	45.0	47.5	48.0	46.4	48.8
Attainability	Yes	60.4	54.3	62.8	59.1	63.8	65.2	56.1
	No	39.6	45.7	37.2	40.9	36.2	34.8	43.9
Emphasis	Values	39.6	39.4	39.6	39.8	41.2	39.2	39.9
	Policy	60.4	60.6	60.4	61.1	58.8	60.8	60.1

about as likely to be substantial as insubstantial. In other words, promises are not the monolithic disasters they are thought to be. Consider, for example, the following passage from George W. Bush's acceptance speech at the 2000 Republican convention:

> We will extend the promise of prosperity to every forgotten corner of this country. To every man and woman, a chance to succeed. To every child, a chance to learn. To every family, a chance to live with dignity and hope. For eight years, the Clinton/Gore administration has coasted through prosperity. And the path of least resistance is always downhill. But America's way is the rising road. This nation is daring and decent and ready for change. Our current president embodied the potential of a generation. So many talents. So much charm. Such great skill. But, in the end, to what end? . . . We have seen a steady erosion of American power and an unsteady exercise of American influence. Our military is low on parts, pay and morale. If called on by the commander in chief today, two entire divisions of the Army would have to report . . . "Not ready for duty, sir." This administration had its moment. They had their chance. They have not led. We will.[16]

In some ways this is stock rhetoric, but it is also interestingly layered. Most notable is its balance: a promise made and a promise forsaken; opportunities given and opportunities missed; leadership grasped and leadership denied. Not all political rhetoric is this symmetrical, but the Bush passage shows that most promises are not made in the abstract but always in a specific political context, a context often containing the shadow of one's opponent. Political promises usually embrace some grand vista, but they also have implicit warnings: to act now or to lose the initiative, to move forward lest one slide backward. There is, in short, a complexity to promises often missed by their critics.

Table 11.1 also shows that political promises feature attainable more than unattainable goals, goals lying within the purview of the president. In the passage cited, for example, Bush does not promise instant wealth; he promises his fellow citizens a chance to attain such wealth. Presidents alone cannot make everyone rich, but they can initiate legislation that will make some richer than others. Bush does not pledge to rid the nation of mortal sin or to make cosmetic surgery more popular. He focuses instead on building the military, something that all Republican presidents do, in part because it is something they can do.

On balance, then, political promises defy their caricatures. No doubt, individual politicians veer off in their own directions when promising things but, taken as a whole, promises are fairly prudent. Why, then, are they so often parodied? Part of the answer lies in the Locus variable, a measure of whether candidates offered personal promises or analyzed those of their opponents. As we see in Figure 11.1, the latter tendency has been on the rise in recent years. So it may not be promises per se that are the problem but *how they are managed* by candidates. Perhaps because of the media pressures bear-

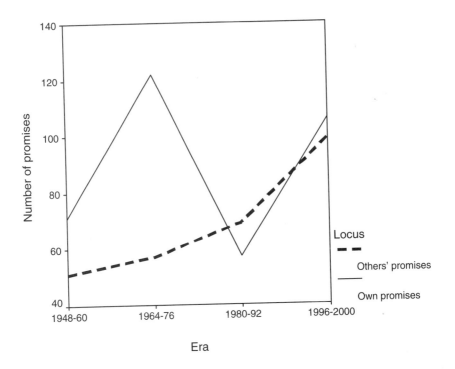

Figure 11.1 Promissory Locus over Time.

ing down upon them, the campaign season's brutal length (and its travel demands), or the increasing difficulty in getting voters' attention, candidates more often focus on their opponents' promises than their own. As a result, voters come to believe that negative campaigning is the only sort of campaigning possible. Each election season, candidates and the media presume that as well, confirming each other's expectations and thereby accelerating them.

PROMISSORY RESTRAINT

Political promises are surprisingly careful, especially when featuring the candidate's personal goals (versus those of an opponent). We found that candidates were six times more likely to be positive than negative in such cases and that they nicely balanced policy and value concerns as well. In other words, despite the high-profile promises we sometimes hear discussed—Walter Mondale's pledge to raise taxes in 1984 and George Bush's not to do so four years later—most promises are fairly banal: "I do not promise the millennium in the morning"; "I don't promise that we can eradicate poverty, and end discrimination, eliminate all danger of war"; "I do promise action on a new policy for peace abroad; a new policy for peace and progress and justice at home."[17]

Political scientists regard these optimistic, nonpolicy promises as rhetorically self-sealing. To conceive of their linguistic counterpart ("I promise to dishonor the Lincoln Memorial") is absurd.[18] Economists are even rougher on them, terming all costless, nonbinding, nonverifiable utterances as *cheap talk*, messages "sent from one party to another that are payoff-irrelevant to both."[19] Economists cannot understand why such pledges would influence anyone to do anything because they are so intangible. Economists also cannot explain why voters expect, and even demand, them from their leaders (one is reminded of George W. Bush, standing in the ashes of the World Trade Center, pledging that the nation would be avenged even though he hardly knew how at that time). The most generous observation economists can make about cheap talk is that, because people like it, politicians must provide it to maximize their utilities.[20]

While economists discount promises, cultural scholars are intrigued by them, knowing that human relationships are often guided by feelings that can neither be weighed nor measured. Such scholars know that a politician's perceived character, for example, can override empirical factors. So, for example, Dwight Eisenhower was asked to run for office by the Democrats in 1948 and by the Republicans in 1952 because of his transcendent popularity, not because of his specific political beliefs. The television era exacerbated those tendencies, allowing personality to sometimes override a whole patch of nastiness (e.g., Bill Clinton's ability to escape the hangman's noose when his affair with Monica Lewinsky was discovered). In a mediated world, charisma can become a commodity, odd and irrational though that may sound.[21] In a campaign, promises exploit "existing and often unstated obligations" people have for one another, thereby becoming an "indirect payoff" for voters' communal or party or national loyalties. By doing so, they become eminently functional.[22]

Consider the cases of two candidates who needed relational help to win the presidency. While public memory of the martyred president is now generous, a little historical sleuthing reminds us that John F. Kennedy was perceived, in July 1960, as an upstart from New England who had parlayed a good war record, family wealth, and an undistinguished congressional career into his party's nomination for president. He was not a long-time party loyalist, and, although he had amassed some impressive primary victories, he still needed to make a case for himself. He did so by connecting himself to both a tradition and a platform at his party's national convention. And he did so by making promises:

> The New Frontier of which I speak is not a set of promises, it is a set of challenges. It sums up not what I intend to offer the American people, but what I intend to ask of them. It appeals to their pride, not their pocketbook. It holds out the promises of more sacrifice instead of more security. But I tell

you the New Frontier is here, whether we seek it or not. . . . It would be easier to shrink back from that frontier, to look to the safe mediocrity of the past, to be lulled by good intentions and high rhetoric and those who prefer that course should not cast their votes for me, regardless of party. But I believe the times demand invention, innovation, imagination, decision. . . . There may be those who wish to hear more promises to this group or that, more harsh rhetoric about the men in the Kremlin, more assurances of a golden future, where taxes are always low and subsidies ever high. But my promises are in the platform you have adopted.[23]

Sixteen years later, Gerald Ford also needed to tend his relationships. He did not have to introduce himself to his party, like Kennedy, but he did have to make his party proud once again and to purge Republicanism of the Nixon onus. Ford began by acknowledging he had "seen the polls and the pundits who say our party is dead" and was resolved to change those perceptions. He ended with a promise: "[A]s we go forward together, I promise you once more what I promised before: to uphold the Constitution, to do what is right as God gives me to see the right, and to do the very best that I can for America."[24] The economists would wretch at a promise this vague, but few Republicans wretched that evening.

Speech act theorists report that people make their most powerful promises in intimate circumstances with someone they know well. That hardly sounds like modern politics, where personal and spatial distance prevail. Those conditions put pressures on promises, as does the media's ability to make local things national and specific things general. Consider, for example, what would happen if a candidate made a promise in a particular place (say, Bob Jones University) to a particular group (say, conservative Republicans), prior to a particular political event (say the South Carolina primary of 2000). Because of the mass media, the world would soon become witness to that promise. The fact that a seasoned candidate like George W. Bush forgot that possibility shows (1) how powerful the desire to make promises can be and (2) how carefully people attend to the promises politicians make.

Speech act theory might have saved Bush the grief of the Bob Jones speech. When telling students he looked forward "to publicly defending our conservative philosophy," his vision seemed cramped and sectarian to many Americans. The *act* of making that commitment became a cause célèbre for Bush because Bob Jones U. had banned interracial dating. To guard against such miscues, candidates are usually careful about their promises. One way they do so is by calling an audience's attention to what they are doing and not doing. The following fragments show such meta-talk in action:

- *I know that promising is not performing:* "It is easy enough to promise. It is harder to perform. There is a good reason why voters are suspicious of politicians. Over the years politicians have made *promises* they knew they couldn't carry out and the people knew that the politicians knew they couldn't carry them out." (Adlai Stevenson)[25]

- *I know that promising is measurable:* "For these past two years, I have been careful never to promise what I could not deliver. It has been my goal to inspire your confidence in America through solid performance rather than through mere words." (Gerald Ford)[26]

- *I know that promising can be abused:* "We must always be careful not to over promise, but we also should never underestimate our potential in our nation to correct our mistakes, to root out hatred and discrimination, to enhance equality of opportunity, to insure personal freedom and to carve out for ourselves and our children a better life." (Jimmy Carter)[27]

In sum: Promises operate as bonding devices, putting the self at risk in the presence of the other. Because that is so, promising is done carefully so as many people as possible will feel included in the candidate's (and the promise's) embrace. Promises help a candidate cut through the campaign noise, but, having done so, their notoriety creates a new set of problems. That is what happened to George H. W. Bush in 1988. Reflecting on that event, political pollster Richard Wirthlin said that Bush's statement constituted "the six most damaging words in the history of politics." One of Bush's aides agreed, observing "there is no one speech, no magic move, no silver bullet that will persuade them that this time Bush means it."[28] Promises are utterances that act with special force.

PROMISSORY CONFLICTS

Although their personal promises are careful, candidates throw caution to the wind when discussing those of their opponents. In such circumstances, candidates are five times more negative than positive, resulting in an increasingly sharp campaign dialectic. With challengers being twice as likely to talk about promises as incumbents and with Republicans doing so three times more often than Democrats, those two groups account for much of the negativity of recent campaign discourse.[29] In other words, the out-party and the party interested in hierarchies of values try to set the campaign agenda, findings that dovetail with what scholars have been saying about U.S. political culture lately.[30]

Figure 11.2 makes these findings especially clear. Here we see Republicans consistently topping Democrats in the use of promissory tokens. In addition, with relatively few exceptions, challengers talked about promises more than did incumbents. In races where there were no incumbents (1952, 1960, 1968, 1988, and 2000), the out-party candidate typically stressed the failed promises of the previous administration. One exception to those patterns was the 1984 election, in which Ronald Reagan successfully re-ran the 1980 campaign, joining Walter Mondale and Jimmy Carter at the hip, reminding Americans of the long gas lines four years earlier.

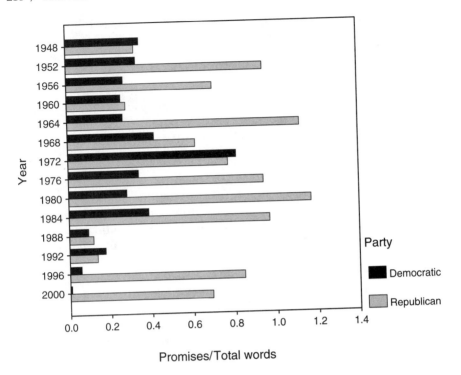

Figure 11.2 Promises by Party over Time.

Scholars tell us that challengers criticize "freely and in exaggerated terms."[31] The language of promises is perfectly suited to that task. Political promises operate in a kind of netherworld between the abstract and the concrete, giving voters a sense of specificity without real tangibility. A promise like "I pledge to never again let the United States become the laughing stock of the free world" can sound specific in 1984 when voters still have memories of downed American helicopters in Iran, or in 2004 when memories of terrorism in New York City were still fresh. Naturally, measuring the extent to which the United States is, or is not, a "laughing stock" is impossible. Nonetheless, such language (1) makes promises sound like completed actions, (2) lets candidates take advantage of recent cultural events, and (3) encourages voters to fill in the gaps between an attractive future and a sorry past.

Promises also even the playing field for challengers. With no history of accomplishment to stand on, challengers use their opponents' promises to cantilever onto some dire state of affairs. That gives challengers momentum that would normally lie with the incumbent, the mass media usually being willing to publicize promises made by any major candidate. Such language also lets the challenger contrast the incumbent's earlier promises with what actually resulted, thereby taking advantage of the (inevitable) gap between anticipated and empirical reality. For these reasons, revisionism becomes the challenger's stock-in-trade. Also helpful is the challenger's ability to make predictions without fear of immediate contradiction. No challenger is likely to claim, for example, "Before this election is over, my opponent will raise your taxes."

It is not altogether clear why Republicans have such a fondness for promises, but they do. Table 11.1 hints at why. Republicans were more likely than Democrats (1) to offer Insubstantial (fairly theoretical) promises than tangible ones and (2) to take an "inherentist" approach to the presidency, restricting their promises to the office's traditional prerogatives. These qualities gave Republican promises a formality, even a preachiness, not seen among the Democrats. Richard Nixon's discourse had both qualities. Notice in the following passage how much pleasure he derived from savaging Democrats' promises. His own plans not only seem tidier in contrast but morally superior as well. And the beauty of all this is that Nixon made no real promises himself other than to avoid the Democrats' inflationary rhetoric:

> [The Democrats] promised everything to everybody with one exception. They didn't promise to pay the bill. And I say tonight that with their convention, their platform and their ticket they composed a symphony of political cynicism which is out of harmony with our times today. Now we come to the key question: what should our answer be? And some might say, why, do as they do. Out promise them, because that's the only way to win. And I want to tell you my answer. I happen to believe that their program would be disastrous for America. It would wreck our economy; it would dash our people's high hopes for a better life. And I serve notice here and now that whatever the political consequences, we are not going to try to out promise our opponents in this campaign.[32]

Over the years, Republicans have increasingly made character attacks on their opponents. When Dwight Eisenhower declared in 1952, "I don't come before you, ladies and gentlemen, to make any long list of promises. All the promises, the political promises, have been used up in the last 20 years anyway," he only gently chided the Roosevelt and Truman administrations for extending government services too far. He was courtly when doing so, naming no names and citing no specific cases of overreaching: "What I bring to you is a pledge, a pledge couched in the kind of thing that you people have a right to demand and expect of your government. There will be no concealing of crookedness and dirt in the new administration."[33]

Thirty-two years later, Ronald Reagan folded his opponent more prominently into the mix, invoking Walter Mondale's name five times in four sentences at one campaign stop. Eisenhower's stately rhetoric contrasts sharply with Reagan's more personal tone: "But this year he's outdone himself. He's already promised, of course, to raise your taxes. But if he is to keep all the other promises he made, he'll have to raise taxes by the equivalent of $1,890 for every household in the United States. That figures out to about $150 a month." To be sure, Reagan's was a policy-based argument and a substantive one at that, but it also contained an implied moral claim, one that Reagan camouflaged with his aw-shucks demeanor. He went on to talk about the future impact of the "Mondale mortgage" and concluded thusly: "But I'll give [Mondale] this. He gave me an idea for Halloween. If I could find a way to dress up as his tax program, I could just scare the devil out of all the neighbors."[34]

Bob Dole had a sharper bite than Ronald Reagan. Known for his savage sense of humor, Dole was constantly on the attack during the 1996 presidential campaign. Like Reagan, he assailed his opponent's excesses but, unlike Reagan, he drove the dagger in more deeply. Part choir boy at times ("The only promises I make are promises I will keep"), Dole nevertheless kept his opponent in the crosshairs of his rifle:

> No wonder so many Americans have been worried that our country is on the wrong track. Even Bill Clinton felt it. That's why in the last election he promised of course, he promised everything in the last election. But he promised an $800 child credit. Sadly, he never got it. And I've been saying to people, everybody who got that tax credit Clinton promised you in Pennsylvania last year, you ought to vote for him again. You ought to vote for him again twice if you can. But he didn't do that. He broke his promise, as he's broken so many other promises time after time and day after day.[35]

Humanizing promises in this way makes sense, with research on political cognition showing that personal anecdotes can drive out less tangible information. These postulates are central to Samuel Popkin's theory of shortcuts and gut rationality.[36] "Because we generate narratives about kinds of people," says Popkin, "it is easier to take personal data and fill in the political facts and policies than to start with the political facts and fill in the personal data."[37] Whether they understand Popkin's theory or not, challengers and Republicans (and especially Republican challengers) operate as if they do. In a cultural analysis of U.S. political parties, Jo Freeman suggests that Republicans regard themselves as "representing the core of American society" and "as the carriers of its fundamental values."[38] For these reasons, Republicans take promises seriously. They talk about them more often than Democrats, positing a world of constant betrayal, a kind of finger-pointing that works well for party loyalists. For agnostics, however, such a rhetoric can be tiring; for others it can be deflating. History shows that voters often prefer people like Roosevelt, Kennedy, or Clinton, candidates whose promises have, in the language of the cliché, "the lift of a driving dream." Exactly why we like such people, and when, are mysteries not yet solved.

PROMISSORY SUBSTANCE

Many casual observers assume that campaign promises are "empty," by which they mean irrelevant and unattainable (e.g., "I pledge to cure the moral sickness of this nation"). But that is an unfair characterization. Table 11.1 shows that fully 60 percent of the promises we tracked dealt with issues

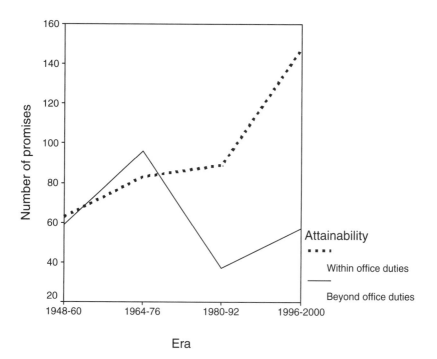

Figure 11.3 Attainability of Promises by Era.

over which the president had direct responsibility (e.g., declare war, sign a bill, etc.). Moreover, as we see in Figure 11.3, that tendency has increased over time. During five of the last six elections (1988 being the exception), attainable promises outnumbered unattainable promises by a factor of two to one.

Our data suggest that promissory tokens have reigned in campaign rhetoric, forcing candidates to discuss institutional issues—taxes, trade, healthcare, employment, Social Security. This last issue appeared in sixty-eight of the speeches under examination, with all but five of the twenty-four candidates plighting their troth to the program.[39] Although they were hardly children of the New Deal (ideologically, at least), even Bob Dole and George W. Bush walked that path, with the latter declaring in his notoriously abrupt way: "I will keep the promise of Social Security. No changes, no reductions, no way."[40]

Issues like Social Security lie in the policy domain, but even when discussing values candidates focused on the duties of office. For example, although homiletic by nature, Jimmy Carter stuck to the issues when describing the tone he wanted in the White House. His statement at that time was a prepolicy statement, but a pointed one:

I don't want to mislead you, because you've endorsed me and because this is a happy day for me to be here. There will be times when I as President, even in spite of what I've said about partnership, will not always agree with you. That's obvious. I can't agree with every proposal you make and also agree with every proposal that other groups in this country make, as President. I cannot promise you that there'll be unlimited Federal resources to meet every demand that's presented to my desk in the Oval Office. I can't promise that every new program will be passed through the Congress without delay, even if you and I agree that it ought to be done. I can't promise you that there will not be difficult challenges in the future and tough decisions to be made. But I do tell you that we share the same goals and the same ideals and the same hopes in the future.[41]

Figure 11.4 adds another piece to the puzzle: The making of promises has gone down in recent years. That will shock many Americans who nurture the idea of Washington being filled with bafflegab. But politicians have husbanded their promises lately, distinguishing between what they could and could not do. Here is another irony: The year in which George H. W. Bush made his famous pledge not to raise taxes was the very year when promises

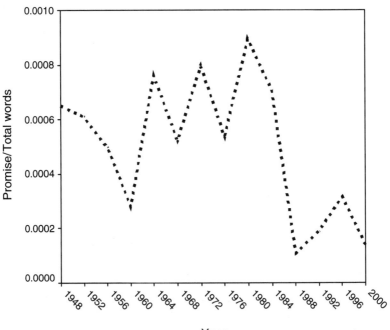

Figure 11.4 Promises Made over Time.

began to fall. Within our admittedly limited sample, Bush made but five promissory statements; compared to the two dozen other candidates in our study, only Bush's opponent, Michael Dukakis, made fewer. After a steady ratcheting-up for thirty years, campaign promises have dwindled. Why?

Several answers come to mind. The press has become increasingly ornery, holding Republicans and Democrats to every statement made during a campaign. Opposition research has also gotten better. Databases of candidates' former statements are now fully searchable, allowing candidates to disentomb an opponent's ill-considered remarks (a problem that bedeviled Pat Buchanan—a professional writer—during his lonely run for the presidency in 1996). Campaigns are also tightly coordinated, with a candidate's speeches becoming sound bites on the evening news and then ad copy the next day. That has caused campaigns to operate with military-like coordination, nary a word out of place. Too, the American people have become disaffected with politics, and that puts pressure on candidates, requiring them to say only what they can prove.

One wonders if the recent aversion to promises has taken the spontaneity out of politics. After all, a promise is a hope, not a prediction. It is a way for people to share their intentions with others and to celebrate their relationships. In the everyday world, after all, we forgive one another when noontime traffic makes us tardy for a lunch date. We do so because we realize that no one can control every contingency. We do so because we feel lucky to have been asked out in the first place, that someone wanted to spend time with us. We do so because living in the present is not enough for us and because promises stake a claim on the future.

What does it mean that political promises have become scarce? Does it suggest that leadership has gotten too timid? That political imagination has dried up, causing candidates to say only what they can prove? Should we be asking for more promises rather than fewer promises to get a better idea of how our leaders reason? Because they come to fruition only in the future, promises are inherently fragile. And yet they are flattering, a speech act that says I care enough about you to imagine a future with you. Promises have their limitations but, it must be asked, would we be happy without them?

CONCLUSION

Our survey of political promises shows them to be comparatively careful, comparatively self-risking, comparatively positive, and increasingly based on the institutional prerogatives of the presidency. Political candidates are rougher on their opponents' promises, and that has become truer over time. For a host of strategic and cultural reasons, promises have dropped off in recent years. In our data, promissory rhetoric is not bloated as charged.

We began this chapter by reflecting on George H. W. Bush's memorable pledge not to raises taxes. The story behind that promise is an interesting one. The phrase was born amidst a conflict between Bush's economics advisor, Richard Darman, and his speechwriter and media consultant—Peggy Noonan and Roger Ailes. Whereas Noonan and Ailes viewed "read my lips" as "central to refashioning Bush's image," positioning the vice president as bold and principled, Darman thought the line "stupid and irresponsible," a silly stratagem in light of a growing budget deficit and divided government in Washington.[42]

Bush's advisors were not really arguing over words, per se, but over a speech act designed to show Bush as a man of resolve. Bush's promise was meant to counteract images of his being, as they said at the time, a "wimp." Somewhat earlier in the campaign (on January 25, 1988), Bush had pursued a similar strategy when getting into a nasty fight with Dan Rather on a rare live broadcast of CBS Evening News. Rather pummeled the vice president over the Iran-Contra affair, being so discourteous in some people's eyes that the incident quickly became known as "Rather's AmBush."[43] Subsequent analyses, however, indicate that Bush knew quite well what he was getting into and that this was but another speech act for making him appear presidential. He succeeded in both cases, but his promissory success was short-lived.

Because promising is a unique speech act it captures attention. In a competitive media environment, opponents listen for an opponent's unwise promises, the press listens for fresh and memorable pledges, and voters listen for commitments that will reveal a candidate's values. Promises are risky because they get something done when getting something said. According to Republican strategist Richard Wirthlin, after the "read my lips" pledge there was nothing the Bush team could do to regain the trust of the American electorate. Six short words, one significant act.

Why do we punish politicians so severely for mis-promising? In Bush's case, were his words egregious enough to discount sixty-four years of public service? After all, just a bit of reflection shows he was basically just saying that taxes were too high, government waste too grand, and that he would do something about it. A little reflection also shows that we ourselves have made a thousand such pledges to our friends, many of which did not work out as expected. "But politicians should be kept to a higher standard," the bromide goes. Perhaps, but one wonders why. Why should the average politician be any better than the average citizen at mapping the future? A promise is not a prediction, after all, it is a statement of intention. A prediction is the product of science or religion; a promise is the product of relationships. That seems a good distinction to keep in mind.

Promises pose an interesting dilemma: If voters become too scrupulous about them they will disappear entirely. Without politicians' promises, we will be unable to imagine the future. Asking where a candidate currently stands is one thing; asking where they will stand is quite another. All politicians should be required to answer the first question. No candidate can possibly answer the second. Promises ask us to conflate two moments in time—today and tomorrow—but that is never really possible. So perhaps we should ease up a bit on our leaders, encouraging them to share their dreams with us—to make their promises—and telling them in return that we will treat their dreams as dreams. Unless we do, we will hear them no more. Can we live without dreams?

NOTES

1. G. H. W. Bush, "Acceptance Address to Republican National Convention," August 18, 1988, *Annenberg/Pew Archive of Presidential Discourse,* CD-ROM (Philadelphia: Annenberg School for Communication, 2000).

2. See, for example, A. Kiewe and D. W. Houck, *A Shining City on a Hill: Ronald Reagan's Economic Rhetoric, 1951–1989* (Westport, CT: Greenwood, 1991).

3. G. Pomper with S. Lederman, *Election in America* (New York: Dodd, Mead, 1976).

4. M. G. Krukones, *Promises and Performance: Presidential Campaigns as Policy Predictors* (Lanham, MD: University Press of America, 1984); J. Fishel, *Presidents and Promises: From Campaign Pledge to Presidential Performance* (Washington, DC: Congressional Quarterly, 1985); C. M. Shaw, "President Clinton's First Term: Matching Campaign Promises with Presidential Performance," *Congress and the Presidency,* 25 (1998): 43–65.

5. P. E. Kinberg, "Presidential Fulfillment of Party Platform and Campaign Pledges," unpublished doctoral dissertation, University of Maryland College Park, 1997.

6. M. Korcok, "Health Promises Scarce Among U.S. Presidential Candidates," *Canadian Medical Association Journal,* 162 (2000): 1032–34.

7. F. Wykoff, "An Election Year Opportunity for Journalists," *Quill,* 84 (1996): S1.

8. K. H. Jamieson, P. Waldman, and J. Devitt, "Mapping the Discourse of the 1996 Presidential General Election," *Media, Culture & Society,* 20 (1998): 323–28.

9. T. E. Patterson, *Out of Order* (New York: Vintage Books, 1994), 11.

10. See the following studies, respectively: S. Jacobs and S. Jackson, "Speech Act Structure in Conversation: Rational Aspects of Pragmatic Coherence," in *Conversational Coherence: Form, Structure and Strategy,* ed. R. T. Craig and K. Tracy (Beverly Hills, CA: Sage, 1983); M. Z. Rosaldo, "The Things We Do with Words: Ilongot Speech Acts and Speech Act Theory in Philosophy," in *Cultural Communication and Intercultural Contact,* ed. D. Carbaugh (Hillsdale, NJ: Lawrence Erlbaum Associates, 1990), 373–408; L. Abbeduto, "The Development of Speech Act Comprehension in Mentally Retarded Individuals and Non-retarded Children," *Child Development,* 59 (1988): 1460–73; R. M. Nischik, "Speech Act Theory, Speech Acts, and the Analysis of Fiction, *Modern Language Review,* 88 (1993): 297–307; K. Riley, "Telling More Than the Truth: Implicature, Speech Acts, and Ethics in Professional Communication," *Journal of Business Ethics,* 12 (1993): 179–97.

11. J. L. Austin, *Philosophical Papers* (London: Oxford University Press, 1970), 99.

12. J. Searle, *Speech Acts: An Essay in the Philosophy of Language* (Cambridge: Cambridge University Press, 1969).

13. In focusing on these tokens only, we operated as strict constructionists. Other keywords could also have been used such as *plan, swear, assure, guarantee, vow,* and so on. We ignored these terms to make our project more manageable, ultimately focusing on textual fragments in these proportions: *promise* (n = 226), *promises* (n = 155), *promised* (n = 99), and *pledge* (n = 139).

14. See Pomper, *Election in America,* Fishel, *Presidents and Promises,* and Shaw, "President Clinton's First Term," for discussions of "empty" and "substantial" promises.

15. According to political scientist Clinton Rossitier, the President of the United States performs several roles, including Chief of State, Chief Executive, Commander in Chief, Chief Diplomat, Chief Legislator, Chief of the Party, and Voice of the People. Yet many scholars (notably, Cronin) note that the public's understanding of the presidency has stretched well beyond the official duties of the position. In the Attainability variable, we examined how the promises offered in campaigns match the job description of the President of the United States. See C. Rossitier, *The American Presidency* (New York: Harcourt, 1960). See also T. J. Cronin, "The Textbook Presidency and Political Science," in *Perspectives on the Presidency,* ed. N. S. Bach and G. T. Sulzner (Lexington, MA: D.C. Heath, 1974), 54–74.

16. G. W. Bush, "Acceptance Speech at the Republican National Convention," Philadelphia, PA, August 3, 2000, in *In Their Own Words: Sourcebook 2000,* CD-ROM (Stanford, CA: Political Communication Lab, 2000).

17. R. Nixon, "Speech at the Republican National Convention," Miami Beach, FL, August 8, 1968, *Annenberg/Pew Archive of Presidential Discourse,* CD-ROM (Philadelphia: Annenberg School for Communication, 2000).

18. See Pomper, *Election in America.*

19. S. A. Matthews, "Veto Threats: Rhetoric in a Bargaining Game," *The Quarterly Journal of Economics,* 104 (1989): 348. See also J. Farrell, "Cheap Talk, Coordination, and Entry," *The RAND Journal of Economics,* 18 (1987): 34–39.

20. J. Farrell and J. Rabin, "Cheap Talk," *The Journal of Economic Perspectives,* 10 (1996): 103–18.

21. For more on the influence of the media, see M. McCubbins, "Party Decline and Presidential Campaigns in the Television Age," in *Under the Watchful Eye: Managing Presidential Campaigns in the Television Era,* ed. M. McCubbins (Washington, DC: Congressional Quarterly, 1992), 30.

22. R. W. Gibbs, Jr., and S. M. Delaney, "Pragmatic Factors in Making and Understanding Promises," *Discourse Processes,* 10 (1987): 107–27.

23. J. Kennedy, "Acceptance Address to the Democratic National Convention," Los Angeles, CA, July 15, 1960, *Annenberg/Pew Archive of Presidential Discourse,* CD-ROM (Philadelphia: Annenberg School for Communication, 2000).

24. G. Ford, "Acceptance Address to the Republican National Convention," Kansas City, MO, August 19, 1976, *Annenberg/Pew Archive of Presidential Discourse,* CD-ROM (Philadelphia: Annenberg School for Communication, 2000).

25. A. Stevenson, "Think About Tomorrow, Campaign Address," Cincinnati, OH, October 3, 1952, *Annenberg/Pew Archive of Presidential Discourse,* CD-ROM (Philadelphia: Annenberg School for Communication, 2000).

26. G. Ford, "Campaign Address to Mutual Radio Network," November 2, 1976, *Annenberg/Pew Archive of Presidential Discourse,* CD-ROM (Philadelphia: Annenberg School for Communication, 2000).

27. J. Carter, "Campaign Address, First of the General Election Campaign," Warm Springs, GA, September 6, 1976, *Annenberg/Pew Archive of Presidential Discourse,* CD-ROM (Philadelphia: Annenberg School for Communication, 2000).

28. "Bush Message Emerges; Less Government and Clinton Draft Issue," *Washington Post,* September 19, 1992, A1.

29. Here it is important to note the breakdown of Democratic and Republican incumbents and challengers. Between 1948 and 2000, there were seven Democratic

incumbent candidates, seven Democratic challengers, seven Republican incumbents, and seven Republican challengers. In terms of victories, six Democrats won during those years, eight Democrats lost, eight Republicans won, and six Republicans lost.

30. See, for example, J. Freeman, "The Political Culture of the Democratic and Republican Parties," *Political Science Quarterly*, 101 (1986): 327–56.

31. J. S. Trent and R. V. Friedenberg, *Political Campaign Communication: Principles and Practices* (Westport, CT: Praeger, 1995), 82.

32. R. M. Nixon, "Acceptance Speech, Republican National Convention," Chicago, IL, July 28, 1960, *Annenberg/Pew Archive of Presidential Discourse*, CD-ROM (Philadelphia: Annenberg School for Communication, 2000).

33. D. Eisenhower, "Campaign Train Address," Vancouver, WA, October 7, 1952, *Annenberg/Pew Archive of Presidential Discourse*, CD-ROM (Philadelphia: Annenberg School for Communication, 2000).

34. R. Reagan, "Campaign Address," Glen Ellyn, IL, October 16, 1984, *Annenberg/Pew Archive of Presidential Discourse*, CD-ROM. (Philadelphia: Annenberg School for Communication, 2000).

35. R. Dole, "Remarks at Elizabethtown College," October 2, 1996, *Annenberg/Pew Archive of Presidential Discourse*, CD-ROM (Philadelphia: Annenberg School for Communication, 2000).

36. S. Popkin, *The Reasoning Voter* (Chicago: University of Chicago Press, 1991), 73, 79. In what he describes as Gresham's Law of political information, Popkin outlines how a small amount of personal information can dominate a large amount of historical information about a candidate's past record.

37. Ibid, 78. Popkin continues, "Presidential appearance, particularly in the short run, can seem to voters to be an adequate basis for predicting presidential success in the future. This can occur because in comparing personal information with political behavior, one is comparing stories with facts. Personal data gathered from observing the candidate generates a story about the candidate—what he or she is like, and is likely to do if elected. The information about votes, offices held, and policy positions taken in the past does not generate a full story and may not even be joined with the personal data. Narratives are more easily compiled and are retained longer than facts" (78).

38. See Freeman, "Political Culture."

39. In our textbase, the five candidates who deviated from this pattern were John Kennedy in 1960, Richard Nixon in 1972, Michael Dukakis in 1988, and, astonishingly, Bill Clinton in 1992 and 1996.

40. G. W. Bush, "Campaign Speech," Langhorne, PA, October 12, 2000.

41. J. Carter, "Annual Convention of the Civil Service Employees Association," Niagara Falls, NY, October 1, 1980.

42. "Bush Message Emerges," A1.

43. For more on this matter, see M. Plissner, *The Control Room: How Television Calls the Shots in Presidential Elections* (New York: Free Press, 1999).

12

The *Consultant*
A Synecdoche for All of Politics

With John Handy Bosma

As George W. Bush's presidency neared its hundredth day, journalists from news outlets across the country prepared their assessments of what has now become an important milestone in any presidential administration. Not surprisingly, given the trends of the last fifty years, one of the key figures mentioned at that time was Karl Rove. As *Time* magazine declared, "No one, with the possible exception of the President, will be more responsible for the success or failure of Bush's presidency."[1] Karl Rove was not, it must be remembered, the Speaker of the House or the Secretary of Defense. He was not even the head of the Republican National Committee. Karl Rove was a political consultant and campaigner extraordinaire, a fellow who got his start with the Young Republicans as a nineteen-year-old delegate from the state of Utah. Over the years, his encyclopedic mind grew so large that it can now parse west Texas alone into four distinct political regions. The *New Yorker* magazine calls Rove "The Controller," a person who has a "plan to take over politics" as we know it.[2]

Why would Karl Rove, a mere political strategist, receive the lion's share of the credit for a president's success? Bush, after all, was no pushover himself, nor was his svengali of a vice president, Dick Cheney. It must also be remembered that the hundredth day of the Bush presidency fell around the first of May, hardly an election season. How did a campaign strategist become a governance strategist? (Some commentators even had Rove calling the shots on the war in Iraq as well as on abortion and Medicare.) One answer is that of Sidney Blumenthal, who declares there is now a "permanent campaign" in the White House, a campaign run, not surprisingly, by specialists like Karl Rove and his Clinton-era predecessor, James Carville.[3] How did all this happen? Is it good for us?

In reporting their fascination with Rove, *Time* and the *New Yorker* revealed the tip of an iceberg that has been growing for decades. Such stories contained the tonalities of their age: a president keeping a faithful eye on the poll numbers, hidden meetings to decide political strategy, policy announcements designed to achieve partisan ends. The topic du jour in the *Time* article, for example, was global warming and the president's decision to back away from the Kyoto Accords, but the subject could have been almost anything. *Time* profiled its protagonist this way:

> Setting priorities and delivering bad news to friends is just a sliver of what Rove does as Bush's top political gun. It was Rove who shaped the agenda, message and strategy that got Bush—the least experienced presidential nominee of modern times—into the White House. Now it is Rove's job to keep him there through 2008. "My job," Rove told *Time* last week, "is to pay attention to the things that affect his political future."[4]

The *consultant*, we shall argue here, is a new keyword in American politics and an important one. Our thesis is that political consultancy has become a prism through which all politics is now viewed. It is in the classical sense a synecdoche—a part of politics that stands for the whole of politics. It has come to structure people's perceptions of how, when, and why politics is conducted. The consultant is an iconic force, a mysterious (sometimes dark, always complex) figure in whom extraordinary powers are located. Consultants are the computer engineers and gene splicers of their profession, persons who can "run the numbers" in their heads and order the right ad buy in less than a second. They are the seers of politics. They help set its rationale.

Who can compete with them? Certainly not the candidates—they are flotsam and jetsam on the consultant's tides. Certainly not voters—they are too uncerebral for the new business of politics. And certainly not journalists— both the *Time* and *New Yorker* articles reek with the unmistakable smell of envy. No, only the consultant can explain the nuances of politics, and, today, politics is nothing but nuances. All roads lead to and from the *consultant*.

THE POWER OF THE CONSULTANT

Presidential campaigns are no longer the madcap trek through the nation they once were. Rather, they have become military campaigns—carefully planned, brilliantly coordinated, enormously expensive, highly mechanized. Many of the components of these campaigns—political polling, database management, focus group testing, opposition research, voter demographics—have become scientific specialities in their own rights. The people who once ran campaigns were anonymous, but that has changed as well. Gurus like Karl Rove have become celebrities, and they superintend virtually all campaign decision-making. Some feel that even the minds of the candidates are now in the thrall of the consultants.

The gradual acceptance of these premises over the last dozen or so presidential elections is a fascinating story. It is the story of a new kind of politics and a new kind of America. According to some experts, consultants have succeeded in wresting control of the political system from candidates, parties, and voters as well.[5] But why is the consultant's story compelling to so many? Why does it overwhelm or repel still others? After all, consultants' core activities—advising candidates, plotting strategies, and fashioning messages—have always existed in some form or fashion.[6] If there has been a revolution in politics during the last fifty years it has been in part a rhetorical revolution, a revolution featuring people's fascination with efficiency, technocracy, control, and expertise. The story of the consultant is the story of our life and times.

As we will see, the *consultant* trope has a certain openness to it that has let it incorporate multiple meanings over time. People who are fascinated by the machinations of politics are fascinated by the consultant. People who detest the manipulativeness of campaigns detest the consultant. If a candidate loses a campaign he or she is said to have listened to the wrong consultant. If the candidate wins an election it is because of the consultant's dexterity. The candidate's brilliance or vision, what he or she stands for, inevitably takes a back seat in such a scenario.

Only a moment's reflection reveals how odd this story really is. As Larry Sabato observes, to become a political consultant (unlike becoming a brain surgeon or a corporate attorney) one need only hang out a shingle.[7] Although many observers declare the 1930s to be the beginning of political consulting in the United States, others are less sure of its date of origin, in part because "the profession" itself is so vague. Once it began, however, its sins became legion. Jay Rosen and Paul Taylor have declared, for example, that political consultancy has changed fundamental journalistic routines.[8] Lance Bennett says it has compromised the party system.[9] Edward Schwartzman describes the consultant as the main reason campaign spending has increased so prodigiously.[10] Stephen Ansolabehere and Shanto Iyengar argue that consultants have infected the minds of both the voting and nonvoting public.[11] And David Chagall observes that consultants have changed the electoral fortunes—and sometimes the lives—of public officials at both the national and local levels.[12]

As we saw in chapter 10, political campaigns are now candidate-centered, and that, too, has been attributed to consultants, who often hail from the marketing industry, where branding has become an art form.[13] Other observers note that campaigns have become more voter-centered, with the electorate being sliced into finer and finer elements to assist in message targeting.[14] In the early days, consultants would draft a press release or write a speech for a candidate and then let the fates take hold. That is no longer true, with "spin control" having changed the very phenomenology of politics, its essential message to the voter being: "You did not see what you saw; you saw what I saw."[15] Most ominous of all, however, is the charge that consultants have moved into the policy arena itself, helping the candidate decide what to *do* as well as what to say. During the 1996 campaign, for example, it was common knowledge among journalists that Dick Morris helped formulate the policy initiatives Bill Clinton pushed during the campaign.[16]

Despite political consultants' alleged power, hard data about those effects are difficult to come by. But we are less interested in such empirical effects here than in the *consultant story*. In the remaining pages, we will lay out that story, basing our observations on the news coverage archived in the Campaign Mapping Project's database between 1948 and 1996. We found over ten thousand instances of the *consultancy* trope and its cognates (e.g., *campaign advisor, strategist, press secretary, spokesperson*, etc.), with references starting out gradually and then building to a crescendo beginning in the 1970s.

Although we analyzed the text surrounding these tokens in several ways, our central questions were basic: What cultural interpretations of the consultant are encouraged by the text? Do the images of the political consultant change from era to era? What activities and specializations within consultancy are emphasized, and what do those specializations tell us about politics writ large? What social and political effects are ascribed to consultants by working journalists?

In inspecting the news coverage, we concentrated on (1) the actions or functions attributed to consultants, (2) the time horizons in which they were said to operate, (3) their relationships to other campaign personnel (as well as to politicians, voters, and the media), (4) the images and schemas implied by the *consultant* trope, (5) the actions and states-of-being ascribed to the consultant, and (6) the generic imperatives imposed on the consultant story by the news text.[17] To the best of our knowledge, this is the first systematic study of reportage featuring the political consultant, although we are indebted to qualitative work previously done in this area. Our general finding is that, as with other keywords, the *consultant* tells a story larger than itself.

THE RISE OF THE CONSULTANT

During the last fifty years, interest in backroom politics has become so prodigious that the consultant now typifies modern politics. The transformation was gradual, but the consultant moved from an unknown to a known quantity, continually absorbing new ideas about political work. The boundaries delimiting such work were, however, unclear in 1948. At that time, party organizations had primary responsibility for raising funds, planning campaigns, and stumping on behalf of candidates. Presidential aspirants relied on an informal network of "advisers" or "strategists" who were often lower-level office-holders themselves. Too, in 1948 the political consultant was a generalist who did a bit of this and a bit of that. Technology had not yet caught up to politics (or politics to technology), so even the direct mail specialist had yet to be imagined.[18] And while there were many keen political operatives working in the United States in 1948, they were invisible to the American public.

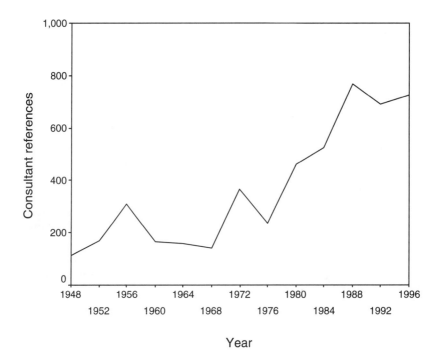

Figure 12.1 Consultants Referenced Across Time. (Includes advisory, strategic, and organizational roles.)

Figure 12.1 shows the sudden acceleration of the *consultant* token during the last quarter of the twentieth century. These data include every reference in our sample to individuals working on (or alongside) a campaign staff during each presidential election. The number of consultants profiled by the press more than doubled between the 1950s and the 1980s, a trend that has not abated since then. All of this is rather odd since the political work performed fifty years ago was often similar to that being performed today. Over time, however, specializations developed and the amount of political work done by nonparty personnel rose dramatically. As these new professionals came on the scene, their personal images rose as well. Consider, for example, how energetically the *Los Angeles Times* described the psychodrama of the 2000 Republican campaign, a campaign that featured political turncoat Mark McKinnon:

> Mark McKinnon's old photos fit together like a mosaic of Democratic idealism. There's a shot of him hunched in a strategy session with Ann Richards, the acid tongued former Texas governor, and legendary Democratic advertising consultant Bob Squier. And here he's mugging for the camera next to James Carville and Paul Begala, two architects of Bill Clin-

ton's 1992 White House victory. The images only suggest the chasm Mc-Kinnon crossed when he took his current job. He is the media consultant to Republican presidential candidate George W. Bush. That makes him a traitor in the eyes of one political party and a stranger in the eyes of another. By the standards of the insular fraternity of presidential campaign consultants, McKinnon's jump is almost unheard of. The biggest names in the business still are die hard loyalists to one party. Those who switch, including McKinnon, are viewed with suspicion by both sides.[19]

The McKinnon story was reported on October 7, near the end of a campaign featuring such issues as the death penalty, campaign finance reform, environmental degradation, defense spending, national health insurance, military operations in the Balkans, corporate malfeasance, and much else. Less than thirty days before that campaign ended, however, the *Times* only had eyes for the McKinnon story. The reasons are obvious: colorful protagonists, ideological realignments, traitorous relationships, legends fighting legends. How could a toxic waste dump compete with that?

During the past fifty years, the lexicon of consultancy has grown as well. New work and role terms were hatched, thereby adding specificity to reporters' stories. Core work terms described knowledge domains—press, media, finance, advance, polling, and so on—while core role terms reflected the "vertical" aspects of the campaign organization—aides, staffers, advisers, strategists, consultants, and so on. In the early days, these personae were often mixed and matched, creating a patchwork image of the campaign staff. The early descriptions of consultancy were vague as a result. The 1948 phrase "strategists of the Republican party" hits the modern ear awkwardly. It is too collective a term for individualists, too bland a term for readers of *People* magazine. The phrase has an insulting, clandestine quality. Today, we want to be behind the scenes behind the scenes.

Over the years, the shifting lexicon of consulting signaled the increasing complexity of the modern campaign. No longer was a lone candidate grabbing random hands along a rope line. It now took an entire cast to run a campaign. As we see in Figure 12.1, advisory, strategic, and organizational roles did the lion's share of the work. This is not only a mathematical fact but a qualitative one as well. In the 1948 election, for example, only a few generic tasks were mentioned: campaign director, party official, presidential press secretary, campaign strategist, and so on. The 1972 election added more technical roles: chief media adviser, advertising campaign director, national field director, television consultant. By 1980, the campaigns had directors of political affairs, professional pollsters, creative directors, and political media specialists. Campaign staffers soon became indistinct from Madison Avenue types.

The 1996 election was newer still, as consultancy became hybridized. The parallel to trends in the modern corporation are intriguing. Increasingly, that is, American companies have gotten away from rigid specification of roles and, even, rigid specification of the workplace (e.g., telecommuting). Company workers must now be as "proactive" as possible, "leveraging" their skills in a thousand ways. This sometimes results in "scope creep," as more duties are thrust upon them, but an employee with a broad enough "skill set" should be able to "take ownership" of all relevant duties. Campaign coverage also reflects these conglomerating trends. The work of the fund raising and direct-mail specialist is now discussed alongside the White House aide and campaign director, who should not be confused with the political director and senior administration strategist. This lexical salad reflects new employ- ment patterns for campaigns, but it also reflects changing cultural motifs, as people try to cope with a hyper-fast, hyper-mediated age.

Not only are consultants seen regularly today, but they are heard from more often as well, as we see in Figure 12.2.[20] This is ironic since, as we saw in chapter 5, candidates themselves have been allotted shorter sound bites over time. But the emergence of the consultant also makes sense for a reporter since a quote from Karl Rove will usually be more interesting than one from his boss. Rove, after all, works in a world of symbols where every- thing is always possible. The president, in contrast, works in a world of guns and butter, where there are always too many of the former and never enough of the latter. Because the law requires him to be reasonably transparent, Bush

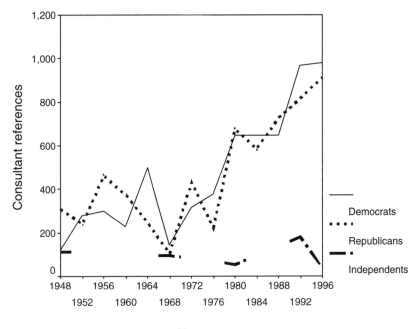

Figure 12.2 Consultants Quoted Across Time.

will usually exercise caution when speaking. Karl Rove, in contrast, can be pleasantly specific when he wants to be.

During the 1992 and 1996 elections, consultants were quoted three times more often than they were in the 1948 and 1952 elections. Reporters have become dependent on consultants for obvious reasons—they are in touch with campaign details—but also for nonobvious reasons—they have intimate knowledge of the candidate-as-person. Consultants know things, but they also certify things, thereby adding authenticity to the news text. Sometimes, the media's credentialing of the consultants is itself captivating. For example, the *Christian Science Monitor* once described Karl Rove as "a mild faced man who looks more like an accountant than Machiavelli. The political consultant famously met Bush over 25 years ago, when George the father, then head of the Republican National Committee, summoned a low ranking aide (Rove) to hand his son the keys to the family car." Having established Rove's expertise, the *Monitor* went on to describe the other main Bush advisor, Karen Hughes: "A former political reporter for KXAS TV in Dallas, Ms. Hughes is Bush's longtime spokesperson. He reportedly told her that if she did not join his presidential campaign, he was not going to run. Her main job: damage control for Bushisms." Finally, the *Monitor* quoted one consultant to authenticate another consultant: "'When Bush is in a public setting, and says something that's a little bit off, Karen knows how reporters are going to read it,' says Bill Cryer, who was press secretary for Ann Richards, Bush's first gubernatorial opponent."[21]

As we see in Figure 12.2, political workers were ignored as recently as 1968. Even when quoted directly they were quoted anonymously. That made campaign work seem an exercise in civic virtue. In part it was, since early campaign advisors were either volunteers or minimally paid. The professionalization of politics changed that, as did the media's growing need to describe the "campaign scene." As we see in Figure 12.3, this need for a richer media text relegated the ordinary political workers to the sidelines. By the 1980s, politics had gone upscale. To look for the name of a volunteer in news coverage today would be as frustrating as looking for the name of a consumer in *Business Week*.

These trends stand in stark contrast to earlier coverage, where reporters seemed interested in lay political work. "In Los Angeles, Cleveland and the boroughs of New York," said one story from the 1972 campaign, "in storefront headquarters, bagel shops and meat markets, ordinary and largely unpaid citizens are trying to spread the word that Mr. Nixon and not Senator McGovern, better understands the fears and aspirations of the Jewish community."[22] Twenty years later, consultants not only dominated the news text, they also dominated the headlines:

- "Inventing Clintonomics; Spectrum of Advisers Debates Goals, Priorities"[23]
- "Atlanta TV Is a Battleground: Bush Being Outspent in Ad War"[24]

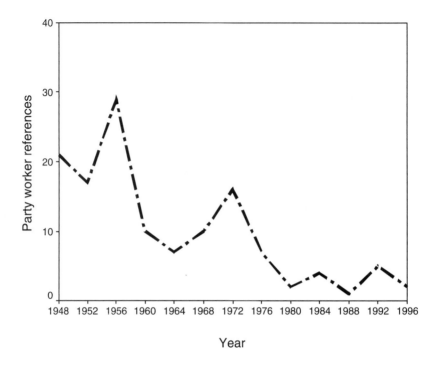

Figure 12.3 Party Workers Referenced Across Time.

- "Smoother Bush Campaign Shows Baker's Famous Touch"[25]
- "White House Staff Deeply Frustrated by Campaign"[26]

Why has politics become more patrician? Money is one reason. Campaigns have become more expensive, requiring bigger staffs to do the needed work, which in turn ballooned the campaign budget. Expertise is another reason. Campaigns have become more technologically dependent, and that has ushered in a new breed of campaign worker—a computer specialist, not a door-knocker. Hierarchy is a third reason: The campaign entourage provides an attractive cast of characters, the Downstairs to the candidates' Upstairs. Mystery is a final reason. Dark spaces are a constant source of intrigue and the press has a flashlight, ready to reveal all. For these reasons and others, consultancy has become the trope of our age.

Was all of this inevitable? In part it was. For one thing, in the postwar environment the presidency itself changed. Modern complexities mandated greater decentralization in the White House (as well as in the rest of society) and that resulted in advisers with increasingly distinct portfolios. The National Security Advisor and Council of Economic Advisors, for example, could not have been imagined in the days of Teddy Roosevelt, never mind Abraham Lincoln. In addition, people came to accept the notion that presidents need political as well as policy advice, a gratuity that led to the "continual campaign" mentioned earlier.

We also found that the press offered *attributed* quotations from consultants twenty times more often than unattributed statements, a tendency that has steadily increased over time. This suggests either an increasing boldness on the parts of consultants or an increasing interest in them by journalists—or both. While in the early days campaign staffers retreated behind generic labels and offered anonymous comments on the campaign, consultants now stand at center stage. It is not surprising, then, that three years after the Clinton presidency ended, Paul Begala had a popular talk show and James Carville was making commercials for Nike.

But here is an equally intriguing finding: *Unattributed* quotations from consultants have also increased dramatically. News stories between 1968 and 1976 were twice as likely to offer such remarks as they were between 1948 and 1972. That tendency increased fivefold between 1980 and 1996. To be sure, unattributed speech grew at a slower rate than attributions, but the media's increasing willingness to reference "background" sources attests to their fascination with subterranean politics.[27] We also found some subtle differences: While the remarks of *spokespersons* were almost always properly attributed, strategic staffers (advisers, counselors, and campaign personnel) were quoted anonymously, a practice that also added to the campaign's mystique. In short, we now hear from consultants constantly and we hear from them even when we do not hear from them directly. Consultants have become the ether of politics.

One wonders about the effects of all this. The optimist would argue that any device that leads to greater interest in politics is a social good. If it takes political intrigue to lead people to the voting booth, so be it. The pessimist would, appropriately, be more pessimistic: Why would a citizen want to vote when politics is a business run by unelected persons for undeclared reasons? Ultimately, the pessimist might continue, a democracy depends on amateurism, not professionalism, for its vitality and voting are the supreme acts of amateurism. If professionalized politics undermines voters' senses of efficacy, it is dangerous. The pessimists clearly have a point.

THE RISE OF SPECIALIZATION

To this point we have treated the *consultant* broadly, finding it to be an increasingly dominant trope in news coverage. But there are details to the consultant's story and these details make the story richer. For example, we found ten different kinds of political workers described in the reportage; eight were specialists and two were generalists.[28] For efficiency's sake, we have grouped them according to function. A perusal of these functions provides an interesting glimpse of how politics has changed in the United States.

Campaign Strategy

The *adviser*, the *strategist*, and the *pollster* have become more and more prominent in news coverage, especially after the 1968 election. That is ironic since the 1968 campaign is remembered more often for its passion than its detachment. But the 1960s was also the decade of science. It began with *Sputnik* and ended with a man on the moon. Politics, like much else in American society, got caught in the scientific undertow.

There is also a second irony: 1968 was a year in which leaders were especially asked to lead (stay in Vietnam or abandon it?) as well as a year when ordinary Americans were asked to express their political attitudes (which they did via mass marches in Washington, San Francisco, and, memorably, Chicago). The fact that politics was being professionalized at that same moment shows how comprehensively the times were changing.

The strategist treats the campaign as a competitive, zero-sum environment and quantifies things as well. Politics has always been about quantities—How far is it to Korea? How much will a war cost?—but voters have rarely thought of it that way. They do now, with the strategist increasingly making politics demographic, deconstructing the idea of a single electorate by enumerating its imbedded constituencies. In 1948, these subgroups were standard ones and the strategists well disguised: "Dewey strategists, however, still believe the Governor can fight it out with Mr. Truman on even terms for the 'conservative' trade union vote."[29] At the turn of the century, strategy became four things it was not in 1948: (1) It was no longer anonymous, (2) it was no longer simplistic, (3) it was no longer univocal, and (4) it was no longer terse:

> Gore strategist Tad Devine said Gore had decided not to waste money in a state [Illinois] where he has the lead and where Bush appears to be pulling out. Bush campaign officials maintained that their prospects had brightened this week in other states where Bush had been struggling, including Missouri and Ohio. "The cumulative effect of this week has been very good for us," said Matthew Dowd, the campaign's polling director. However, Devine said that, on the basis of his analysis of the race, there are opportunities for the vice president that did not exist a month ago. Beginning Tuesday, the Gore campaign will launch its first ads of the campaign in Nevada, a small but symbolic step designed to send a signal in a state that Bill Clinton narrowly won in 1992 and 1996 but where Bush has held the advantage this year. "We are looking to expand the playing field and not contract it," Devine said. "If we pull media from states it's because we feel we're in very good shape there, or [because] our opponents have come down there. We're going to make the playing field bigger this week, not smaller." Gore's foray into Nevada is part of the cat and mouse game between the two campaigns as they try to bait each other into spending time and money defending their own territory, as both of those resources become increasingly precious.[30]

The *strategist* is a centerpiece of horserace coverage, a journalistic trend decried by many.[31] But horserace coverage still intrigues readers with its promises of inside information and second-guessing. The preceding coverage looks like baseball coverage—players jostling, bunts faked, runs scored, innings yet to be played. The analogy to baseball is apt since baseball is the most statistical of games, with fans often turning the RBI race into a sport-within-a-sport. As with politics, the great danger in doing so is that fans will miss the action on the field when filling out their scorecards.

In politics, *pollsters* are the primary keepers of the tally sheets, but they also perform an adumbrative function, explaining what the numbers mean. *Political* pollsters, however, are also advocates because they are often hired by the campaigns themselves. They must keep partisan spirits up when the numbers are down. As we see in the following, there is science in polling but there is heart in it as well: "Robert S. Strauss said that recent surveys by presidential pollster Patrick Caddell show Carter in excellent shape in the state. 'He [Caddell] thinks Anderson is going down rather substantially,' Strauss told a group of reporters. 'We could win New York today.' "[32]

Advisers are the campaign graybeards. If strategists know psychology and if pollsters know numbers, advisers know history and hence have a grander vision. Advisers lay out the game plan and suggest courses of action. Advisers also tell the press when they are correct and when they are not. Advisers are often cloaked in secrecy, conferring behind closed doors with persons known and unknown. People like this, people who live in the shadows, insult us with their absence, but they also intrigue us by knowing things we do not know. A background story on Walter Mondale's 1984 campaign shows why we read such stuff. "Many of the party elders," said the *Washington Post* at that time, "have been jarred by the prospect of a Mondale defeat so large that he could take much of his party down with him." Accordingly, a new economic platform was laid out, a strategy "aimed at recapturing Democratic voters—older voters and blue collar voters who seemingly should be Mondale's by now but who are telling pollsters they are for Reagan." "The changes did not come tranquilly, according to some high level campaign advisers" continued the *Post*, "there was a struggle within."[33] Reading a story like the *Post*'s does not really make one smarter, but it makes one *feel* smarter. In a cynical age, feeling smart can feel especially good.

Campaign Operations

Not surprisingly, given the rise of mass communication, *press secretaries, spokespersons*, and *media advisors* began to surface, respectively, in the 1970s, 1980s, and 1990s, paralleling the campaigns' needs to (1) establish formal relationships with press personnel, (2) centralize the dissemination of campaign information, and (3) lay out broad strategies for coordinating media approaches, approaches that now include ad placements, op-eds, cable buys, web enhancements, and, increasingly, email strategies. Because they deal so directly with the media, these individuals are far better known than *campaign managers*, persons who keep the big picture in mind. Peter Knight, Don

Evans, Donna Brazile, and Scott Reed are hardly household names, even though they ran the most recent presidential campaigns for the Republicans and Democrats. But these individuals were quoted heavily in the press at the time, especially when the going got tough. Compared to the 1950s and 1960s, campaign managers are now four times more likely to be quoted in the media. References to them have increased linearly since 1976.

This is somewhat surprising since campaign managers deal with the nuts-and-bolts of campaigns, leaving the rhetorical flourishes to the communications people. That managers now appear so often attests to the media's insatiable appetite for details. Such details make campaigns paeans to efficiency and organization, supreme American values. Campaign reportage takes on military trappings as a result, emphasizing administration, supervision, and authority. Interestingly, despite their frequent appearance, campaign managers were not personally characterized. They remained visibly invisible. In a random check of twenty-five *manager* tokens, not a single adjective was used to describe them. Instead, they were identified, quoted, and then ushered off the stage. Campaign managers run things. They do not have human qualities.

Thinking of campaigns as rational events is appealing on many levels. The everyday world is filled with chaos, so some voters prefer to think of campaigns as well-oiled machines. But the coverage we examined was so top-heavy, so strategically oriented, that it seemed antiseptic. Therein lie several dangers. When the media extract the emotion from politics it does politics a disservice. Every four years, Americans by the tens of thousands work for political candidates, suffering the indignities of sleepless nights, dank hotel rooms, poorly digested food, and, when they are lucky, insultingly small paychecks. They do so because they believe in things—the candidate, the platform, the political process.

The media rarely cover ordinary workers. They emphasize management and strategy instead, encouraging us to think of campaigns as commodities that manufacture commodities. That makes it hard to draw voters into the campaign but easy for them to reject the "suits" who skulk around plotting plots. By emphasizing campaign machinery, the press fails to challenge us. By emphasizing campaign officials, the press fails to engage us. By emphasizing campaign strategy, the press fails to motivate us. Although journalists have wondrous abilities to tell a good story, they too often diminish us when making politics seem bloodless.

THE IMPACT OF CONSULTANCY

What difference does it make that consultants have become prominent in campaign coverage? Could this be just a passing fad with no long-term implications? Our argument is that these changes dovetail with larger cultural trends and they have accelerated those trends as well. Even if one could ignore the consultant's role in modern journalism it would be unwise to do so. The *consultant* has a larger story to tell.

For one thing, focusing on political consultancy has allowed the press to depict itself as being on the cutting edge. A newspaper, after all, promises readers each day they will find something new in it. Focusing on the back-rooms of politics helps newspapers establish what critic Paul Starobin calls the "conceptual scoop," documentation of a trend with important implications.[34] Consider, for example, one such scoop reported in the *Washington Post* in 1988:

> Puzzling over the wild gyrations in presidential polls this summer, Republican consultant Robert Goodman has come up with a theory: "If the Constitution didn't require it, we wouldn't be having an election this year." In Goodman's reading, the jitterbugging polls depict an electorate that is disengaged and fickle—its attention span short, its investment in both candidates shallow, its mood malleable and its sense of urgency about public affairs at a low ebb. The campaign about which the voters keep changing their minds, he noted, offers neither the great issues nor the vivid personalities to compel sturdy commitments. His forecast, widely shared by political professionals in both parties, is that swing voters will keep shopping right up until nearly Election Day and finally will make their choices on the weight of gaffes yet uncommitted, national and world events yet to unfold, and 30-second punches and counterpunches yet to be thrown in a slugfest of attack ads that could start as early as this week.[35]

The strategy here is obvious: The *Post* uses the consultant's experiences to document incipient trends that cannot really be documented because they are so incipient. Accordingly, the reporter treats the consultant as an oracle, telling readers what they cannot possibly know because they must live life one day at a time. In this case, for example, the reporter moves from the consultant's presuppositions to evidence from opinion polls to commentary by unnamed professionals—a self-sealing paradigm of fact and conjecture. This is a useful approach since it allows the consultant to tiptoe into the future while the journalist stays rooted in the present (should the prediction not work out). Tomorrow's paper can always set the record straight, or, as often happens, it can drop the matter entirely.

Because politics is symbolically driven, news coverage can be speculative without objections being raised. Faced with incomplete evidence—as is often true in politics—consultants can offer their guesses and reporters can turn those guesses into knowledge itself. That is why candidates' personalities are so often emphasized. A "personality" is a vague and mellifluous thing, something that people can sense without really understanding. Psychological coverage is thus an ideal genre: It lets something be said when facts are unavailable. Adding consultants' thoughts to news coverage even lets reporters say something about the enigmatic George H. W. Bush: "'Deep down, he's still Clark Kent,' said Democratic pollster Peter Hart. 'The bumbling, the awkwardness, the uncertainty—my sense is that they're going to reappear.' "[36]

The impact of all this on media operations seems clear: Over the years, journalists have come to think like consultants. The image of the hard-bitten reporter looking askance at all things political has given way to the scribe tracking down some grand new theory. Reporters and consultants have become colleagues of sorts, reading the same tea leaves. That has caused news coverage to preference the strategic, the professional, and the surreptitious. This approach draws readers into the story but it also distances them from politics. As one observer remarks, abandoning policy for psychology gives readers "the sort of intimacy that once-marrieds still retain for one another, a deep-knowledge that produces a knowing glance and a snarl simultaneously."[37]

The consultant's view affects reporters' "interpretive frames." One result of that framing is that voters are constantly invited to examine why politicians say what they say. And it is only one small step from deconstructing candidates' motives to deconstructing politics itself. With reporters writing like consultants and with readers reading like consultants, who is left to think about the purposes of governance—building highways, solving crimes, curing AIDS, caring for the elderly? To be sure, the Watergate era has made Americans suspicious of government, and that is not altogether a bad thing. But suspicion should activate citizens to fix what is wrong. The consultancy frame, in contrast, turns them into armchair quarterbacks.

People's interpretations are susceptible to change. A sofa that looks good in the showroom on Saturday can seem less appealing on Wednesday when the invoice arrives in the mail. But people's interpretive frames are tied to their presuppositions, and so they are more enduring. Voters who distrust the sitting mayor will warm up to the mayor's replacement only if voters retain a sense of political efficacy. A steady drumbeat of strategic campaign coverage puts a strain on those feelings, especially when they are reinforced by media authorities. A community loses something important when the news immobilizes people.

The media coverage studied here was not monolithic. We examined thousands of stories written by hundreds of reporters. Much of the coverage was thoughtful and compelling; it told readers what they needed to know and why they needed to know it. But the steady incorporation of the *consultant* token changed the tone of those reports, encouraging readers to think more about less. In the early years of the coverage, the mythic aspects of the presidency—the greatness and prestige of the office—were dutifully laid out for the reader but never in a fawning way. Writers of the 1950s and 1960s were often hard-hitting, describing why governance had gone wrong. But when politics became professional, the news shifted as well.

There are chicken-and-egg questions here: Did reporting change because the parties had become more hierarchical, or did the parties react to how they were being described in the press? Too, did candidates become more receptive to strategic questions because they wanted to be helpful or because those questions were less problematic than ones about farm subsidies or war in the Middle East? We must also ask why news organizations have opened up their own polling operations. Were Roper and Gallup doing such a bad job of handing out questionnaires that CBS and the *New York Times* needed to lend a hand? From what we have seen here, a more likely explanation is that we have all become consultants—candidates, journalists, and citizens alike.

How has the rise of consultancy affected consultants themselves? In many ways, they have become the primary mediators of politics, translating voters for candidates and candidates for voters. Consultants are now asked to identify the pathways of influence that will bring people to the ballot box. They do so by framing voters as the products of media influence rather than party influence, replacing patronage with persuasion as the dominant political force. Such perspectives have given rise to entirely new political strategies. The 2002 off-season elections, for example, saw hordes of election workers prowling about America's neighborhoods with BlackBerrys in hand, instantly sending (and receiving) information about how they were being received on the nation's front stoops. This "narrowcasting" of the campaign was a consultant-inspired innovation. It was as if candidates themselves were knocking on people's doors.

As a result of these new approaches, consultants are now filled with themselves. And with good reason. A few years ago, 507 different firms were paid consulting fees in the state of Florida alone for just one election cycle.[38] When Mary Repper started her political consulting business in California in 1980, she had "a hard time getting the Yellow Pages people to understand what I did, so they put me under public relations. Now they have a whole category for political consultants."[39] In addition to their normal fees, consultants get hefty bonuses if their candidates win. The market is also expanding: Hank Sheinkopf, a pollster in the 1996 Clinton campaign, found that even a county commissioner candidate in Indiana could afford to hire him. With 513,200 elected offices now in the United States, business is booming for consultants, with one source estimating that $14 billion was spent on consultants in a single four-year election cycle in the United States.[40] One of the luckiest was San Francisco–based Clint Reilly, who alone received more than $7 million from the insurance industry for his work on a California ballot initiative. The initiative lost, but Reilly was paid.[41]

All of these anecdotes came from the nation's newspapers. Reporters love describing consultants and have done so increasingly during the last fifty years. Some might argue that such coverage costs us little, that anything that makes politics more interesting to readers is useful. We disagree. When consultants rather than candidates are featured in the press, we learn less about what the candidates believe. When consultants rather than parties are featured, politics becomes a game rather than a policy struggle. When consultants rather than voters are featured, we are invited to see politics as irrelevant to our lives. And when consultants rather than the media are featured, the press becomes less introspective. These are four very different consequences of featuring the *consultant*, and none is unimportant.

CONCLUSION

The kind of textual analysis attempted here cannot determine with certainty how consultancy affects the nation, but it does prompt some uncomfortable questions. As we have seen, such coverage emphasizes professional rather than grassroots politics and campaign strategy rather than campaign platforms. These emphases do not alone make such reportage inadequate, nor do they make political consultancy a supreme evil. Understanding such concepts as "margins of error" can help us digest poll reports intelligently, and attending to "political spin" can make us discerning about political communications. Too, consultants sometimes provide an important service when keeping candidates informed of demographic changes in their districts, thereby allowing them to better serve their constituencies. The opposition research they provide can keep scoundrels out of office, but it can ruin the careers of good people as well.

There is nothing inherently wrong with consultancy-based coverage except when it is the only coverage available. Despite the changes observed in this chapter, the nation's newspapers still do a fine job of political reporting and they still keep candidates' feet to the fire. But they can do more. In addition to lionizing consultants they can tell us what consultants are paid and how that affects the cost of doing political business in the United States. Fortunately, the records of such payments lie in the public domain since a democracy is still a democracy, even when it costs several million dollars to get a $65,000-a-year job as governor of Nebraska. Perhaps all of this money is wisely spent in an increasingly diverse, mediated, society. But it is also possible that consultants have gotten out of hand and that voters should cut off some of their air supply. Perhaps we need to know more, rather than hear more, about consultants.

One of the great dangers of consultancy gone wild is that politicians will think less about what they want to say and more about how they say it. Poll-driven State-of-the-State addresses do nobody any good. Consultancy makes governors think less carefully about what should be done for the electorate or how they can validate the public trust they have been given. Similarly, when voters think like consultants by paying too much attention to the governor's shock of red hair they miss a chance to see what is in store for them in the upcoming year. Focusing on political strategy transforms communication environments into a meta-communication environments where judgments are layered on judgments and where politicians give speeches about their opponents' ads featuring misleading survey results. That creates a topsy-turvy world where candidates say little of importance and where voters declare a pox on all politicians' houses. That would be fine if all of us—candidates, reporters, consultants, and voters—did not have to live in those houses. They are, alas, the only ones available.

NOTES

1. J. Carney and J. F. Dickerson, "The Busiest Man in the White House," *Time*, April 30, 2001, 32–36.

2. N. Lemann, "The Controller: Karl Rove's Plan to Take Over Politics," *New Yorker*, May 12, 2003, 68–83.

3. S. Blumenthal, *The Permanent Campaign* (New York: Simon and Schuster, 1982).

4. Carney and Dickerson, "Busiest," 34.

5. Specialties such as *campaign advisor, strategist, press secretary,* and *spokesman* were known quantities even in 1948, but the term *political consultant* did not appear in the news texts studied here until the 1968 presidential election.

6. This study of thousands of examples of campaign reportage from 1948 to 1996 shows that the political culture sees consultancy as perhaps the most crucial organizing principle in campaigns. From consultants comes the campaign's strategy. From strategy comes the various political specialties. From these specialties come the many campaign artifacts and political events that define campaigns.

7. L. Sabato, *The Rise of Political Consultants: New Ways of Winning Elections* (New York: Basic Books, 1981).

8. J. Rosen and P. Taylor (eds.), *New News vs. the Old News: Press & Politics in the 1990s* (New York: Century Foundation, 1992).

9. W. L. Bennett, *The Governing Crisis: Media, Money, and Marketing in American Elections* (New York: St. Martin's Press, 1992).

10. E. Schwartzman, *Political Campaign Craftsmanship: A Professional's Guide to Campaigning for Public Office* (New Brunswick, NJ: Transaction Publishers, 1989).

11. S. Ansolabehere and S. Iyengar, *Going Negative: How Attack Ads Shrink and Polarize the Electorate* (New York: Free Press, 1995).

12. D. Chagall, *The New King-Makers* (New York: Harcourt Brace Jovanovich, 1981).

13. For more on this, see S. Salmore and B. G. Salmore, *Candidates, Parties, and Campaigns: Electoral Politics in America* (Washington, DC: CQ Press, 1985).

14. See B. Newman, *The Marketing of the President: Political Marketing as Campaign Strategy* (Thousand Oaks, CA: Sage, 1994); B. Newman, *The Mass Marketing of Politics: Democracy in an Age of Manufactured Images* (Thousand Oaks, CA: Sage, 1999).

15. For more on this matter, see J. A. Maltese, *Spin Control: The White House Office of Communications and the Management of Presidential News* (Chapel Hill: University of North Carolina Press, 1992).

16. See, for example, D. Maraniss and J. F. Harris, "Unusually Resilient Ties Unravel: Political Brothers Separate at Birth of Sex Scandal," *Washington Post*, August 30, 1996; D. Maraniss, "The Comeback Kid Is Back—Again," *Washington Post*, August 29, 1996.

17. Only a portion of these data will be reported here. For a more complete presentation, see J. Handy-Bosma, "Images of Political Consultancy in American Presidential Campaigns," unpublished Ph.D. dissertation, University of Texas at Austin, 2000.

18. Sabato, *Rise of Political Consultants.*

19. "For One Ad Man, a Leap of Faith," *Los Angeles Times,* October 7, 2000, 1.

20. Includes all instances in which consultants are described with core consulting terms, and either quoted or paraphrased by name. Consultants need not have made the claim for the reference to be counted; if the text indicated that a particular consultant held a particular view the reference was considered a paraphrase even if that view was suppressed.

21. "A Supporting Cast in the Spotlight," *Christian Science Monitor,* August 2, 2000, 1.

22. "G.O.P. Intensifies Drive to Attract Jews to Nixon," *New York Times,* October 9, 1972, 1.

23. "Inventing Clintonomics; Spectrum of Advisers Debates Goals, Priorities," *Washington Post,* October 15, 1992, 1.

24. "Atlanta TV Is a Battleground: Bush Being Outspent in Ad War," *Atlanta Constitution,* October 9, 1992, 8.

25. "Smoother Bush Campaign Shows Baker's Famous Touch," *Atlanta Constitution,* September 5, 1992, 6.

26. "White House Staff Deeply Frustrated by Campaign," *Christian Science Monitor,* October 15, 1992, 1.

27. The data referenced here include only quotations and paraphrases from unnamed consultants. For example, if the clause included the attribution, "a senior consultant said . . . ," the instance was counted as an unattributed quotation or paraphrase.

28. Labeling and describing various kinds of political work was a central preoccupation of the texts studied here. The texts studied typically combined already familiar terms, thereby offering an ever-expanding sense of the term *consultant.* A close inspection of how consulting work is labeled reveals that seemingly disparate terms are employed to communicate common themes. We examined the activities consultants engage in, cross-referencing them with labels, descriptions, and job titles in the texts studied. The result, we argue, is a clearer understanding of the "building blocks" out of which new tropes of consultancy emerged.

29. "Dewey Tour Looks Like Hot Pursuit of Truman," *Washington Post,* September 10, 1948, 1.

30. "For Bush, Difficult Choices Ahead," *Washington Post,* September 24, 2000, 1.

31. See, for example, J. Cappella and K. H. Jamieson, *Spiral of Cynicism: The Press and the Public Good* (New York: Oxford University Press, 1997).

32. "Campaign Notes," *Washington Post,* September 9, 1980, 3.

33. "Mondale Modifies Ads to Recapture Democrats," *Washington Post,* October 8, 1984, 6.

34. P. Starobin, "The Conceptual Scoop," *Columbia Journalism Review,* 34. 5 (1996): 21.

35. "Voters Fickle as Campaign Rounds Labor Day Bend," *Washington Post,* September 5, 1988, 1.

36. Ibid.

37. R. P. Hart, *Seducing America: How Television Charms the Modern Voter* (New York: Oxford University Press, 1994), 29.

38. F. Mays, "Political Consulting Comes into Its Own in Florida," *The Tampa Bay Business Journal*, July 14, 1997, http://www.bizjournals.com/tampabay/stories/1997/07/14/story8.html (July 15, 2003).

39. Ibid.

40. L. Wayne, "Political Consultants Thrive in the Cash-Rich New Politics," *New York Times*, October 24, 2000, http://www.cas.suffolk.edu/berg/msps/consultants.html (July 15, 2003).

41. D. Bernstein, "Lottery Initiative Was One Consultant's Roll of the Dice," *Sacramento Bee*, August 5, 1996, http://www.sacbee.com/static/archive/news/projects/initiatives/takeinitiative.html (July 15, 2003).

CONCLUSION

Language in Retrospect

This has been a book about words and the people who use them. As Kenneth Burke might say, it is also a book about the words that use the people who use them. Words use us constantly, and keywords use us with special force. Words like *patriotism* and *terrorism* do not let us breathe. They exhaust the air around us. We reason less well in their presence, often doing their bidding because they have been spoken in the right place, at the right time, by the right person. Some observers disagree, arguing that words are mere baubles in a world run by chemicals and machinery, money and might. But the families of hundreds of fallen American soldiers beg to differ. They would remind us, between their tears, that a phrase like the *Axis of Evil* could launch a war in 2003 and that sixteen other words ("The British government has learned that Saddam Hussein recently sought significant quantities of uranium from Africa") could thrust their nation deeper into that conflagration.[1] Those sixteen words had these features: past tense, passive voice, a single dependent clause, colorless modifiers, and, as it turned out, the marks of falsehood. But because these words were spoken by the nation's forty-third president and because they contained one of the most powerful keywords of all, *Saddam Hussein*, they did their intended work. As the families of thousands of dead Iraqis would note, their work was grisly indeed.

This book has also been a story of how language writes history. We have examined only a small swath of time—the second half of the twentieth century—and only one nation, the United States. We have looked at only a handful of words, avoiding such lofty abstractions as *liberty* and *human rights* and such propulsive words as *heritage* and *destiny*. We settled instead on the practical words of politics. On their own, these words cannot launch a thousand ships. On their own, they do not conjure up powerful memories or lay out beatific visions. But words like these are never on their own. They are, instead, folded into more complex locutions and hence become part of the textual underworld. Low-visibility words like *party* and *people* insinuate themselves into our lives, asking very little of us. But anonymity can be powerful. When schoolchildren find it hard to think past their *president* to his policies, when the *media* become an ongoing assumption rather than a political afterthought, and when the *consultant* is seen as an all-knowing figure, the world begins to shift. It shifts further when *politics* reaches into our private lives and when the tapestry of *promises* mesmerizes us. When *government* becomes problematic or, worse, an impossibility, unusually potent forces are set afoot. Despite voters' wishes, the keywords of politics will not leave them alone.

We have covered considerable ground here, and it is time to take stock. Stock-taking is especially important in what has been called an "over-communicated" age, an age that bombards its citizens each day with a hundred, nay a thousand, messages from the Home Shopping Network to pop-up solicitations on the web, from the chatty screens in taxicabs to the daily deluge of junk mail. In such an age the news becomes denser, the rap becomes faster, and flags are flown higher. People's fields of attention shift quickly—from peace talks in Israel to the celebrity rape suspect in Colorado; from a wandering object in outer space to the latest Harry Potter book; from scandals in the church to a punishing job market. It is hard to attend to one thing in such an age; in such an age it is hard to attend to anything. Images blur; words become cheap; people shut out the noise.

Governments must still function in such an age, an age that flattens hierarchies and makes legitimacy difficult to achieve. People are easily distracted in such an age, and that affects governance as well. Election turnout rates are now quite terrible in the United States; the audience for serious news is minuscule; activists find it hard to fashion working coalitions; Generation Y voters look at party allegiance with contempt. Oddly, even though it is hard to get messages across in an over-communicated age, people demand more of them, as if the disease were its own best cure.

Such a scenario puts special demands on keywords. Because they are only *words* they must compete for attention in a world of sight and sound, in an electronic, pulsating environment that chews up at Time Two what it has spit out at Time One. But because they are *keywords*, because they are (1) repeated with special frequency in (2) high-profile environments by (3) persons of considerable stature and, especially, because (4) they are easily overlooked (being only words, after all), they can slowly, teasingly affect our hearts and minds. Keywords are at their most powerful when they are taken for granted.

What happens when keywords fail? What happens when, as researchers report, ordinary citizens begin to refer to *the government* rather than *our government*?[2] Is that a sign of trouble? Even as that happened, however, the nation's leaders were steadily increasing their use of first-person plurals—*we* and *our*.[3] A sense of the collective was evaporating in one sector even as it was being heralded in another. What does it mean when keywords are juxtaposed in these ways? What happens when they cease to do their jobs well or when their jobs change? What happens when new voices come upon old language, or when new language is imported from old cultures (*homeland security* is a recent example)? What happens when a nation cannot find a language that fits? when rhetoric and reality clash? This book has touched on all these problems, and it seems useful to touch on them once again.

LANGUAGE AND FUNCTION

Our approach in this book has been a practical one, and that puts us squarely in the tradition of Raymond Williams. As mentioned in chapter 1, Williams returned from World War II determined to "teach young working men how to grasp and hold on to their own future." He did so by calling their attention to the words they consumed voraciously but unthinkingly, words "taken from *Ulysses* or the *News Chronicle*." Williams was keen to show his young charges the spells cast by language, an approach that would soon be taken up by a host of scholars, Edward Said and Michel Foucault among them, scholars who gave "linguistic history . . . a new political edge." Williams approached this new brand of criticism by reading a text slowly (in Terry Eagleton's terms), focusing on individual language components to see how they influenced readers.[4]

Our method has been different. For one thing, we have read faster than Williams in an attempt to grapple with the constantly circulating discourses of modern life. The more a word is used, we have reasoned, the more it accelerates and hence the greater its mass; the greater its mass, we reason further, the more gravity it exerts on an audience. Like all metaphors, this is an imperfect one, but it does capture the importance of linguistic proportions and, hence, of the additive effects of language. Necessarily, counting things has distanced us from the texts being analyzed (a distancing that would have discomfited Raymond Williams), but it lets us see patterns that would have been missed close up. Too, quantifying things lets us make direct comparisons between different moments in time and different spokespersons. Mostly, though, the value of our approach is that it ignores the vivid instance, the distinctive and hence unrepresentative text. Our approach featured the ordinary, the repeated, an approach that—despite our counting—Raymond Williams might have appreciated.

While we have spoken often of power relations in this book we have not employed Williams' materialist assumptions. Our approach has been functional, an approach inspired more by George Will than Raymond Williams. It is Will who reminds us that one cannot understand the game of baseball unless one sees it as "men at work."[5] So we have focused here on the working words of democracy, hoping they will point to society's soft spots, to its various stresses and strains. We have assumed they will point to its revered folkways and remedies as well.

The United States is a fine case study for all of this. For example, because the United States was founded amidst political and social revolution, *questions of identity* have always bedeviled its people: Do I belong here? Who is my neighbor? Is my color, gender, religion, or sexual preference appropriate? All this made the *people* a hardy perennial because everyone always wants to know what 285 million Americans believe about a given issue. The empirical answer is that they believe everything there is to believe— satanism and Christianity, nuclear weaponry and nude beaches. But that is an emotionally unsatisfying answer, and so the rhetoric of a congealed electorate is used to answer questions—who are we? where do we come from?—that cannot be fully answered. Perhaps better, the answers to these questions lie in their continually being asked.

Because questions of identity are so unsettling for Americans, *questions of legitimacy* inevitably follow. The nation's Puritan roots might have predicted that. Puritanism was, to its core, a reactionary religion, rejecting high-church Anglicanism and its attendant worldliness. The earliest settlers in the United States were therefore overcome by issues of rectitude. Those issues quickly took secular form (regarding regionalism, taxation, representation, etc.), but the logic of the village persisted. "Who has the right of command?" the colonists asked, a question that still motivates the Montana Militia. "The president has that right" is an imperfect answer, but it is the nation's best answer thus far. Congress and the Supreme Court are also answers, but they are less compelling rhetorically. The president, in contrast, is fully human, fully imaginable. The *president* token lends itself to narrative, giving school-children and journalists alike easy access to governance. Presidents tend their own institution as well, scouring history for precedent and, when that fails, turning history on its head until it behaves properly. There is some amount of gamesmanship in all of this, but it is a serious game: Such tokens have been used to put troops in harm's way, to quell urban riots, to pass tax legislation, to curb unemployment, and, yes, to fly Americans to the moon. It takes more than the president to establish legitimacy in a nation so large, but, without the president, everything becomes more difficult.

Questions of hierarchy flow directly from questions of legitimacy, but the former adds an element of compulsion. The Puritans' ecclesiastical modes of governance sufficed for a time, but only for a time. As the blacksmiths, boot-leggers, and Baptists disembarked on the nation's shores it became clear that something else was needed. Government was the result, but it carried with it a host of despised connotations—power structures for an egalitarian peo-ple, routinization for a emergent people. As a result, no keyword has come under more fire than *government* has. Indeed, the surest way of declaring oneself a genuine American is to decry the current order. Other people in other nations behave similarly; nobody likes high-handedness or repression. But Americans have institutionalized that rhetoric. Even its own chief exec-utives deconstruct *government* in order to foster it. On the hustings, the peo-ple are promised as little governance as possible and later treated to all the governance needed in a large and complex nation. This is a poststructural enterprise—tearing Washington apart in order to save it—but it lets people have government without having it. As Lawrence Rosenfield observes, such a rhetoric becomes rather "like the ocean's roar," reassuring the citizenry "that things are normal and [that] the public institutions remain healthy."[6]

The free press has flourished in the United States for several reasons, many of which have to do with its people's quarrelsome nature. The press is also a business—historically, a small business—and that appealed to the nation's entrepreneurial instincts. Mostly, though, the press became popular because the nation's diversity bred a special brand of distrust. *Questions of transparency* resulted, and the *press* became both a sainted and a reviled token. It was sainted and reviled for the same reason: It knew more than most people knew. It always knew more than most people knew. As a result, when the press told its readers something they did not know but wished to know—that the president was having inappropriate relations with a White House intern, for example—many Americans rejoiced for reasons prurient and partisan. Others Americans, for reasons protective and partisan, were outraged that the press would stoop so low. But most Americans want to know everything they can know even while simultaneously feeling someone is keeping something from them. The *media,* which know everything and are rich to boot, are therefore a perfect object of opprobrium, the one obstacle to the people becoming omniscient.

One of the most contested of all American keywords is the *party,* and all of the foregoing factors explain why. Parties, said James Madison, are factions and therefore dangerous. They are dangerous because they operate in cabalistic fashion (thus prompting questions of transparency) and they are dangerous because they are gluttonous, drawing all power unto themselves (thus raising questions of hierarchy) in an attempt to establish a new political order (thus raising questions of legitimacy). The political *consultant* is the party individuated; that is both frightening and entrancing. It is frightening because no individual should be able to have so much influence, especially behind closed doors. It is entrancing because few of us can resist being drawn into the flame of celebrity. Focusing as it does on the engineering of consent, the consultant token appeals to the technician in us even as it scares the insurgent in us. The *party,* in contrast, is hardly efficient, but it is troubling for similar reasons: Someone, somewhere, is celebrating something and we have not been invited. Perhaps that explains why the *party* has disappeared from campaign rhetoric in recent years. But the press continues to nurture it because parties are so necessary, so functional. Still, the worries persist.

Questions of destiny also began in the Puritan era and have not abated since. As the Puritans told the story, the United States was to be a New Israel, free of want and free of sin. Preachers from George Whitfield to Billy Sunday to Robert Schuler have told that story and always with gusto. Robert Jewett and John Lawrence have traced the secular manifestations of that myth, showing how a Captain America Complex resulted from these humble beginnings.[7] That complex led to U.S. adventuring in its own western territories, in the Suez Canal and the Bay of Pigs, in Kosovo and Grenada and Baghdad. Matters of destiny have been worked out in less fearsome ways, too—by members of the Peace Corps, by NASA engineers, by AmeriCorps workers, by Fulbright scholars. When America is not on the move it feels less like America. That may explain the persistence of political *promises.* Voters detest promises and crave them at the same time. They detest them because promises are so airy (they would have no lilt were they more sober) and they crave them because they are so substantive (lower taxes, smarter children, longer lives for all). Few Americans believe all the promises they hear, but most Americans, because they are Americans, remain troubled by their unbelief.

Political keywords in the United States work hard each day to grapple with the aforementioned questions, but they expend even more effort to cope with *questions of continuity.* Again for a number of reasons, the United States has been a cauldron of change since its inception. Its cultural pluralism mandated that, its expansionistic nature mandated that, its mercantile fervor mandated that, its love of scientific advancement mandated that, and its resistance to Old World hegemonies sanctified that. As a result, American political slogans have always been trite with newness: New Frontier, New Covenant, Bridge to the Twenty-first Century, New Democrat, Reformer with Results, and so on. The need to be on the cusp, to be ahead of the game, has also fueled American consumerism, resulting in faddishness in dress and entertainment and in a host of eccentricities. Americans are comfortable with change—in part, at least.

American progressivism also prompted the migration of *politics* from one field to many fields. As women's rights were expanded and as the civil rights movement bore fruit, politics was discovered in new and strange places. The pluralists brought politics into the classroom, the bedroom, the boardroom, and into the academic salon as well. Areas that had been previously cordoned off from politics—sports, movies, religion, family life, the neighborhood—had their windows opened wide and a new political breeze blew through. Admittedly, our observations here derive from literary phenomena—book titles—but the transmigration of *politics* to hitherto unexplored lands paralleled wider social trends as well. The latter part of the twentieth century was distinguished by all politics all the time.

But for all of the Sturm und Drang reported in chapter 2, chapter 3 showed a remarkable consistency to the concept of politics. Our metaphorical tracings revealed that, across many fields of study, politics has been seen as a quintessential mode of accommodation. Politics helps people cope with winning and losing, attaching and detaching, changing and maintaining, achieving and imagining, and the demands of nature itself. Writers of every stripe have happened on these problems time and again. A certain essentialism has resulted, with *politics* being found where it has always been found—in the interstices of life, at the crossroads of human interaction.

Other nations have faced the questions outlined here, but few have faced them for so long and in quite the same configuration as have Americans. These questions—identity, legitimacy, hierarchy, transparency, destiny, and continuity—are only some of the problems the United States has encountered in its three centuries of existence, but they have been unusually persistent ones. The keywords detailed in this book were used to cope with these unresolved, perhaps unresolvable, issues. But the American story is not a single story. It permutates in interesting ways. We review those permutations next.

LANGUAGE AND TIME

We have listened to many voices in this book, and all have had something to say. We have seen the *party* lose ground with politicians only to regain it with the press. Political crises have coaxed the *people* from their slumbers; political campaigns have sent them back to bed again. Campaigners have savaged *government*, content in the knowledge that the newly elected *president* will redeem it. The *media* have been decried in print journalism even as the nation's politicians lionize the *press*. Every four years, journalists have denounced the empty *promises* politicians make only to have politicians order up a new supply. Such pushings and pullings have been found throughout this book. When keywords are looked at as a whole, the whole is divided.

Our general argument is that keywords are juxtaposed at the crossroads of change and stability. Keywords are used to create momentum and to adjust to emerging political realities. But they are also used as ballast for the ship of state, keeping its sails trim and its direction true. We have found keywords to be energizing and boring, surprising and expectable. When beginning this project, we did not anticipate that. We assumed we would find clear, linear progressions, distinct political voices, words that served only one purpose. We rarely found such things. We found instead a rhetoric of change located within a rhetoric of stability. Although ours has not been a comparative study, we sense that this dialectic is sharper in the United States than in other nations. The latter part of the twentieth century tells that story, a period that produced progressives like John Kennedy and Bill Clinton and rock-ribbed conservatives like Ronald Reagan and George W. Bush. From a European perspective, these chief executives often sounded alike—talky doctrinaires functioning as centrists. We also find an underlying conservatism to American political discourse, but a conservatism that is more psychological than ideological in nature. When the data reported here are parsed by era rather than by keyword, the contours of that conservatism become clearer.

The 1950s begin that story, a decade that has been stereotyped as placid when it was in fact a period of great change, a muscular and often imaginative time. *Sputnik* made its appearance in the fifties, as did atomic spies, automation, suburbia, and a gaggle of new home appliances, especially (and notably) television. The 1950s also introduced Senator Joseph McCarthy and considerable national panic about communist sympathizers. "Few Americans" in the 1950s, says David Halberstam, "doubted the essential goodness of their society." "Most Americans," he goes on, "needed little coaching in how they wanted to live. They were optimistic about the future. Young men who had spent three or four years fighting overseas were eager to get on with their lives; so, too, were the young women who had waited for them at home." Above all, says Halberstam, "Americans trusted their leaders to tell them the truth, to make sound decisions, and to keep them out of war."[8]

Our data reflect many of these patterns as well. The *people* were still "global citizens" to the nation's leaders, a people haunted by the world's recent hostilities. *Government* was treated as a beneficent thing, a reflection of the comparatively genteel contests between Adlai Stevenson and Dwight Eisenhower. *Politics* was institutional, not cultural, with some women wanting careers but more wanting marriage. The *consultant* was nowhere to be found, the *party* was still a prominent force, and political *promises* were made infrequently. This was a sober age. Children respected their parents, parents their political leaders, and political leaders their God. The 1950s was hardly an idyllic time, but it was an orderly one, a discipline mothered by the demands for new product manufacturing. It was, above all, a religious time:

> Fear, then, was probably the major cause of the phenomenal return to religion. People turned to religion in record numbers to find hope in an anxious world. . . . The insecurity brought on by hydrogen bombs and atomic spies made churches seem the mainstay of traditional values. Despite the diverse denominations between Protestantism, Catholicism, and Judaism, there seemed to be a basic unity to religion in America.[9]

The 1960s began with one of the most exhilarating presidential campaigns in U.S. history, a campaign featuring two bright young men who wanted to lead the nation through what was expected to be a decade of change. It turned out to be just that, with the last presidential campaign of that decade being exquisitely tumultuous. "The legacy of the Sixties should remind us that good intentions are not enough," says Paul Lyons; the era echoed some of the perfectionism that had long been part of the Protestant tradition, a tradition that admitted to certain "radical expressions of an extreme individualism" (do your own thing) but also an enlivened sense of community (mind your brother's business).[10] The 1960s saw both of these antinomian impulses as well as "the rejection of organization, hierarchy and leadership, the critique of intelligibility and coherence, and the call for a 'money-free economy.'"[11] Everything that could have happened in the sixties happened: the Cuban Missile Crisis, a presidential assassination, urban riots, student protests, the erection of the Berlin Wall, the Great Society, a moon landing. The sixties left the nation reeling, its families torn apart.

The 1960s was really two half-decades rather than a single coherent one, with the "hope and optimism of the early 1960s" ultimately "replaced by the darker emotions of the second half of the decade."[12] Our data show that as well. The conservative portion of the sixties found *presidential* allusions a popular commodity, with John Kennedy and Lyndon Johnson constantly looking to the past for ideational support. Such allusions rose sharply in textbooks as well; making good Americans was a topic on everyone's minds. The *people* were turned inward; they were described as taxpayers and jobholders as the economic growth of the fifties took hold. But as the sixties unfolded, new sounds were heard as well. The *people* were increasingly framed as audience members, part of a "demographic" that must be cultivated. The *media* came on the scene to do so, and that changed politics forever. Because of these new forces, *party* workers began to fade and were replaced by jaunty television ads. Political *promises* became headier and more frequent, in part because this was a Democratic era but also because it was an optimistic era (until late in the decade). Keywords continually crisscrossed in the 1960s.

Politics burst on the scene in the 1970s and has not abated since. Political book titles tripled between the 1960s and the 1970s, jumped another 50 percent in the 1980s, and increased an additional 20 percent in the 1990s. For both good and ill, the people of the 1970s were shaped by the turbulence of the previous decade. Watergate separated Democrats from Republicans; Vietnam separated children from their parents; busing separated blacks from whites. Good things happened too. The nation's bicentennial was observed in 1976, overseen by a genial man (Gerald Ford) who helped bind up the nation's wounds. Another genial man, Jimmy Carter, ministered to the nation's psyche, but he could not fix oil prices, the rate of inflation, or problems associated with de-industrialization. The 1970s was an ambivalent decade. A gap between optimism and dynamism opened up relative to *government* during those years: Government was doing more, but it made few people happy. A sharp rise in political *promises* was seen, but politicians sometimes promised things they could not deliver and that led to more disillusionment. A dominant keyword was the *press*, perhaps the only respected icon to emerge from the Watergate affair. On the campaign front, political *parties* became less prominent and, for the first time, one could read about *consultants* in the newspaper, a trend that would rocket skyward in the 1980s.

Much happened in the 1970s, but nobody seemed pleased. "Americans for the first time pierced the veil of secrecy that surrounded the normal exercise of power in their country," observed Peter Carroll. "'You don't get to the top in politics without doing a lot of crooked stuff,'" said a seventy-three-year-old cab driver in Washington, DC, on the day of Richard Nixon's resignation. "Watergate confirmed that truism," says Carroll, "and if anything, threatened to reveal too much about the inner workings of American politics."[13] With conventional politics seeming a dead-end, young people, who already distrusted the corporations and the national government, "flocked to the Sierra Club and Ralph Nader."[14] As the economy went south, says Todd Gitlin, "the general sense of spaciousness withered" (despite the politicians' promises) and the bottom-line message became clear: "Lower expectations, dress up, get down to business."[15] While this may have been practical advice it was not a heady concoction.

Ronald Reagan was the 1980s. He owned the decade. He owned its politics as well as its leitmotifs. Despite his fellow Republicans' earnest platform-writing, Reagan ignored *party* appeals and staked out entirely new political territory. Reagan was also the first "cult" president the nation has known, which is to say he constantly produced *himself*. Kathleen Jamieson says that Reagan employed a "feminine style" to work his magic, a style that relied on heartfelt, personal appeals replete with gentle humor, a style that felt good even to those who detested his politics.[16] Reagan also trolled the history books, using Democratic and Republican *presidents* to advance his programs. He topped all of his predecessors in political *promises*—less government, lower taxes, renewed prosperity, waning inflation. He made good on a few, failed on many, but few seemed to care. This was a popular president.

Reagan understood "electronic eloquence" says Kathleen Jamieson.[17] He was not the first television president (that was Dwight Eisenhower nominally, John Kennedy phenomenologically), but he was the first president to have so many tools at his disposal. Not surprisingly, references to the *media* began a steep ascent in the 1980s; *consultants,* the wizards of the New Political Age, now appeared in full force; the *press* fell off the radar screen (they were too stodgy, too verbal, too confrontational); and warnings about *big government* filled the airwaves. Ronald Reagan was the beneficiary of all these trends. The Left, in contrast, retreated "into stock thought and rhetoric." "It bristled and huffed," says Gilbert Sewall, exacting "loyalty tests, accusing anyone wary of its agenda of 'insensitivity' and 'monoculturalism' and worse."[18] Ronald Reagan sailed past all of this, and the media were his friends. His successor in office, George H. W. Bush, had none of Reagan's rhetorical talents and no appreciation for how profoundly the new media were changing the face of American politics and, in Robert Fogel's terms, destabilizing the prevailing culture.[19]

The 1990s was an apolitical decade. By the time it began, cynicism had taken hold. The number books written about *politics* was at an all-time high, but they featured cultural politics not institutional politics. Everyone seemingly was hip to the tools of deconstruction. The 1990s produced a reasonably popular president, Bill Clinton. But he too was a cult president, and, this time, the culture wars raged about him. Keyword usage showed a clear de-instutitionalization: candidates rarely referred to the *parties;* the *press* was barely mentioned by reporters (although they gleefully shared criticisms of the *media*); and academics seemed uninterested in State and infrastructure *politics* (at least compared to earlier decades).

It was hard to run for political office in the nineties. Political *promises* were at an all-time low, and favorable references to *government* services and operations were nowhere to be found. There was a smarminess to the era. Candidates attacked their opponents' pledges rather than present their own for consideration and, when pressed, were as likely to launch an assault on the *media* rather than propose new policy platforms. When politicians talked about the *people* they framed them as more competitive, watchful, and isolated than in previous decades. Was all of this inevitable? Numerous commentators say it was, but they say so for different reasons:

- *E. J. Dionne—too much ideology:* Liberalism and conservatism are framing political issues as a series of false choices. Wracked by contradiction and responsive mainly to the needs of their various constituencies, liberalism and conservatism prevent the nation from settling the questions that most trouble it. On issue after issue, there is consensus on where the country should move or at least on what we should be arguing about; liberalism and conservatism make it impossible for that consensus to express itself.[20]

- *Haynes Johnson—too complex a citizenry:* It requires no insight to state that the millennial America of more than 280 million citizens is more divided than it is united. The disconnect goes far beyond the political divisions that were so sharply exposed during the last presidential election cycle. In truth, Americans don't really know one another, or, at least, they have relatively little contact with other large segments of their society.[21]

- *Paul Johnson—too many scandals:* The continual fear of prosecution engendered what has been called a 'culture of mistrust' in American government and led to an unwillingness of public-spirited citizens to run for high political office or to accept presidential invitations to serve. . . . Scandal politics were thus part of the process whereby popular democracy was degenerating into "media democracy."[22]

History, as they say, is a text. It can be read in many ways. For our part, we find no single trajectory to our data, no inevitable trend toward chaos or comity. Instead, we find the United States picking its way through the minefields of culture. The keywords we have tracked signal important changes over the years—toward more skepticism, toward more individualism, toward a new sort of interest-group politics. But for every worrisome trend we find counterbalancing forces. For example, it may be unwise that the schools are making a cult of the *presidency,* but it is useful when the *press* reminds a sitting president about his forebears. It cannot possibly be good for voters to hear campaigners carp about *government* constantly, but that seems to change when the new chief executive takes office. It is odd that political candidates are increasingly ignoring the *party* (upon which their candidacies depend and upon which the two-party system is based), but the news media have picked up the slack in recent years. Although some commentators say the nation is unraveling, we find it significant that the *people* were prominently called to witness during two of the nation's moments of stress. We also find it heartening that politicians have become more careful with their *promises,* although they might throttle back a bit when attacking those of their opponents. It is probably healthy that *politics* is being discussed in new and different ways, but it is mournful that so many find it so boring, so toxic.

When taken together, these trends reveal an interesting set of (1) dynamic forces that (2) act as counterweights to one another and, therefore, (3) create a fundamental political stability in the United States. It is noteworthy, for example, that even as the press became more cynical, children's textbooks became more establishmentarian. It is also noteworthy that the Democrats lauded the *people's* sobriety after September 11 while the Republicans did so during the impeachment process. And it is noteworthy, too, that even though the political *consultant* is now a celebrity, that same celebrity may help spur greater interest in politics. Although one can wring one's hands when considering any of these findings in isolation, they seem less worrisome when taken together.

Naturally, too much stability can be troublesome. Congressional debates, as John Hibbing and Elizabeth Theiss-Morse note, regularly stabilize a contentious polity, but that does not endear members of Congress to the people.[23] Too much stability can also lead to an incrementalist politics that satisfies nobody and can foster complacency as well, sapping the energy a political system needs to attract civic volunteers. When stability becomes an end in itself innovation also suffers, which is why some commentators see political friction as central to a healthy system. "The very dominance of the middle-class ethic," says Walter Dean Burnham, has meant that "political oppositions of European clarity and hardness . . . have never had the opportunity to form in this country during the past century."[24] Deprived of these sharper tensions, politics in the United States risks becoming a spectator sport rather than a participant's sport, and that, too, is dangerous.[25]

Stability also has its attractions. Most important, a stable political system can reproduce itself, and that is especially important in a society that has few ethnic, religious, geographical, or tradition-based ways of knitting itself together. Stable systems typically abhor new and untried solutions, and that can help citizens sleep easier at night. Because "poverty is a principal obstacle to democratic development," says Samuel Huntington, stable political systems are overwhelmingly attractive to corporate forces and, hence, to the people they employ.[26] Civil society also prospers in stable polities, as does high culture. Finally, when working optimally, stable systems facilitate civic involvement and civic recruitment as well. Political keywords produce none of these bounties on their own, but they are among the forces that help stabilize things. That is either bad or good depending, again, on one's taste for stability.

LANGUAGE AND CHALLENGE

Keywords call attention to themselves. To mention *politics* at a party is to start a conversation; to mention *government* is to end it. People inevitably have opinions about these and other keywords. Many of them feel, for example, that the *media* have become too self-important. Young Americans are especially distrustful of *parties*, although they are not yet settled on a replacement. The *president*, any president, is either the root of all evil or salvation incarnate depending on one's conversational partner. Everyone thinks they know what the *people* believe—everyone with any "common sense," that is. From morning to night keywords do considerable work.

To identify a society's keywords is to identify its trouble spots. People in the United States love to discuss their *rights*, for example, with those treasuring the *right to work* frequently detesting those promoting the *right to choose*.

Computer scientists interested in open architecture have started a *right to know* movement, but they are not to be confused with the environmentalists pushing the *right to know* or the *right to know* advocates in Houston who speak in behalf of adoptees. There is a *right to read* group pushing phonics in Virginia, a *right to die* movement headquartered in Colorado, a *right to play* outfit in New York, and there are *right to life* groups in all fifty states. Everyone in the United States has rights. None feels they have enough.

Because keywords are so intimately tied to what a society values and detests, what it inspires and what it fears, we might ask how they will affect the national conversation in the future. Certain *ontological challenges*, for example, could confound political communication. As Mary Ann Glendon notes, when the concept of *rights* means too many things to too many people, when the right to get drunk is equated with the right to a speedy trial, danger results.[27] Societies become soft when words mean everything and nothing at the same time. In a hyperkinetic age when so many symbols are hurled at us with so much speed, it is easy to get sloppy with language. These conditions lead, in Glendon's terms, to an "impoverishment of political discourse," with important concepts like *freedom* and *justice* losing their integrity. When that happens, a society makes it easy for people to talk past one another rather than to one another. A semantically lazy society cannot speak well, and it cannot think well either.

We cannot hire language police to solve these ontological challenges. As we have seen throughout this book, words tend themselves, moving and morphing constantly. Keywords are especially likely to invite multiple interpretations. Indeed, part of the fun of being human is discovering what a given concept means to others. Because the United States is so large and because language is so polysemous, the nation will always have an *acculturation challenge* as a result. That is, it will need to teach its sacred truths to a changing population. So, for example, a refugee from a totalitarian society must be taught that *authority* is a pluralized concept in the United States, that the nation admits to many authorities, not all of whom have the same amount of influence. Being respectful, but not sacral, toward language is one of the boons of living in a democracy. Civic education must therefore become a kind of language training as well.[28]

When it comes to keywords, all societies face a *habituation challenge*, the problem of freezing meaning in its tracks. In the United States, where people argue vociferously about so many things, that hardly seems a challenge. But ideas have a way of becoming sedimented, of being taken-for-granted, and that can make a nation unreflective. *Race*, for example, has long been a keyword in American society. But it is also a poorly discussed concept and when it is discussed it is often discussed in tired ways. That tendency will be especially dangerous in the future. During the 2000 Census, for example, 2.4 percent of the U.S. population, or 6.8 million people, checked more than one race box, a fact that pleased the Association of MultiEthnic Americans located in Tucson, Arizona.[29] Those same data irritated traditional civil rights groups (e.g., the NAACP and LaRaza), however, because they foretold a new political calculus. Because young Americans are especially likely to embrace their multiethnic heritage, these data reveal a generational gap as well. The United States will need new ways of discussing *race* in the future.

A bewildering number of *management challenges* may also present themselves in the future. Keywords do not reside in some neutral site set apart from the surrounding culture. They are out in the open, constantly being contested. As we have seen, the concept of *politics* has been variously appropriated in the last thirty years. Writers and scholars are one thing, professional lobbyists are quite another. Each day in Washington they feed at the public trough and work the rhetorical angles as well. The Left, for example, attacks *Pentagon* spending, a metonomy conjuring up images of a wasteful, monolithic bureaucracy taking needed tax dollars from unwed mothers and unschooled children. The Right, in turn, speaks of supporting the *troops*, turning the spotlight on young Americans in uniform. There is word magic here, but there is also much at stake: schoolbooks for children, weapons for soldiers. There is not yet a science of managing keywords, but some are getting good at it. To sell the Gulf War to the American people in 1991, for example, Kuwait employed twenty different New York public relations firms (Hill & Knowlton being the most prominent—it alone received $11 million for its services). With resources like these available to manage public meanings, the world is indeed becoming a different place.

No matter how skilled a manager is, however, it takes two to communicate. Today, fewer Americans seem available when politics comes knocking. Numerous explanations have been offered for this *attention challenge*—people are too busy; their leaders have failed them; politics is too complex; cynicism has become a lifestyle. There are also technical explanations: With three hundred television channels to choose from, citizens are now on overload, making it harder to reach them (some media consultants estimate that a viewer must see a political ad ten times for it to have any effect). Even if a voter watched the *Today* show before work, read the local paper at lunch, listened to talk radio during drive time, surfed the web before dinner, and dialed up cable news shows each evening, what would he or she know about *healthcare* at the end of the day? Keywords can be powerful, but how do people access them in an over-communicated society? For his part, Michael Schudson praises the "monitorial citizen" who does enough "environmental surveillance" to stay up on the issues.[30] But with all the attentional claims made on that individual each day, how is that possible? How can *common* understandings be generated in a "narrowcasted" society where each of us deals with a unique set of messages each day?

Other authors have worried about a *commodity challenge,* of letting certain individuals (e.g., Rupert Murdoch) and certain corporations (e.g., Time Warner) monopolize people's perceptions. In the summer of 2003, for example, the Federal Communications Commission decided (by a 3–2 vote) to ease media ownership limits. Unexpectedly, a firestorm erupted, propelled by an unlikely coalition of conservatives (who worried that unpopular viewpoints would be crowded out) and liberals (who were appalled that a handful of industrialists could tell the nation what to think). From our perspective the issue is this: Can a keyword be purchased? That is, with enough money can U.S. oil interests succeed in equating *environmentalists* with *radicals*? With enough expertise, can General Motors break the unions in the name of workplace *democracy*? With enough "free media," can leftists succeed in reconceptualizing *marriage* by opening it up to same-sex individuals? With enough liberal bias, can newscasters challenge Corporate America by encouraging tort cases in the name of *consumerism*? Given the imbalance of resources available, the former two possibilities are more likely than the latter two, but all are unfortunate for those wanting free expression to remain tolerably free in the United States.[31]

As the world becomes smaller a seventh and final problem is the *insularity challenge*: Will the United States wind up talking to itself? Despite the domestic popularity of the war in Iraq, for example, the nation entered the conflict virtually alone (only Britain, Poland, and a few other countries sided with the United States). Militarily the war was an initial success although its aftermath was gruesome (diplomatically, politically, and culturally). But the war created a rift between France and the United States that was exacerbated by careless rhetoric. Bush almost never mentioned *allies* when discussing the war and overstressed *American* interests. Given the traumas of September 11, many granted him that license but others warned that "He [Bush] does not seem to speak a world language."[32] Instead, Bush invoked images of a *crusade* against terrorists (located in an Islamic country) and said he wanted Osama Bin Laden *dead or alive*, bringing up images of the American Wild West. These tokens played well locally but unnerved many Europeans: "Much of it is the way [Bush] talks, the rhetoric, the religiosity. It reminds them of what drove them crazy about Reagan. It reminds them of what they miss about Clinton. All the stereotypes we thought we had banished for good after September 11—the cowboy imagery, in particular—it's all back."[33]

Any of these challenges is challenge enough on its own. Combined, they create massive difficulties for fashioning a fully functioning society that is enlightened and yet strong, generous and yet self-protective. Such dangers are especially troublesome when there is an imbalance between rich and poor nations, Christian and Islamic nations, industrialized and agricultural nations. In such a world it is easy to misunderstand one another, even easier to hate what one does not understand. Such a world cannot be made smaller or less rivalrous or more egalitarian merely through speech. But one must do what one can do and one can always think harder about how to talk to others. The fact that the world speaks in so many different tongues makes that hard, as do people's tendencies to interpret even the same symbols idiosyncratically. Each nation, each culture, has its own special language. It is probably too optimistic to imagine a new set of keywords being invited to lead the world out of darkness. But if one could imagine such an invitation, one might give *peace* a chance.

CONCLUSION

There will always be those who doubt the possibilities of communication, who think it daft to emphasize words in a world where nuclear-tipped missiles bulge hither and yon. There are also those, the economic determinists, who will argue that money and what it purchases can alone control the world. There are those who will look to the great social movements of the past, finding peasants storming the barricades and students marching, and say only there—in massed assemblage—does one gaze on the full face of power. There will be those, especially those living in a mediated age, who will claim that words are too antique an invention to do much. It now takes pictures and websites and DVDs, they will claim, to arouse the conscience of a nation. And there are those who will say we have now entered a post-structural age in which all symbols embarrass themselves, so replete are they with ambiguity and so filled with jaundice are the people who consume them. In such an age, they will argue, nobody believes anybody any more.

Your authors beg to differ. We believe in language. This book has traced one nation's half-century attempt to find words that fit. Our journey has seen fits and starts, backings and fillings, a cacophony of voices. No single word, no single spokesperson, had all the answers or convinced all the people. The paths we followed found people trying out language, looking for an elixir that worked. The language they used revealed how power is negotiated in the United States and how it is shared. Writers, educators, reporters, and a great many political leaders plied their wares and were stretching all the while, trying to wrap their hands around the prominent words of their culture. Some succeeded, some failed, some succeeded for a time. Intelligent though they were, few knew exactly how keywords worked but they used them anyway, hypothesizing victory in order to achieve it. People who use words think they own them, and that is a special human conceit. But keywords are too complex to be easily disciplined. In many ways, this has been a book about language experiments.

Tomorrow's keywords may differ from today's, but some will persist. Keywords will cluster where they have always clustered—at a society's emotional center, at the intersection of its understandings. People will continue to use these words, and one hopes they will be used well, with discretion instead of bravado and with regard for the whole community. Keywords come in all shapes and sizes and have been used throughout history to launch grand adventures (in the United States it was the *West*) and grand misadventures (for Hitler it was the *volk*). Keywords. Most are short, most are easily remembered, none float gently away. They persist because people persist and cultures persist and problems persist and opportunities persist and politics persists. For these reasons, too, we must give *peace* a chance.

NOTES

1. These are, of course, the notorious words spoken by President George W. Bush in his State of the Union Address, January 28, 2003, http://www.washingtonpost.com (August 12, 2003).

2. From a nationwide poll, "America Unplugged: Citizens and Their Government," conducted by Peter D. Hart and Robert Teeter for the Council for Excellence in Government, http://excelgov.org/publication/excel/pressrelease.htm (July 12, 1999).

3. R. L. Teten, "Evolution of the Modern Rhetorical Presidency: Presidential Presentation and Development of the State of the Union Address," *Presidential Studies Quarterly*, 33 (2003): 333–46.

4. F. Inglis, *Raymond Williams* (London: Routledge, 1995), 117, 119, 278.

5. See G. F. Will, *Men at Work: The Craft of Baseball* (New York: Perennial Press, 1991).

6. L. Rosenfield, "The Terms of Commonwealth: A Response to Arnold," *Central States Speech Journal*, 28 (1977): 89.

7. R. Jewett and J. S. Lawrence, *Captain America and the Crusade Against Evil: The Dilemma of Zealous Nationalism* (Grand Rapids, MI: Erdmans, 2003).

8. D. Halberstam, *The Fifties* (New York: Villard Books, 1993), x.

9. D. T. Miller and M. Nowak, *The Fifties: The Way We Really Were* (Garden City, NY: Doubleday & Company, Inc., 1977) 92.

10. P. Lyons, *New Left, New Right, and the Legacy of the Sixties* (Philadelphia: Temple University Press, 1996), 222.

11. J. Stephens, *Anti-Disciplinary Protest: Sixties Radicalism and Postmodernism* (New York: Cambridge University Press, 1998), 25.

12. M. J. Heale, *The Sixties in America: History, Politics, and Protest* (Chicago: Fitzroy Dearborn, 2001), 90.

13. P. N. Carroll, *It Seemed Like Nothing Happened: The Tragedy and Promise of America in the 1970s* (New York: Holt, Rinehart and Winston, 1982), 159.

14. T. Gitlin, *The Sixties: Years of Hope, Days of Rage* (New York: Bantam, 1993), 421.

15. Ibid., 423.

16. K. H. Jamieson, *Eloquence in an Electronic Age: The Transformation of Political Speechmaking* (New York: Oxford University Press, 1990).

17. Ibid.

18. G. T. Sewall (ed.), *The Eighties: A Reader* (Reading, MA: Addison-Wesley, 1997), viii.

19. R. W. Fogel, *The Fourth Great Awakening and the Future of Egalitarianism* (Chicago: University of Chicago Press, 2000), 43.

20. E. J. Dionne, *Why Americans Hate Politics* (New York: Simon and Schuster, 1991), 11.

21. H. Johnson, *The Best of Times: America in the Clinton Years* (Orlando, FL: Harcourt, 2001), 556.

22. P. Johnson, *A History of the American People* (New York: HarperCollins, 1997), 937.

23. See J. R. Hibbing and E. Theiss-Morse, *Congress as Public Enemy: Public Attitudes Toward American Political Institutions* (Cambridge: Cambridge University Press, 1995).

24. W. D. Burnham, *Critical Elections and the Mainsprings of American Politics* (New York: W. Norton, 1970).

25. For more on this possibility, see R. P. Hart, *Seducing America: How Television Charms the Modern Voter* (New York: Oxford University Press, 1994).

26. S. Huntington, "Democracy's Third Wave," in *The Global Resurgence of Democracy,* 2d ed., ed. L. Diamond and M. F. Plattner (Baltimore: Johns Hopkins University Press, 1996), 3–25.

27. M. A. Glendon, *Rights Talk: The Impoverishment of Political Discourse* (New York: Free Press, 1993).

28. For more on this problem, see N. C. Rae, "Class and Culture: American Political Cleavages in the Twentieth Century," *Western Political Quarterly,* 45 (1992): 629–50.

29. As referenced by the Association of MultiEthnic Americans, http://www.ameasite.org/census/031201censusdata.asp (August 15, 2003).

30. M. Schudson, *The Good Citizen* (New York: Free Press, 1998).

31. For more on these matters, see R. W. McChesney, *Rich Media, Poor Democracy: Communication Politics in Dubious Times* (Urbana: University of Illinois Press, 1999).

32. G. Hinsliff and J. Burke, "Bush Rhetoric Is Scaring Europe, Says Mandelson," *The Observer-Guardian Unlimited,* August 11, 2002, http://observer.guardian.co.uk/iraq/story/0,12239,772584,00.html (August 15, 2003).

33. From the article "To Some in Europe, the Major Problem Is Bush the Cowboy," by *New York Times* correspondent David E. Sanger as quoted in W. F. Buckley, "High Noon in Europe," *National Review,* February 24, 2003, 3.

INDEX

A

Acculturation challenges, 258
Actions
    of consultants, 229
    the people's, 115, 118f, 122
    political, 32, 33
Adams, John, 10, 138, 155, 156
Advisers, 236, 237
Affirmative action, 5, 31
Afghanistan, 124, 131
African Americans, 3–4
Against All Enemies (Clarke), 19
Agnew, Spiro, 97–98, 171
Ailes, Roger, 222
Alcoff, Linda, 36
Alford, John, 69
Almond, Gabriel, 79
American Candidate (television show),
    19
American Civics (Hartley and Vincent),
    137, 138–40
American Freedom Library Database,
    9
American Government, 141
*American Government: Comparing Polit-
    ical Experiences*, 142
*American Government: Principles and
    Practices*, 142
American Idol (television show), 77
American Philosophical Quarterly, 59
American Political Behavior
    (Mehlingher and John), 144
American Political Science Associa-
    tion, 150
American Sociological Association,
    150
Ames, Fisher, 56
Anderson, Benedict, 108
Anderson, John, 191

Anderson, Richard, 5
Ansolabehere, Stephen, 228
*Antonio Canova and the Politics of
    Patronage in Revolutionary and
    Napoleonic Europe*, 25
AOL Time Warner, 94
Arendt, Hannah, 32
Arnold, Carroll, 117
Association of MultiEthnic Americans,
    258
Associations
    with the media, 91, 99
    of the party, 189, 193t
    in *Time* magazine articles, 154
Atlanta Constitution, 91
Atlantic Monthly, 58
Attainability, of promises, 209, 210t,
    211, 218–19
Attention challenges, 259
Austin, J. L., 209
Australia, 187
Authority, political, 32, 33, 35
*Automatic Government: The Politics of
    Indexation*, 57–58

B

Babel, tower of, 3
Bach, Kurt, 34
Baird, Zoë, 172
Balbo, Laura, 37
Balkans invasion, 2
Barber, James David, 159
Barker, Ernest, 76
Bartels, Larry, 186, 189, 195
*Battered Women's Justice: The Movement
    for Clemency and the Politics of Self-
    Defense*, 40
Baym, Geoffrey, 110
Beecher, Henry Ward, 82

Weber, Max, 21
Weber, Vin, 98
Welch, Jack, 153
West's American Government, 135, 137, 140–41, 142
White, James Boyd, 4, 39
Whitfield, George, 137, 250
Whyte, William H., 97
Will, George, 248
Willard, Charles, 110
Williams, Raymond, 2, 6–7, 8, 247–48
Wills, Garry, 68–69, 75, 168
Wilson, Woodrow, 10, 141, 175
Wirthlin, Richard, 215, 222
Women, 24, 35, 36–38, 58. *See also* Feminism
Women's movement, 132
Wood, Kimba, 172

Woodward, Bob, 92
Words
    as answers, 5–8
    as questions, 3–5
    as signals, 8–15
WorldCom, 67, 168
World War II, 2, 7
Wright, Frank Lloyd, 88

Y

Young, Bill, 119–20
Young, Iris, 31, 37

Z

Zavalloni, Marisa, 77
Zelizer, Barbie, 178–79
Zernicke, Paul, 8